WHAT MEN LIVE BY

WORK

PLAY  LOVE

WORSHIP

BY

RICHARD C. CABOT

ASSISTANT PROFESSOR OF MEDICINE

HARVARD UNIVERSITY

BOSTON AND NEW YORK

HOUGHTON MIFFLIN COMPANY

The Riverside Press Cambridge

Published January 1914

TO MY WIFE
INCOMPARABLE LEADER AND COMRADE
IN THE WORK, PLAY, LOVE, AND WORSHIP
OF MANY YEARS

PREFACE

THIS book has been written in many Pullmans and in the homes of many friends. I fear it bears evidence of the Pullmans; I am proudly certain that it shows traces of all the friends, — of Dr. and Mrs. Philip King Brown, of San Francisco; Bruce Porter, of the same impressive city; Maulsby Kimball, of Buffalo; Professor W. E. Hocking, of New Haven; Florence Painter, Rosalind Huidekoper Greene, and Henry Copley Greene, of Boston. The last five have read the entire manuscript, corrected many errors, and put in many improvements; to all I am deeply grateful.

I owe still more to my wife, whose influence appears, I hope, on every page. Other friends, visible and invisible, have also helped, — G. K. Chesterton, Josiah Royce, Ralph Waldo Emerson, and so many others that no title-page would hold their beloved names. I must be content with thanking them for whatever is true and absolving them from whatever is false in the pages to follow.

My title is that of one of Tolstoy's most beautiful stories. Such use of his words is quite in accord with the spirit and letter of his beliefs and with the gratitude which I owe him.

Parts of several chapters have already been printed in the *Atlantic Monthly* and are here reprinted by courtesy of the editor.

CONTENTS

INTRODUCTION

In the spring of 1909, I had been gnawing away at three tough and ancient problems which came to me through the Social Service Department of the Massachusetts General Hospital: What is the best way to care for the tuberculous? How can "nervous people" (neurasthenics) be restored to balance and happiness? Where can we find help that is worth offering to a girl facing motherhood without a husband?

A vacation in England that summer took me far enough away from the surface details of these problems to see that the solutions thus far suggested for them all have a strong family likeness and illustrate three stages of opinion.

An institution is our first idea for all these sufferers. A sanitarium for the tuberculous, a nervine for the neurasthenics, a "Rescue Home" for the unmarried mother. This solution contents us for a time, but further experience shows us how limited is the good which an institution can do. Even at its best it is too artificial, too much of a hothouse existence, to accomplish more than the beginning of a cure. The violent herding of special miseries in one place — disease facing similar disease, day in and day out — makes physical or moral contagion always a danger, sometimes a fact. More individual attention is needed for each body and soul. Mass treatment will accomplish only the first stages of cure.

Personal care, then, personal teaching, personal influence, seem to be the need. We form a small group of consumptives into a "class." The doctor and the nurse not only teach the patients hygiene, but use their Christian names and try to become friendly with each. The nurse visits the tenement and tries to show the poor consumptive how to carry out at home the sanitary régime of the hospital. Personal influence is appealed to for the momentum needed to encourage the sufferer along the barren, ugly path toward recovery.

So with sexual troubles. The reaction against institutionalism brings us to rely on personal influence and personal teaching. Some one must win the affection of each sufferer, penetrate the intricacies of the past, and guide the future better. Not alms or institutions, but a friend is what we hope to provide. Not material aid or mere instruction, but one's self, one's best service, seems now the ideal gift.

But though this is certainly part of the answer, we cannot rest content with it, for any one who tries to give "himself" in this way soon finds out that the gift is pitifully small and weak. We soon use up our slender stock of wisdom. The appeal, "Do this for my sake," soon wears out. No human personality is rich enough to suffice for another's food. Moreover, in proportion as this plan succeeds, we perceive the dangers of dependence. The sufferer must learn to stand upon his

own feet. He must get back into life. "Real Life,"
then, as we now begin to see, is after all the best teacher
and the best doctor. Nothing less fruitful will nourish
body and soul. We do not give up friendship and personal influence; but we see that they must take their
part with the other sanative elements of normal experience.

For the neurasthenic and for those struggling with
problems of sex, this need of "real life" is now pretty
generally recognized. Seclusion in sanitaria or rescue
homes is being replaced by efforts to get the sufferers
back into the industrial world, back into family life,
back to the surroundings which keep ordinary people
a-going. It is not so obvious that the tuberculous need
anything of the kind as a means of cure. Yet, if not,
why do consumptive doctors at a sanitarium like
Trudeau get along better than other consumptive
patients? Because (so Dr. Trudeau once told me) the
doctors are living a more normal life, — they can
sometimes do a little doctoring or microscopy, and so
forget that they are patients. The successful progress
of their work in sick-room or laboratory gives them
courage to be faithful to rules and to force down food.

In three widely separate fields, then, I think I see
a similar evolution, away from institutionalism, away
from dependence upon personal influence, — toward
a plan, the essence of which is to get the sufferer back
to real life: not back to "nature," but back to the best
that civilization has to offer to normal people.

Educators, social workers, and physicians with whom I have talked, seem to agree upon the following mystical prescription: —

Rᴄ

REAL LIFE   an indefinite
                          amount

Take a full dose after meals and
at bedtime.

But what do we mean by "real life"? What are the essentials which we want to secure for consumptives, neurasthenics, and "wayward" youth of both sexes?

Watching like a Boswell the practice of experts in the healing of broken souls and wounded characters, I have noticed that besides work — my own favorite prescription — the experts apply two other remedies: recreation (through play, art, or natural beauty) and affection. They also hope rather helplessly that a fourth resource, worship, will somehow get into the sufferer's life.

Out of the dazzle and welter of modern civilization, which offers a hundred quack remedies for every ill of the soul, work, play, and love emerge as the permanent sources of helpfulness to which parents, educators, and social workers are now turning with confidence, while over their shoulders they glance wistfully toward worship.

"Real Life," then, if it is to mean the nourishing, sustaining, and developing of existence, demands work, play, and love, and so much of the material and spiritual conditions of existence as make these possible.

Though I came to this belief first from a doctor's point of view, and as the result of search for the essential principles of healing within a special field, I have since come to notice that the special groups of people whom I see as patients are not the only ones who need these great medicines. I notice a growing tendency to center all remedial effort upon the same trio of ends, no matter what sort of trouble is at hand. More satisfying and interesting occupation, more refreshment through art and play, deeper and more intense affection, are the life-preservers which one wants to secure about the blind, the maimed, the invalid, the discharged prisoner, the boy who lies and steals but is not yet a prisoner, the orphan, the deserted wife, the discouraged, down-at-the-heel family, the neglected or abused child, the alcoholic, the convalescent, the insane, the feeble-minded, the morphinist, the boy who has inherited millions, and the society girl who has got through "coming out." In genuine emergencies and for those overdriven in their industrial harness, material relief (food, rest, air, sleep, warmth) may be the first necessity, but unless we can give the vital nourishment which I am now advising, all material relief soon becomes a farce or a poison, just as medicine is in most chronic diseases a farce or a poison. Vitality and resisting power are what we most need, and these must be created for the sick out of the same nourishment which keeps the well people well.

I made just now a long list of sufferers. Did I mention all who need the essentials of real life? Obviously not, for those who are going right need these life-saving activities as much as those who are going wrong. It is the stake in life given us by our work, our play, and our love that keeps any one from going wrong. The conservative needs them to leaven his conservatism; the radical needs them to hold him down to solid ground. Young and old need them, for by these three principles we are helped to grow up and saved from growing old.

In this style I was sailing confidently along when one day a friend asked me: "How do you distinguish Work, Play, and Love from Drudgery, Frivolity, and Lust? You have made saints of your favorites and put halos around their heads, but not every one can see the halos or can believe in them upon your say-so."

"True!" I should answer, "not on my say-so, but on your own. You believe in them now." Everybody sees halos and worships saints of some kind, though many have learned to hide the habit even from themselves. Work, play, and love are my saints, and in this book I want to draw their lineaments and make their halos visible to others. The religion of work, or art, and of love is not the strongest or the truest, but it is a good beginning. There one finds outlet for devotion and gropes toward God. One can do all but speak to God. One fails only when it comes to worship, which is to-day so unfashionable a habit that one must be prepared to shock the modern ear and to violate all the scientific proprieties if one confesses belief in it. Civilization is supposed to have carried us beyond the need of rites and forms and to have fused the demonstrative and emotional side of religion into daily work, play, and affection.

But this is theory, not observation. As a matter of fact the doctor, social worker, or teacher who believes that all true religion can be woven into work, play, or affection falls into the same fallacy as those who think English composition can be taught by weaving it into the courses in history, science, and philosophy. Experience shows, I think, that vital religion and the ability to write good English are not acquired in this incidental way. Scientists, economists, and historians often write barbarously. We must practice the art of writing directly as well as incidentally, else we shall duplicate the catastrophe of our public-school system, wherein the conscientious effort to avoid proselyting, to abolish sectarian teaching, and let religion take care of itself, has now brought us perilously near the French secularism.

There is no originality in my suggestion that we should focus our efforts upon work, play, love, and worship. For though we talk a great deal about "efficiency," economics, hygiene, and other matters of secondary importance, at bottom we all know well enough what we need, and what all the paraphernalia of civilization, money, health, and education, are really meant for. If I were not persuaded that, in our right minds, we know the fundamental reasons for all this hurry and bustle, I should not venture to write a reminder. We know where we are traveling, but we need a time-table to remind us of details.

I do not say that every one *wants* only the ends which I have named. He usually wants fame, riches, wisdom, talents, personal beauty, and an easy time of it generally. He may be too sleepy and comfortable, or too tired and miserable, to want anything but Nirvana or release. Yet, enervated by heat, calloused by routine, steeped in sin, crazed with pain, stupefied by luxury or by grief, still he needs four inexorable blessings.

The interplay of these four is the end of life, and the sole worthy end, in my creed. This is the fruit of the "life and liberty" which are guaranteed under our Constitution. This is the goal to be secured through efficient and progressive governmental machinery. This is the end of all education and all moral training. This is the food of the soul in health or in disease, needed by the doctor, the social worker, the teacher, and the statesman, to feed their own souls as well as to prevent and to cure social ills. This is our justification for the enormous machinery and the costly ugliness of civili-

zation. This is the essential of that "more abundant
life" which many modern prophets [1] extol without
defining.

Every human being, man, woman, and child, hero
and convict, neurasthenic and deep-sea fisherman,
needs the blessing of God through these four gifts.
With these any life is happy despite sorrow and pain,
successful despite bitter failure. Without them we
lapse into animalism or below it. If you want to keep
a headstrong, fatuous youth from overreaching
himself and falling, these must be the elements of
strength. When you try to put courage and aspiration
into the gelatinous character of the alcoholic or the
street-walker, you will fail unless you can give responsibility, recreation, affection, and through them **a**
glimpse of God.

I do not believe that evolution, revolution, or de-
cadence have power to change these elemental needs.
For all I know, we may be this instant in the position
of the French court before the Revolution. At this
very moment we may be lurching over the smooth
bend of a cataract that is to overwhelm us; but if so,
it is because we have not enough of that unchanging
valor which has preserved us so far, and will reconsti-
tute us after our downfall. For work, play, love, and
prayer are open to rich and poor, to young and old;
they are of all times and all races in whom character
is an ideal.

[1] For example, Ellen Key.

On each of these gigantic forces I have particular designs: I want to show the sacredness of work and love; I want to show the accessibility and the universality of play and worship. That despite our secular habits, we are so close to worship that we may at any time abruptly fall into it; that play and art can be closely woven into the fabric of work, till drudgery is reduced to a minimum; that work is our key to the sacredness of material nature, and that affection can be disciplined only by consecration. These are my theses.

This book has still another motive: gratitude for the good things that have come to me through work, play, love, and worship. Is it not churlish to make no attempt at hearty applause for all that is given us in this world? Grant that I am shielded from much that makes others curse God or nature; shall I not praise my side of the shield?

"On the 19th of July, 1857," says Tolstoy, "in Lucerne before the Schweizerhof Hotel, where many rich people were lodging, a wandering minstrel sang for half an hour his songs and played his guitar. About a hundred people listened to him. The little man in the darkness poured out his heart like a nightingale in couplet after couplet, song after song. Near by on the boulevard were heard frequent murmurs of applause, though generally the most respectful silence reigned. *The minstrel thrice asked them all to give him something.*

Not one person gave him anything, and many made fun of him." (The italics are Tolstoy's.)

There is no sin that I would not rather have upon my soul than to have displayed to the universe such ingratitude.

Do you say that the universe cares as little about our praise as the ocean for Byron's command to "roll on"? Well, I vote against you. I believe the universe does care, and needs our gratitude.

WHAT MEN LIVE BY

PART I: WORK

WHAT MEN LIVE BY

CHAPTER I

WORK, PLAY, AND DRUDGERY

A CAMPER starting into the woods on his annual vacation undertakes with enthusiasm the familiar task of carrying a Saranac boat upon a shoulder-yoke. The pressure of the yoke on his shoulders feels as good as the grasp of an old friend's hand. The tautening of his muscles to the strain of carrying seems to gird up his loins and true up his whole frame. With the spring of the ground beneath him and the elastic rebound of the boat on its resilient yoke, he seems to dance over the ground between two enlivening rhythms. It is pure fun.

In the course of half a mile or so, the carry begins to feel like work. The pleasant, snug fit of the yoke has become a very respectable burden, cheerfully borne, for the sake of the object in view, but not pleasant. The satisfaction of the carry is now something anticipated, no longer grasped in the present. The job is well worth while, but it is no joke. It will feel good to reach the end and set the boat down.

Finally, if in about ten minutes more there is still no sight of the end, no blue, sparkling glimmer of distant water low down among the trees, the work becomes drudgery. Will it ever end? Are we on the right

trail at all? Is it worth while to go on? Perhaps not;
but to stop means painfully lowering the boat to the
ground and later heaving it up again, which is the
worst task of all — worse than going on as we are.
So we hang to it, but now in scowling, stumbling,
swearing misery, that edges ever nearer to revolt.

In varying proportions every one's life mingles the
experiences of that carry. At its best and for a few,
work becomes play, at least for blessed, jewel-like moments. By the larger number it is seen not as a joy
but a tolerable burden, borne for the sake of the children's education, the butter on the daily bread, the
hope of promotion. Finally, for the submerged fraction
of humanity who are forced to labor without choice
and almost from childhood, life seems drudgery, borne
simply because they cannot stop without still greater
misery. They are committed to it, as to a prison, and
they cannot get out.

It is not often, I believe, that a whole life is possessed
by any one of these elements, — play, work, or drudgery. Work usually makes up the larger part of life, with
play and drudgery sprinkled in. Some of us at most
seasons, all of us at some seasons, find work a galling
yoke to which we have to submit blindly or angrily for
a time, but with revolt in our hearts. Yet I have rarely
seen drudgery so overwhelming as to crush out altogether the play of humor and good-fellowship during
the day's toil as well as after it.

In play you have what you want. In work you know what you want and believe that you are serving or approaching it. In drudgery no desired object is in sight; blind forces push you on.

Present good, future good, no good, — these possibilities are mingled in the crude ore which we ordinarily call work. Out of that we must smelt, if we can, the pure metal of a vocation fit for the spirit of man. The crude mass of "work," as it exists to-day in mines, ships, stores, railroads, schoolrooms, and kitchens, contains elements that should be abolished, elements that are hard, but no harder than we need to call out the best of us, and here and there a nugget of pure delight.

I want to separate, in this book, the valuable ingredients from the conglomerate loosely called work, especially those ingredients which preserve a "moral equivalent" [1] for the virtues bred in war, in hunting, and in the savage's struggle against nature. For in battle, in the chase, and in all direct dealing with elementary forces, we have built up precious powers of body and of mind. These we are in danger of losing in our more tame and orderly civilization, as William James has so convincingly shown.

His warning is echoed in different keys by President Briggs,[2] and by others, who fear that kindergarten

[1] William James, "The Moral Equivalent for War," *Memories and Studies.* Longmans, Green & Co., 1911.

[2] LeBaron R. Briggs, *School, College, and Character.* Houghton Mifflin Company, 1901.

methods in education are making children soft and spiritless, and that all sting and stubbornness has been extracted from modern school work. President Briggs quotes, apparently with approval, the opinion of James Martineau that "power to drudge at distasteful tasks is the test of faculty, the price of knowledge, and the matter of duty."

This conception blurs, I think, the most vital distinction in the whole matter, that, namely, between work and drudgery on the one side and that between work and play on the other. Work, like morality and self-government, differs from play because play is spontaneous and delightful, while work is done soberly and against resistance. Nevertheless we work because we want the fruit of work — not from pure dogged determination. To force ourselves along without any desire for a goal of attainment is drudgery. Work is doing what you don't *now* enjoy for the sake of a future which you clearly see and desire. Drudgery is doing under strain what you don't now enjoy and for no end that you can now appreciate.

To learn how to work is so to train our imagination that we can feel the stimulus from distant futures, as the coast cities of California get heat, light, and power from distant mountain streams. In all work and all education the worker should be in touch with the distant sources of interest, else he is being trained to slavery, not to self-government and self-respect.

Defined in this way, work is always, I suppose, an acquired taste. For its rewards are not immediate, but come in foretastes and aftertastes. It involves postponement and waiting. In the acquisition of wealth, economists rightly distinguish labor and waiting, but in another sense labor is always waiting. You work for your picture or your log house because you want it, and because it cannot be had just for the asking. It awaits you in a future visible only to imagination. Into the further realization of that future you can penetrate only by work: meantime you must wait for your reward.

Further, this future is never perfectly certain. There is many a slip between the cup and the lip; and even when gross accidents are avoided, your goal — your promotion, your home, the degree for which you have worked — usually does not turn out to be as you have pictured it. This variation you learn to expect, to discount, perhaps to enjoy, beforehand, if you are a trained worker, just because you have been trained in faith. For work is always justified by faith. Faith, holding the substance (not the details) of things unseen, keeps us at our tasks. We have faith that our efforts will some day reach their goal, and that this goal will be something like what we expected. But no literalism will serve us here. If we are willing to accept nothing but the very pattern of our first desires, we are forever disappointed in work and soon grow slack in it. In the more fortunate of us, the love of work includes a love of the unexpected, and finds a pleasant spice of adventure in the difference between what we work for and what we actually get.

Yet this working faith is not pure speculation. It includes a foretaste of the satisfaction to come. We plunge into it as we jump into a cold bath, not because the present sensations are altogether sweet, but because they are mingled with a dawning awareness of the glow to follow. We do our work happily because the future is alive in the present — not like a ghost but like a leader.

Where do we get this capacity to incarnate the future and to feel it swelling within us as a present inspiration? The power to go in pursuit of the future with seven-leagued boots or magic carpets can hardly be acquired, or even longed for, until we have had some actual experience of its rewards. We seem then to be caught in one of those circles which may turn out to be either vicious or virtuous. In the beginning, something or somebody must magically entice us into doing a bit of work. Having done that bit, we can see the treasure of its results; these results will in turn spur us to redoubled efforts, and so once more to increased rewards. Given the initial miracle and we are soon established in the habit and in the enjoyment of work.

But there is a self-maintaining circularity in disease, idleness, and sloth, as well as in work, virtue, and health. Until we get the result of our work, we cannot feel the motive for exertion. Until we make the exertion (despite present pain and a barren outlook), we cannot taste the delightful result, nor feel the spur to further effort. The wheel is at the dead point! Why should it ever move?

Probably some of us are moved at first by the leap of an elemental instinct in our muscles, which act before and beyond our conscious reason. Other people are tempted into labor by the irrational contagion of example. We want to be "in it" with the rest of our gang, or to win some one's approval. So we get past the dead point, — often a most alarming point to parents and teachers, — and once in motion, keep at it by the circular process just described.

Various auxiliary motives reinforce the ordinary energies of work. Here I will allude only to one — a queer pleasure in the mere stretch and strain of our muscles. If we are physically fresh and not worried, there is a grim exhilaration, a sort of frowning delight, in taking up a heavy load and feeling that our strength is adequate to it. It seems paradoxical to enjoy a discomfort, but the paradox is now getting familiar. For modern psychologists have satisfactorily bridged the chasm between pleasure and pain, so that we can now conceive, what athletes and German poets have long felt, the delight in a complex of agreeable and disagreeable elements. In work we do not often get as far as the "selige Schmerzen" so familiar in German lyrics, but we welcome difficulties, risks, and physical strains because (if we can easily conquer them) they add a spice to life, — a spice of play in the midst of labor.

Work gets itself started, then, by the contagion of some one else's example, or by an explosion of animal energies within us. After a few turns of the work-rest cycle we begin to get a foretaste of rewards. A flavor of enjoyment appears in the midst of strain. Habit then takes hold and carries us along until the taste for work is definitely acquired.

CHAPTER II

MOST doctors have set a good many women to work and taken a good many men out of it. Doctors have, therefore, a doubly fortunate opportunity to see what work can do for people, and a better right than any one else to speak (if, alas, they cannot sing!) of its blessings.

We all of us see something of the man out of work, thanks to strikes, freaks of fashions, and shifts in trade currents. But in these crises it is the pressing need of the work's wage that holds our attention — not the desire for work itself. Because the doctor's angle of vision is different, he sees another type of suffering. He sees men to whom the pinch of hunger is unknown languish, chafe, and fret when forcibly removed from their daily work. I recall the illness of an old stage-driver. He had no need to work. His children were eager and willing to supply his wants. But despite good medical care he would not or could not convalesce till his sons lifted him into his wagon-seat and put "the lines" into his feeble hands. Then you could see him gain every day.

In an old man, shaped and warped by his work through seventy years, this tug of habit is perhaps only natural. But such habits of work are often early formed.

The schoolboy usually wants to get back to school as fast as he can after an illness, and if he finds something besides pure work to attract him in school, he is like his elders in this also. For work is seldom "pure," — rarely separated or shut away from the other elements of sociability, exciting variety and fun.

I want to set down what I can of the good which I have seen accomplished by work for two classes of people: — for men temporarily deprived of it, and for women who are experiencing its rewards for the first time.

Many times I have seen work pull people out of the misery of a self-centered existence. Without work many a woman has thought herself fundamentally selfish, or if she was not so rough with herself, her relations have vented a similar lament. For almost all people think about themselves when they are not enticed by the call of the world's work into thinking of something else. To get busy is the way out of most cases of self-centeredness. We are like wells. When our life is full, the dregs of shallow selfishness at the bottom do not often rise to consciousness. But when we are empty, our selfishness is necessarily exposed, and we are to blame only if we have made no effort to fill up the aching void with what we know belongs there, — especially work.

The nervous sufferer or the chronic invalid is often no more to blame for his selfishness than for the piti-

ful meagerness of his muscles. The long and the short
of it is, he is not nourished; his vitality has been
emptied out. Till he gets back into life he cannot help
staring at the four blank walls of his narrow self. But
to get back into life, or to get into it for the first time
(as many women have to) is practically what work
means. For the world is primarily a working world.
From the insects to the angels, creation hums with
work, and through work fits us for play.

Idleness is corrosive. Human energies, like human
stomachs, turn inward perversely and self-destructively
if they have not material to work on. Deprived of work,
people exhaust themselves like crazed animals beating
against their bars, even when the cage is of their own
making. Thoughts, that should run out in path-finding,
path-making labor, circle round and round within the
mind, till it is dizzy and all distinctions are blurred. By
work you straighten out such cramped and twisted
energies, as you shake out a reefed sail.

Healthy people deprived of the outlet and stimulus
of work are in danger of getting into one or another
sexual muddle. For we are many of us creatures who
can be purified only by motion, as the running stream
drops out its pollutions when its current grows swift,
but gets defiled as soon as it stagnates in shallows.
Consciousness, if not kept fully occupied with its proper
business, is pretty sure to upset the whole human machine by turning its light on what ought to be in dark

unconsciousness. A person is normally unconscious of his eyes, of his heart's action, of his stomach, his intestines, and all the rest of his separate and serviceable organs. But the moment consciousness gets focused on any one bit of the human body, we get disaster like to that of the dancer who becomes conscious of his feet. He becomes, as we mistakenly say, "self-conscious." We mean that he is narrowly and painfully conscious of a very small piece of himself, and forgetful of a very much larger area. A workingman's "self" is the whole *milieu*, the whole "proposition" in which he is normally engaged. Because he is the engineer of his train, the policeman of his beat, his "self" is enriched and employed by the extent, the variety, the dignity and worth of his job. The awareness of his separate organs and functions, a torture to him in idleness, vanishes as soon as he gets actively busy.

But sedentary and emotional occupations are impossible for some people because of the sexual tension which they tend to produce. One of the justifications of the apparently wasteful and unintelligent "hustling" in our modern world is here. What Tolstoy seeks to accomplish on his country estate by exhausting labor out of doors, the city man brings to pass by rushing and hurrying about like a June-bug. He works off superabundant energy in irrational ways, because he is not bright enough to work it off otherwise. But it is surely a good thing to work it off somehow.

Work dispels discouragement because it turns consciousness away from our disheartening littleness and lights up the big world — our world — of possible achievement. Consciousness cannot voluntarily extinguish itself. Its light must beat upon the inner walls of our narrow self and illumine them with an unnatural glare unless we have windows into the world's great interests. Through these consciousness can escape. Without them it is turned upon itself. There is no fault in that. The self-centeredness of the invalid, of the man out of work, or of the rich female loafer is a necessary consequence of the fact that consciousness, like a lighted lamp, must illumine something. It will hit with false intensity on the nearest thing if outlets are cut off.

Now that "nearest thing" in the case of consciousness is our own bodies: — hence the bodily miseries, the over-sensitiveness and the squeamishness of the idle. The next "nearest thing" is our poor scanty outfit of powers and virtues. Small and cheap they look in their naked isolation, and the one big thing that they can produce is shadows. The shadow of whatever is crowded up close to the light of consciousness is big enough to blacken the whole world. Hence discouragement is a natural and blameless consequence when idleness blocks the light of consciousness. To be idle is to be shut in, and in such confinement one feels powerless and insignificant.

The platform speaker whose audience is deserting him hears his own voice pronouncing words which hitherto have sounded valuable and potent; — now they seem tawdry and foolish. He has been left high and dry, alone with his naked self. Before the exodus he had courage because he could lose himself in his subject. He had an audience and a message for them. They clothed him, dignified him, gave worth to his vocal gymnastics and meaning to his oratorical labors. But without the response of his audience he is merely a voice, a ghost haunting a world that has forgotten him.

Work gives every man an audience and a message. Through work his personality, small enough in itself, gets out of itself and acquires a strange and blessed ownership of fruitful soil. For his job certainly belongs to him in some sense. It is his spiritual property, and thus, like all property, it gives courage because it enriches personality. Deprived of work and its comradeship, we are lonely and therefore discouraged, for loneliness is so close to discouragement that it is hard to slip the knife-blade of a definition between them.

To find one's work is to find one's place in the world. Most discouragement means homelessness; when downcast there seems to be no place for us in the world. Everybody else seems to be needed and to belong somewhere. But in idleness no one is needed. Idly to watch the busy people in one's own country or abroad is a heart-breaking business. Hence prolonged travel is bearable only if one adopts some plan of work, makes a business of sight-seeing, or in some other way earns every day one's appreciable share of knowledge.

I have said that a job is a special form of property. One gets a right to it, as to any form of property, in proportion as one works it up, by making it fruitful for some community, visible or invisible. The scientific investigator, the inventor, the unappreciated artist, the martyr, works for an invisible community not yet born, or hidden on the other side of the earth or elsewhere. If he escapes discouragement, it is because he has learned to see an audience invisible to others. Without this he is hopeless. Whoever is forced to work where he cannot see with the spirit's sense this invisible community and cannot "paint the thing as he sees it for the God of things as they are," becomes disheartened and may have to seek some smaller but more tangible piece of property, some task bringing with it an heartening social recognition.

Courage for life, then, comes when one gets out of isolation, owns, surveys, and fences in a bit of the uncharted world. Such a place-in-the-world is a job. It matters little whether others see it or not, but if you cannot see it yourself, you are lost in the wilderness. The courage given us by our work is like the self-reliance which Emerson has made forever glorious. Like self-reliance, courage is ultimately a reliance on widening concentric circles of property which reach to God.

As a physician I have had the happiness of seeing work cure many persons who have suffered from that trembling palsy of the soul which results from overmastering doubts, hesitation, vacillation, and fear. Work often cures this kind of skepticism ("*solvitur ambulando*"), which is not thinking but worry. It comes from thinking in a circle instead of thinking straight.

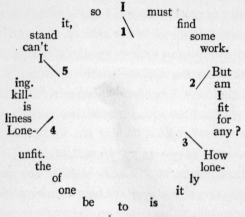

Vacillation (*folie de doute*) has the same circular character, or pendulous swing.

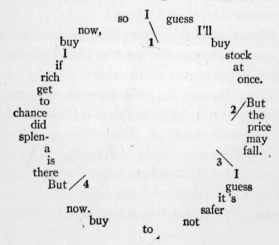

"Break away," says the wise world. For this sort of thing is checked by breaking out anywhere into the real world and going straight in any direction. The "pale cast of worry" was what Hamlet miscalled "thought." Thought is good, and so is action, but circularity is neither thought nor action, nor anything but a round dance of badly trained brain cells.

Many doubts and fears of the circular type are cured by work, because it gives us the evidence needed to banish the fear. "Mr. Accomplishment" is the witness whom we must secure, because the doubts and fears that we are talking about now are doubts of one's own powers, or fears of one's own weakness. A doctor or friend may asseverate till he is black in the face: "You have this power; you need n't fear that weakness." But nothing convinces, or ought to convince in such a matter, except waking up to find one's self actually doing the thing for which one could not, by taking thought, conceive one's strength sufficient.

In all such healing of worry through work we begin with a plunge and a submersion of consciousness. For "action," when we contrast it with "thought," means an amazing descent into the arms of the elemental which supports us and carries us to achievement across a gulf of unconsciousness. In singing one throws the voice at a high note wisely oblivious of just how one gets there. One measures the stream before leaping it, but not in the moment of the leap. In enthusiasm, *élan*, and the most successful flights of invention or creative art, we shut our eyes, and surrender ourselves into the hands of some force that we trust but cannot watch. How does this differ from recklessness and jumping at conclusions? It differs in its preparation. The life that we have lived before we thus surrender ourselves guides us even in our passivity. Training and conscious practice lead us up to the brink of the gulf and fix the direction of our leap. But the final plunge, the miracle of fresh achievement, cometh not during observation, but in darkness when the sun has set.

CHAPTER III

THE JOY OF WORK

SUNDAY, September 15, 1907, I could not find a seat in Faneuil Hall, Boston's colonial relic, where President Dennis Driscoll, of the Boston Central Labor Union was to answer what President Eliot had said on the previous Sunday on the rights, duties, and privileges of the manual laborer. With manual laborers the hall was so crowded that I found standing-room only in the middle aisle. President Driscoll finished what he had to say about the "closed shop" and turned to another topic: —

"President Eliot spoke last Sunday to us workingmen about The Joy of Work!" said the speaker, and paused. Then as he lifted his head from his manuscript and looked out over the crowded hall, a sound of derisive laughter spread in wave after wave over the audience. There was but one thing to think of such an idea as "The Joy of Work." It was a bitter joke. To the workmen present, it was really ludicrous that a man could be so foolish, so ignorant of manual work as to believe that there is any enjoyment in it.

To me that laughter was one of the saddest facts that I have faced. This audience of manual workers was instantly and instinctively of one mind. Their leader had no need even to express his thought. It

was enough to put together in one sentence the idea of
joy and the idea of work; the absurdity, the contradiction, was then self-evident. Any joy that was to come
to them must come out of working hours. Their work
was drudgery to which they were bound by the ancient
curse: "In the sweat of thy face shalt thou eat bread."
But though necessity bound them, their minds were
still free to protest. If work were already full of joy,
would they, the manual workers, be united to change
and improve the conditions of labor? Their very
existence as members of "organized labor," their very
presence in that hall, meant that they were vehe-
mently dissatisfied with their work and with one whom
they viewed as a soft-handed academic professor, ignorant of the actual conditions of modern manual work,
and therefore deluded enough to suppose that there is
joy in it. How little they knew President Eliot!

I have told this incident to sharpen further the previously defined distinction between work and drudgery.
Even if drudgery has its blessings,[1] it is surely no blessing to him whose life contains little or nothing else. For
President Driscoll's audience the satisfactions of
drudgery (though President Eliot called it work) were
nonexistent. They did not know what he was talking
about, and he (they felt sure) did not know their lives.
His "work" was their "play." In the zest of their
labor-union discussions (never thought of as "work"),
they perhaps got nearer to the enjoyment of something

[1] W. C. Gannett, D.D., "Blessed be drudgery."

which he would have called work than at any other time; but they never imagined that he could mean anything like that.

Much, perhaps most, that is called work in modern industrial society weighs upon the laborer as a blight and a burden, something to be hated and so far as may be banished out of life. Now we can all agree, can't we, that whatever feels like this ought not to be praised and cultivated? We may say that this is slavery, not real work, that it is the abuse, not the fruition, of man's labor. But then we must not extol indiscriminately all that goes by the name of work.

A rich man may find it very good fun to task his muscles now and then with wood-chopping or horse-shoeing, but he is a fool if he supposes that the wood-chopper or the horse-shoer gets this amateur's pleasure out of his trade. "Arizona is a delightful place to live, is n't it?" I said to a consumptive doctor whom I met on his daily rounds near Flagstaff. "Oh, yes," he answered, "if you don't *have* to live here." The tourist's, the greenhorn's, the amateur's view of manual work dwells on its picturesque, its novel, and exciting aspects. But this is rightly rejected by the day laborer. Who can blame him for indignation against those who praise manual work because they have never done any?

But is it so bad, even in present-day factory conditions, — is it so joyless as President Driscoll's audience felt it to be that Sunday afternoon? Was there not something of pure misunderstanding and cross-purposes in that lamentable mirth at President Eliot's expense? Question any prosperous, hustling American male (who would sooner work than eat); put to him the question, "Do you find joy in your work?" he will deny it with an oath or with a good version of the derisive laugh which I heard in Faneuil Hall.

For in the first place "joy" is too "hifalutin" a word for him to take upon his lips. It recalls to him some pink-and-blue-ribboned frivolity, or the grotesque frenzy of a religious camp-meeting. If you asked: "How do you like your job?" or if you got him talking about its technicalities, there would ooze out in his talk something of his solid satisfaction in it, some of its spice and variety, even some genuine emotion about its rewards and adventures. I have asked that question of a great many workingmen under conditions of intimacy when mutual understanding was to be relied upon, and I never received more than two or three negative answers. If we ask about "joy," then national peculiarities, masculine shyness, and fear of emotion play a part in the discouraging answers. There is an instinct, too, against the vivisection of this fragile element, — joy, — from out the tissue of working life.

Yet, even in manual labor, just as it is in America to-day and with all our sins and blunders upon its head, there is still, I believe, much satisfaction to the workman. Else why is it that when he is sick he complains in that most pregnant phrase: "Doctor, I've lost all my ambition"? By *ambition* he means zest and spirit for work. A mere slave, a hopeless drudge, would not know what this "ambition" meant. One cannot lose one's appetite for life and work unless despite their monotony and strain they once tasted good. The sense of competence, the conscious possession of skill that the apprentice cannot learn in many months, — there is almost always some satisfaction in that. Then the comradeship in work, the gossip and jokes over it, the twist and turn of the unexpected in every day's work, the appreciation of friends and onlookers, all these weave about the monotonous job a web of genuine interest. The job itself, — parts of it, anyway, — may then become as automatic as breathing or eating. Only the invalid is oppressed by the curse of labor in his physiological functions, as he draws his breath, chews his meat, or handles his knife and fork.

Yet President Driscoll's speech, his audience, and their scorn of President Eliot's "joy of work" are facts which we must take seriously to heart. For any other audience of manual laborers would doubtless have laughed just as bitterly at the idea that there was joy in their work — partly, as I believe, from dislike of the word "joy," partly from misunderstanding of the speaker's motive, but largely because they believe that they have been forced, without any choice of their own, into work in which they do not believe they are getting their fair share of return, in which they cannot recognize their own achievement, and in which they get no human touch with their employers. It is not so much the work itself, nor even its unhealthful conditions that wage-earners resent. It is rather the state of society by reason of which (as they believe), someone no better or wiser than they, someone whom they never chose to lead them, has usurped the right to force work upon them under unsanitary conditions and at low wages. Social and political leaders they can choose. "Captains of industry" they must find and follow, too often, with bitter protest.

To remedy these great evils economic readjustments, — socialism or some halfway house on the road to it, — will doubtless be tried within the next few decades. But no one will like his job any better unless not only the economic but the psychical conditions are notably improved. Above all, our personal relations and personal ideals must improve, else economic reforms will amount to nothing. Things are bad; but it is people, not mere things that make them so. Economic reforms, better hours and wages, will do good if they mirror and accompany an improvement in your character and mine; not otherwise. As fast as we grow more honest, more generous, and more ambitious, we shall make a better industrial system and a new form of government to clothe our larger powers. Meantime "class consciousness," which means class hatred, delays our advance.

CHAPTER IV

THE POINTS OF A GOOD JOB

In the crude job as we get it there is much rubbish. For work is a very human product. It is no better than we have made it, and even when it is redeemed from brutal drudgery it is apt to be scarred and warped by our stupidities and our ineptitudes. Out of the rough-hewn masses in which work comes to us, it is our business, it is civilization's business, to shape a vocation fit for man. We shall have to remake it again and again; meantime, before we reject what we now have, it is worth while to see what we want.

What (besides better hours, better wages, healthier conditions) are the points of a good job? Imagine a sensible man looking for satisfactory work, a vocational adviser guiding novices towards the best available occupation, and a statesman trying to mould the industrial world somewhat nearer to the heart's desire, — what should they try for? Physical and financial standards determine what we get *out* of our work. But what shall we get *in* it? Much or little, I answer, according to its fitness or unfitness for our personality, — a factor much neglected nowadays.

Among the points of a good job I shall name seven: (1) Difficulty and crudeness enough to call out our latent powers of mastery. (2) Variety so balanced by

monotony as to suit the individual's needs. (3) A boss.
(4) A chance to achieve, to build something and to
recognize what we have done. (5) A title and a place
which is ours. (6) Connection with some institution,
some firm, or some cause, which we can loyally serve.
(7) Honorable and pleasant relation with our comrades in work. Fulfill these conditions and work is
one of the best things in life. Let me describe them
more fully.

We want a chance to subdue. Boys like to go stamping
through the woods in thick-soled boots. They like to
crush the sticks in their path and to jerk off the
branches that get in their way. If there is need to clear
a path, so much the better; the pioneer's instinct is
the more strongly roused. For there is in most of us
an ancient hunger to subdue the chances which we
meet, to tame what is wild. As another's anger calls
out ours, so the stubbornness of nature rouses our determination to subdue it. We want to encounter the
raw and crude. Before the commercial age, war, hunting, and agriculture gave us this foil. We want it still,
and for the lack of it often find our work too soft.

Of course, we can easily get an overdose of crude
resistance. A good job should offer us a fair chance of
our winning. We have no desire to be crushed without
a struggle. But we are all the better pleased if the fish
makes a good fight before he yields.

Not only in the wilderness, but wherever we deal

with raw material, our hands meet adventures. Every bit of wood and stone, every stream and every season, has its own tantalizing but fascinating individuality; and as long as we have health and courage, these novelties strike not as frustration but as challenge.

Even in half-tamed products, like leather or steel, there are, experts tell me, incalculable variations which keep us on the alert if we are still close enough to the elemental to feel its fascinating materiality. When a clerk sells dry-goods over the counter, I suppose he has to nourish his frontiersman's spirit chiefly in foiling the wily bargain-hunter or trapping the incautious countryman. But I doubt if the work is as interesting as a carpenter's or a plumber's. It reeks so strong of civilization and the "finished product" that it often sends us back to the woods to seek in a "vacation" that touch with the elemental which should properly form part of daily work.

We want both monotony and variety. The monotony of work is perhaps the quality of which we most often complain, — often justifiably. Yet monotony is really demanded by almost every one. Even children cry for it, though in doses smaller than those that suit their elders. Your secretary does not like her work if you put more than her regular portion of variety into it. She does not want to be constantly undertaking new tasks, adapting herself to new situations. She wants some regularity in her traveling, some plain stretches in which she can get up speed and feel quantity of accomplishment; that is, she wants a reasonable amount of monotony. Change and novelty in work are apt to demand fresh thought, and to reduce our speed.

Of course, there is a limit to this. We want some variety, some independence in our work. But we can easily get too much. I have heard as many complaints and felt in myself as many objections against variety as against monotony. I have seen and felt as much discontent with "uncharted freedom" as with irksome restraint. Bewilderment, a sense of incompetence and of rudderless drifting, are never far off from any one of us in our work. There is in all of us something that likes to trot along in harness, — not too tight or galling, to be sure, — but still in guidance and with support. That makes us show our best paces.

Nor is there anything slavish or humiliating in this. It is simply the admission that we are not ready at every moment to be original, inventive, creative! We have found out the immense strain and cost of fresh thinking. We are certain that we were not born to be at it perpetually. We want some rest in our work, some relief from high tension. Monotony supplies that relief. Moreover the rhythmic and habitual elements in us (ancient, labor-saving devices) demand their representation. To do something again and again, as the trees, the birds, and our own hearts do, is a fundamental need which demands and receives satisfaction in work as well as in play.

For the tragedies and abominations, the slaveries and degradations, of manual labor, we cannot put all the blame on the large element of monotony and repetition which such labor often contains. We should revolt and destroy any undertaking that was not somewhat monotonous. But the point is that work ought to offer to each worker as much variety and independence as he has originality and genius, no more and no less. Give us either more or less than our share and we are miserable. We can be crushed and overdriven by too much responsibility, as well as by too little. Our initiative as well as our docility can be overworked.

We want a boss, especially in heavy or monotonous work. Most monotonous work is of the sort that is cut out and supplied ready to hand. This implies that some one else plans and directs it. If we are to do the pulling, some one else should hold the reins. When I am digging my wife's garden-beds, I want her to specify where they shall go. We all want a master of some kind, and most of us want a master in human shape. The more manual our work is the more we want him. Boatmen poling a scow through a creek need some one to steer and to tell them which should push harder as they turn the bends of the stream. The steersman may be chosen by lot or each may steer in turn, but some boss we must have, for when we are poling we can't well steer and we don't want the strain of trying fruitlessly to do both. This example seems to me to typify a large proportion of the world's work. It demands to be bossed, and it is more efficient, even more original, when it is bossed,—just enough!

Monotony, then, and bossing we need, but in our own quantity and also of our own kind. For there are different kinds (as well as different doses) and some are better than others. For example, to go to the same place of work every day is a monotony that simplifies life advantageously for most of us, but to teach the same subject over and over again is for most teachers an evil, though it may be just now a necessary evil.

We must try to distinguish. When we delight in thinking ourselves abused, or allow ourselves the luxury of grumbling, we often single out monotony as the target of our wrath. But we must not take all complaints (our own or other people's) at their face value. A coat is a misfit if it is too big or too small, or if it puckers in the wrong place. A job can be a misfit in twenty different ways and can be complained of in as many different tones. Let us be clear about this. If our discontent is as divine as it feels, it is not because all monotony is evil, but because our own particular share and kind of monotony have proved to be a degrading waste of energy.

We want to see the product of our work. The bridge we planned, the house we built, the shoes we cobbled, help us to get before ourselves and so to realize more than a moment's worth of life and effort. The impermanence of each instant's thought, the transience of every flush of effort, tends to make our lives seem shadowy even to ourselves. Our memory is a sieve through which most that we pick up runs back like sand. But in work we find refuge and stability, for in the accumulated product of many days' labor we can build up and present at last to our own sight the durable structure of what we meant to do. Then we can believe that our intentions, our hopes, our plans, our daily food and drink, have not passed through us for nothing, for we have funded their worth in some tangible achievement which outlasts them.

Further, such external proofs of our efficiency win us not only self-respect, but the recognition of others. We need something to show for ourselves, something to prove that our dreams are not impotent. Work gives us the means to prove it.

I want to acknowledge here my agreement in the charge often brought against modern factory labor, — namely, that since no workman plans or finishes his product, no one can recognize his product, take pride in it, or see its defects. Even when factory labor is well paid, its impersonal and wholesale merging of the man in the machine goes far to make it unfit for men and women.

"Goes far," I say,—but not the whole way. For division of labor means specialism, and specialism, as we know in the professions, has its glories despite its dangers. A specialty, as Professor G. H. Palmer has told us,[1] can be a window through which we look out on all the world. One subject, deeply studied, gives us clues and analogies to many others, gives us membership in the freemasonry of those who have mastered something, develops the power to respect and the right to be respected. I have known as patients men who, through their mastery of one small process in watchmaking, had developed a liberal outlook on other difficult arts, a just pride in good workmanship and an inventor's energy. This is not common or easy in any sort of specialism, but it is never impossible.

We want a handle to our name. Every one has a right to the distinction which titles of nobility are meant to give, but it is from our work that we should get them. The grocer, the trapper, the night-watchman, the cook, is a person fit to be recognized, both by his own timid self and by the rest of the world. In time the title of our job comes to stand for us, to enlarge our personality and to give us permanence. Thus it supplements the standing which is given us by our product. To "hold down a job" gives us a place in the world, something approaching the home for which in some form or other every one longs. "Have you any place for me?" we ask with eagerness; for until we find "a place" we are tramps, men without a country.

A man with a job has, at least in embryo, the kind of recognition from his own gang which we all crave. He

[1] G. H. Palmer, *The Teacher*, chap. VI. Houghton Mifflin Co.,1908.

has won membership in a club that he wants to belong
to and especially hates to be left out of. To be in it as
a member in full standing gives a taste of self-respect
and self-confidence.

Despite certain puritanical traditions there are many
people who like to accent the fact of their membership in the great club of job-holders by some scrap of
uniform, partly because this distinguishes them still
further from the untitled. A decidedly amateurish
pastry-cook of my acquaintance shifted from his bakery into private service at the first opportunity, but
the flat-topped white cap which he had acquired in the
bakery he cherished still when he was set to work in
the tiny kitchen of a mountain shanty. It was his badge
of office and he was proud of it. Why should nurses
and naval officers have uniforms and rejoice in them,
while bankers and professors remain undistinguished?
I see no good reason for the arbitrary decrees of fashion
in such matters. While on duty I think every trade and
every profession should have its distinguishing dress.
Our common citizenship while off duty would then be
all the better expressed.

I have been trying to point out the features which
ought to dignify and enrich our work. Mastery, tangible
achievement, and the title which goes with even the
most unsatisfactory job enlarge our personality by
making us stand for something permanent and recog-
nizable. So does connection with a firm, a college, a
municipality, a labor union, a trade association. The

consciousness of membership takes away something of the self-seeking character of economic effort. Even when we feel hostile to the people or the policies just now in control of our working group, we find both a stimulus and a wholesome restraint in the membership.

We want congeniality with our fellow workmen. One of the few non-physical "points" which people have already learned to look for in selecting work is the temper and character of the "boss." Men, and especially women, care almost as much about this as about the hours and wages of the job. Young physicians will work in a laboratory at starvation wages for the sake of being near a great teacher, even though he rarely notices them. The congeniality of fellow workmen is almost as important as the temper of the boss. Two unfriendly stenographers in a single room will often give up their work and take lower wages elsewhere in order to escape each other.

All this is so obvious to those who look for jobs that I wonder why so few employers have noticed it. The housewives who keep their servants, the manufacturers who avoid strikes, are not always those who pay the best wages and offer the best conditions of work. The human facts, the personal relations of employer and employee, are often disregarded, but always at the employer's peril. The personal factor is as great as the economic in the industrial unrest of to-day.

Are not even the "captains of industry" beginning to wake up to this fact?

The psychical standards which I have now tried to enumerate, — balanced variety and monotony, initiative and supervision, the chance to subjugate nature or personally to create something, pleasant companionship, a title and an institutional connection, — go far to give us happiness in work. But even if we have the ideal job there is much in the temper with which we take it. Our temperament may be one of those incurably sad or anxious ones that can never pluck any values out of daily existence or draw them from the future by anticipation. The remedies for this are hard to seek. They can rarely be found in work, sometimes in play, in love, or in worship.

CHAPTER V

THE REPROACH OF COMMERCIALISM: THOUGHT AND ACTION IN WORK

IF any one tells me that Modern America is lamentably, even dangerously, weak in the capacity to appreciate the accumulated treasures of literature, to learn the lesson of history, and to distinguish true from shoddy goods in philosophy and art, I have to agree. Nor can I deny that we are ludicrously unaware of the exuberant life of the trees and flowers, so close around us, so full of their own kind of ingenuity, skill, and strength, as well as of beauty. We don't know much about animals, clouds, mountains, or rivers, — which could give us pointers about our jobs as well as a shiver of admiration at the way they do theirs. We are dunces at music, sculpture, poetry, religion. The only arts we appreciate are drama, dancing, and baseball, the only "literature" we read is in the newspapers.

Yet, when my old friend Thomas Davidson[1] used to rail at the commercialism of our time and compare our life disdainfully with that of Athens, its temples with our factories, its Platonic and Aristotelian wisdom with our cheap newspaper sensationalism, its art with our ugliness, I always wondered what would become of a people all of whom sat under apple trees writ-

[1] C. W. Bakewell, *Thomas Davidson: A Memoir.*

ing poetry. We can no more live by admiring each other's sculpture than by taking in each other's washing. It would be an awful fate to live among a nation of artists and philosophers, or to read nothing but epics and sonnets in the morning paper. Like most of those who hanker after Greek perfection, Davidson seemed to ignore the fact that only a vast subterranean foundation of slave labor and trade made possible the precarious superstructure of Greek art and philosophy.

At Brook Farm, where in the early forties the reformers tried to abolish commercialism, the result was that a few devoted people nearly slaved themselves to death while the rest of the party felt themselves "called" to comparatively easy tasks. Take away our "commercialism" and we should obviously starve; but even while the provisions lasted we should be bored and miserable. Poets and prophets leaven the lump of ordinary humanity; but to live with a townful of them would be as insufferable as eating twenty dinners on end. Most art and most philosophy ought to be the by-product or the holiday adventure of lives soaked through by the teaching of more humdrum occupations. The artistic, philosophic, literary, or scientific specialist ought always to be as rare as a jewel or a high light, getting his meaning and power from his setting.

Without commercialism, most folks, while waiting for starvation, would have to loaf or tramp. They would be far more unhappy as well as far more vicious than they are now. For Satan is still on the job. The human world has always been a commercial world, busy for the most part like the birds in getting its living.

Whether we are socialists or apostles of art, culture, and the spiritual life, all that we have a right to object to in modern commercialism is that while centralizing industry it has also partially crushed individuality. The man who made a whole house and who lived in a whole house must have developed in the process more human nature, more skill, ingenuity, and resource than the man who specializes on window blinds and lives in a tenement.

No one admires the type of man who lives on bananas in a tropical island and usually can't be hired to work, because a few days' labor each year will feed him. We all agree, I take it, that we should n't want (even if we could get it) a planet peopled with beautiful child-like loafers such as Stevenson and LaFarge found in the islands of the Pacific. We agree that men need regular work, with hardship, responsibility, and strain, not as their chief reward, but as an element in their daily occupation. The robust, the resourceful, the venture-some, the tough, persistent characteristics which we all prize in men and women don't develop (so far as anybody knows) *in vacuo*, — without the pressure and drive which if overdone beget slavery. As long as we prize these characteristics we shall always need to keep a sharp lookout lest industry make slaves of us. There is something fearful about the industry of great and fruitful workers, something ascetic and at times

almost barbaric. They narrowly escape being conquered by their work.

But such narrow escapes for the soul are not peculiar
to commercialism. The advancing organization of
science is always close to pedantry; the possessor of
good habits is always on the verge of becoming a creature of habit, the person of acute sensibility is always
on the brink of sentimentalism. No age and no organization of society can escape such dangers. Any one who
thinks we can get more of the benefits of organized industry with less of its dreadful by-products must show
us how to do it. Meantime, it is idiotic for us to
reproach ourselves and our age for being commercial.
We can blame ourselves only for not being more of
something else beside commercial, or for being commercial in so unintelligent a way; for a man without
muscles would be no more of a monstrosity than an
age without commerce. I think that commerce, like
muscles, can be made beautiful, intelligent, and resourceful as well as powerful. To make it so is our
present need.

Many of those who decry "commercialism" are
fond of accenting the contrast between those who work
with their brains and those whose work they suppose
to be merely manual or muscular. In their desire to
exalt the spiritual powers of man they are fond of making a hierarchy in which lawyers, writers, teachers,
poets, philosophers, preachers, and statesmen come at

the top, while those who use their senses and their muscles come at the bottom.

But is head-work nobler than hand-work? Should we all strive to become brain-workers as far and as fast as we can? Or at the other extreme is Tolstoy right when he insists that every one should do "bread-work," something that directly increases the amount of food upon the earth?

The important distinction which these phrases are meant to mark is that between *thought and action:* — thought plans action; action executes thought. The instant that thought relinquishes its task of exploring the future and closes the office where various plans and alterations are being appraised, a relatively mechanical "carrying-out" process begins. Simply to carry out a fixed and detailed plan is so machine-like that a machine will probably be devised to do it better. For the new machines that carry out the logical consequences of any proposition, the machines that copy or that perform the arithmetical process of adding, subtracting, multiplying, and dividing, are not the less machines because they do what is often called "clerical" work. They do not call up the past, they do not plan or choose between future alternatives.

It would seem, then, as if all labor were tending to become more and more motionless and mental while many machines and a few unskilled machine-tenders take from the skilled workers and the *entrepreneurs* the monotonous, exhausting, mindless portions of the world's work. But while this is something like the truth, there are some further facts, rather shy and unnoticed, that make the separation of thought and action even less wide.

Mr. Greenhorn's plans have this form: "I will say to Nature x; she will answer y; I will then rejoin with z"; and so on. For example, "I will get an axe and chop into the base of that tree. It will fall toward the stream and I will then tow it down." Or: "I will put this patient in a sanitarium. She will get rested. I will then take out her appendix." Or: "I will buy some of this railroad stock offered me as a special favor. I will go in 'on the ground floor,' and when the railroad flourishes, I shall get rich."

The second step in each of these processes, the spontaneous maturing of our project, is the one on which labor men suppose "capitalists" are resting. Nature carries out our plan: we sit back and cut the coupons when they mature. But do things work out so? The tree we planned to fall into the stream gets caught overhead in a most unforeseeable way. It can be worked free; but a new plan, modifying the old one, must be made first. The patient's "rest cure" may not rest her at all. I may find that nothing rests her but work, and meantime the appendix quiets down and does n't have to be removed.

The material into which our plan burrows like a tunnel under construction, is always more or less refractory. Whether it is the actors of our cast, the

characters of our novel, the voters of our district, the
members of our week-end party, the steel of our cast-
ings, the wood we are carving, — in any case the "material" resists more or less. Hence we are forced to
feel our way and to form while in action a considerable
part of our plan.

Though this is trite and obvious, we often forget it
when we are declaiming about the divorce of manual
labor from mental work, or the chasm between thought
and action. *Good thinking feels its way by action. Good
manual work is full of thought.* Is the sculptor's task
manual or mental? Of course bad sculpture may be
purely manual (that is, purely imitative or conventional). There is also an opposite kind of sculptural
monstrosity, which looks as if it were gnawed out of
the stone by a man without hands. Does a man sing
with his soul or with his vocal cords? Some "vocal
artists" seem to be all vocalization and nothing else;
some voiceless sentimentalists seem to be trying to sing
without opening their mouths. But is n't it clear as day
that brain and muscle wait each upon the other for the
opportunity to do what God meant them to do? The
wise thought, the successful plan says: "I'll say to
Nature x, and then see what she says. My next step,
y, will depend upon her answer." Her answer comes to
us through our muscles and our senses, and keeps us
alive from head to foot. It is married to our thought
and completes it.

We cannot value manual work, — what Tolstoy

calls "bread-work," — merely because it is *not* brain-work. Yet his warnings may be greatly needed. He is right in telling us that we may get warped and neurasthenic, cold-hearted and footless, if our muscles are never used, our vitality never husbanded by the monotony of routine and the simplicity of the elemental. Yet farmers are not all wise and virtuous. Tolstoy's solution of our difficulty is too simple. If the race is getting stunted and neurotic, puny and degenerate, because it is tied down to any particular kind of work, disproportionately manual or mental, it is time for revolution or reform. Somewhere in our life, in our play, if not in our work, every part and element in us ought to find a chance to praise God in its own fashion.

If indoor work, machine work, literary work, farm work, or any other job leaves a large part of us unserviceable, then we ought either to find some outlet for that strength during the hours away from work or to change the work. But I don't find that agriculture has turned out any better type of man than railroading and shopkeeping. That it weakens health is a serious indictment of any trade; but so far we have no proof that the health of manual workers is any better than the health of those of us who use our brains as well as our hands.

Tolstoy does not convince me that we are always kinder, more neighborly, more comradely in the more elemental and manual trades than in brain-work. A touch of nature does make all the world kin, but it is a touch rather than prolonged pressure. The elemental, impinging in the form of sharp, brief illness, may bring a family together. But chronic illness, prolonged and infiltrated through days, nights, meals, and holidays, may estrange and embitter a family. A party of people cruising on a yacht get wonderfully friendly and even intimate during a week's trip, provided the yacht is not so luxurious as to exclude them from the work of sailing her. But this is true just because the contact with elemental life is a passing one. A shortage of food or even the long continuance of comfortable cruising life sometimes wears out nature's power to make our souls kin. When we are tied to such a life, as Dana was in his "Two Years before the Mast," we do not appear to treat each other more kindly than the city folk.

Action staged always among elemental conditions cannot be trusted to make us wise. But neither can we depend upon slippered "thinkers" for wisdom. If the problem is to know what's wrong with a business, what people will buy, how an election is to be won, or when the psychological moment for action has arrived, he is most likely to be right who can muster the widest range of human experiences, hold them fairly before him in review, like a hand of cards, and then judge.

A state superintendent of education might seem to be as much emancipated from the need of manual work as any one could be. He deals with mental and spiritual problems, with the course of study, with the personalities of teachers and pupils, the humor of parents, school committees, and legislatures. True; but that is not all. He has also to test out courses in music, drawing, physical culture, hygiene, manual and industrial training, and even if he decides to rule them all out of his curriculum, he must know just what they are before he can exclude them wisely. He will be unfair to athletics, to drawing, to forge-work, to folk-dancing, nature study, or sex hygiene, unless he is an all-round man and not merely a pedagogue. He must have done enough work with every sense, with every muscle, to know its worth and its dangers.

Just what dose of original planning and what stint of executing other people's plans is good for each individual is never a fixed quantity. But every one needs both, and therefore no one can make a hierarchy with the "mental" or "spiritual" tasks at the top and the "manual" ones at the bottom. The proportion of thought and of action which is proper to each of us depends somewhat upon our age. Hence the ordinary process of promotion from less responsible and simpler to more complex and difficult positions as men get older is, I think, somewhere near what it ought to be. For old men are apt to be wiser in counsel; to use and balance their energies they need less of a grapple with the elemental than when they were young. They ought not to be hustling like the youngsters, for if they really were youngsters once and were not born old, all the old activities of eye, ear, and hand, all the crudities and the elementals will sit as representatives in the chamber of their minds and contribute their vote when called for.

Commercialism, then, should not be used as a term of reproach. Like romanticism or asceticism it has its good and its bad side. What it needs is reshaping to fit our actual needs rather than the accidents of development. Remembering how intolerable a world of poets and philosophers would be, we should never say or imply that work which deals largely with material objects is any lower in the scale of worth than the calling of the thinker or the scholar. For science and art are most intimately concerned with the material world and derive from it their expressions of truth and beauty. The practice of any art or craft cuts clean across the distinctions between "mental" and "manual" work and weaves both into a truer whole.

Let us abolish terms like "physical culture" or "mental training." To be concerned either with one's mind or one's body is a morbid practice. One should be occupied with tasks that make us forget both mind and body in a higher union of both.

Thought is not nobler than action. It is the first or last stage of action and its worth depends on the act which it plans or mirrors. Good thinking is reshaped again and again by contact with the obstacles and demurrers of its material. The proportions of thought and action, of commerce and poetry, in any life, must be worked out by each person, each nation, and each age to fit individual needs.

Action, manual work, Tolstoy's "bread-work," are not nobler than the practice of art, science, and government. Tolstoy was right in insisting that morally and intellectually we need to use our muscles as well as our minds, wrong in supposing that his own noble scheme of life is ordained for all.

CHAPTER VI

THE GLORY OF RAW MATERIAL

THE material side of life may be enjoyed, scorned, endured, investigated, or ignored. We may wallow in it luxuriously. We may try to forget it and live above it. We may bear with it (sullenly or stoically) as the coal-heaver does. We may turn it into physics and chemistry. We may not notice it at all. These five ways of behavior towards the cruder facts of life are familiar enough to all. We all know sensualists, idealists, day-laborers, and scientists, — besides many who are not concerned in any way with our present problems.

But I am especially interested in another type, one which has figured brilliantly in the writings of Charles Ferguson and Gerald Stanley Lee, yet is still too little appreciated. I mean the man who genuinely respects and even loves the material world, but is very silent about it. The object of the present chapter is to describe this man, and the world as he sees it. He belongs in this section of my book, because he is not only a worker, but *the* typical worker of the present day, soaked with the spirit of work and therefore with respect for matter and with knowledge of its nature. He is incarnate in some of the best doctors, scientists, and business men of my acquaintance, but I shall begin with his most superficial and forbidding aspect, the face that he turns, in self-defense, to an unsympathizing world.

To match his mood of incessant industry there has grown up in him a certain "set" of the spiritual muscles. His mind is bent down and inward like the prehensile hands of the day-laborer. Outwardly he is stoical and grim, not because he is low-spirited, but because he wants to protest against sentimentalism and gush. He abhors a book like this because he is sick of all theorizing. "Tall talk, but mighty little performance," is his favorite phrase of reproach. Vividly conscious of his own limitations and of the world's vast and dangerous power, he is like a burnt child who fears life's fires.

Most of all, perhaps, he fears the flames of emotion, of love, worship, and hot faith. He sees fools hovering about those flames, eager, boastful, and reckless. He has his own type of enthusiasm, — well hidden beneath a stoical exterior, — but his work has taught him chiefly humility. Indeed, he is humble not only for himself, but for the whole race; too humble to expect progress, divinity, or immortality. Absolute assurance on all such matters has been knocked out of him by nature's stubborn resistance to his attack. He bows before the world with a shrug and a patient stoop.

Silence is characteristic of the man whom I am describing, and therefore I am all the more eager to describe him. He is taciturn, partly because he has little aptitude for words as a medium of exchange, partly because he never forgets Booker Washington's story of the Negro who found the cotton he was picking so "grassy" and the sun so powerful hot that he guessed he had a call to preach. People who give up work and turn to talking about socialism or religion, because talking is easier than working, excite in him a holy horror. The smooth drawing-room ideals which they teach so glibly are sure to end as they began, in talk. "Those who can, do; those who can't, teach," he says with scorn.

I agree with much of this indictment. Idealism does often begin in talk the tasks that it never finishes in action. The discouragements encountered as we approach the later and harder places of an undertaking lead many of us to glide out of it and start a new one. Our devious and scrappy lives follow Chesterton's revised version of Longfellow: —

"Toiling, rejoicing, sorrowing, so I my life conduct.
Each morning sees some task begun, each evening sees it chucked."

Reformers love to talk and think, for in thought we can freely shape the early stages of great projects. But when we begin to carry them out, we get into regions not so malleable by thought, — regions full of obstacles that make us feel ignorant and helpless.

Such obstacles the creative worker whom I am here describing has often fought and conquered. When he remembers the blood and sweat which he has expended in the struggle, he feels a deep respect for the enemy who made him work so hard, and deep disdain for those who are always lisping out the beginnings of campaigns in high-sounding phrases, but never completing their sentence in action. A legislative campaign, for instance, often begins in eloquent and glorious discussion. That is easy and pleasant. But in its later complications, among the quick thrusts and parries at close range, the glory goes out of it; it becomes sheer work. The fight to a finish is the best test of sincerity and strength. Then it is that contact with hard facts begins to knock the conceit out of us.

For the pioneer whom I describe the world is colored by memories of many such fights. He thinks of it and attacks it as a mass of resistance, a huge and humbling opponent. The knots in lumber, the frost which spoils crops and orange trees, the aridity and barrenness of soils, earthquakes which devastate cities, fires that wipe out forests, are obstacles that make us respect the enemy and remember our littleness. But the pioneer whose praises I am now celebrating, the creative worker and subduer of nature, is merely humbled, not crushed, by his contact with the material world. Its crude, tough resistance nerves his spirit's leap. For matter is the sire of necessity, as necessity is the mother of invention. The defiance of unbridged streams and devastating disease kindles his fighting spirit to subdue them. They are whip and spur to his imagination. Inventiveness and valor are born of the contact. The lure of the unconquered, the threat of death and disaster, draw out of him resources of ingenuity which could never have been born unaided. The shock of raw nature's adventures and incalculable chances string him taut like a cold bath. He sees his work fronting him, and runs to meet it with fierce joy.

He knows that he need not run far. He need not always be venturing into the wilderness. The raw material of creative work is close at hand. There is plenty of elemental resistance to be met in homely facts like the stupidity of school children, male voters, and un-enfranchised women, the recalcitrancy of old habits, the anarchy of warring elements within us, the resulting vice and crime of cities, the resulting languor and de-gradation of country districts. Plenty of virgin soil for cultivation here. Plenty of untrodden wastes to be explored.

For the "material world" is not only outside us. It is inside us as well. We can recognize it everywhere by the familiar marks of crudity, resistance, disorder, and darkness. Rhapsodies about the universe may seem less poetical to conventional minds if we cross out the word "nature" wherever it occurs, and substitute "my body" or "my cross old aunt," or "my own stupidity." But there is poetry enough in all these tragic facts, and work enough, too. No one can deny that our own uncivilized impulses, organs, and relatives are part of nature and afford ample food for wonder, for ingenuity, and for taming the wild. We need not take ship for distant lands or hark back to savagery. There is chaos enough close at hand; there is beauty enough also.

The pioneer is well aware of this. He begins at home and in the back yard. In his rôle of engineer he has been recently offering us advice in matters of health and education. He will not be confined to spanning deserts and torrents. He knows that the terror and havoc of raw nature oppress us just in proportion to our ignorance, our forgetfulness, and our dullness. *These* make volcanoes terrific, climates deadly, and soils sterile. *These* crowd our foreground with dull pupils, venal corporations, and applicants for divorce. So long as we are too stupid to conquer it, the material world is a perpetual menace to our false security. The best flowers of art, science, and virtue are always in danger while ignorance grumbles underground in volcanic unrest.

But is not this very danger a temptation to better work? Like a prophet, and in the spirit of Carlyle, the material world summons us to be up and doing. To defend our homes and our civilization we must fight the inroads of chaos upon our little trim corner of the cosmos. But we must also fight against our own self-satisfaction, and in this campaign the creative worker with bent back and stern face is still our leader. He teaches us to see our civilization as all too human and man-made. Fresh from contact with elemental forces, he finds our civilization reeking of our littleness as well as of our valiant endeavor. He finds it tame, academic, formal; for it repeats itself and every one's self.

In contrast with all this smugness of so-called civilization, the creative worker sees nature as the vast store-house of the undiscovered. What is now "brute fact," crude matter, animal instinct, contains all the future possibilities of discovery and of creation. Reverence for the material is the recognition of this infinite resourcefulness on the part of nature, together with a manly welcome for the buffets which come to us in work, — "turn earth's smoothness rough," and shape our faculties to learn new truth.

This reverence becomes love in those who realize that the material world provides what most of all their spirits crave: an outlet for the adventurous, the romantic and heroic impulses. To set them afire, the initial check and friction of the elemental are just what is needed.

Why have I linked the material side of existence with work rather than with play, love, or worship? Because play, love, and worship do not so often force us into humbling yet ultimately refreshing contact with what is crude. So long as it is play to shingle a roof, we do not notice the ache of our cramped legs, nor the strain upon our back muscles. When these elemental discomforts force themselves upon our notice, the shingling-game begins to feel like work. When love meets resistance, when it is thwarted by the screens of flesh, forgetfulness, distance, misunderstanding, and rivalry, it too begins to seem like work. It becomes a loyalty worth working for, or else a hateful and hopeless drudgery.

Because this is so, — because work forces us to stare almost incessantly at the material world and gives us, despite its fascinations, so huge a slice of humble pie, — we are always in danger of biting off more than we can chew, imbibing more ugliness than we transform and assimilate. But that is a chance which we must take, all the more cheerfully because history has taught us that honest pessimism, and even honest atheism, bring about precious reforms in conventional religion, purifying it by revolt against its all too easy solution of the riddle of existence. If you become a "materialist" in the popular sense, you may arouse the dormant faith of your age, as the resistance of a tough wad adds force to the ignited powder behind it.

Nevertheless our long bondage to the elemental and to earth is not always good for us. Our self-abasement in work may become barren and dreary because the work has become the extinguisher of the soul which it was meant decently to clothe. To be spiritually abased by work is virtue; to be spiritually squashed by work is failure. Common sense should teach us to take off the kettle when it boils, rather than humbly wait and be scalded when it spits.

Of course I am speaking here not of the low-paid wage-earners who are often weighed down and blighted by the burdens of our industrial system. I am concerned here and throughout this chapter with the "pushing man," relatively well-to-do, strong, sound-sleeping, and of voracious appetite. His danger is to be squashed or scalded not by reason of poverty or overstrain, but because he does not raise his head from work to notice the ancient and beautiful world in which he lives. Industrial reform will not help him much. What he needs is common sense.

CHAPTER VII

THE RADIATIONS OF WORK

THE good intentions with which hell is paved are those that we offer as excuses for inaction, not the intentions which remain unfulfilled despite our best efforts to make them good. If you say, "No, I have not done anything this month, but I have had the best of intentions," you have condemned all the days which you describe. But if you say nothing about your intentions, make no apologies, but do your level best, then your unfulfilled intentions speak for you with the tongues of men and angels. Sincere intentions left unfulfilled despite our best efforts are perhaps the most valuable parts and the best fruits of character.

In any action we may distinguish two parts: First, what the person himself knowingly and intentionally does. Second, and most valuable, the unconscious radiations which emanate from any one in full activity. These unconscious products, which are by far the best of our output, are like the quiet by-effects of a college, — what students get "just by rubbing against the walls of college buildings." Likewise unconscious are the best teachings of the mother who serves high ideals and intends to impart them to her children. She does not deliver just those goods, yet her intentions are not fruitless. The good which she does may issue in quite another direction from that which she planned, yet if she had not made that apparently futile plan, she would not have achieved her unconscious but beneficent influence.

This explains part of Luther's insistence that of himself a man can do nothing, that his efforts are *nil* and God's grace all. A literal reading of this logic would make us give up trying, as some misguided teachers have advised. But the truth seems to be that we should give up expecting to accomplish anything just as we plan it, and should not be disappointed if

"All we have hoped for and darkly have groped for
Come not in the form that we prayed that it should." [1]

Luther's insistence that no man can be "saved" (i.e., can accomplish anything that he really wants to accomplish) by "good works," and that works without faith are dross, can be justified if we are not too literal in our understanding of his terms. Your "works" are what you do self-consciously and with the effort to assume a virtue though you have it not. But your real success is not attained, your real merit is not limited, by the pitifully small results which you thus achieve. From the standpoint of achievement we are all failures, although, as Stevenson says, we can be "faithful failures" and through faithfulness attain such success as we deserve.

I want to exemplify the value of our unconscious

[1] From Gelett Burgess's stirring poem, "Here 's to the Cause."

output in four different fields: in morals, in music, in business, and in science.

. The unconscious radiations of *moral* "example" don't work when the man is trying to set an example. Character talks when we are silent. A doctor wins confidence, not by what he says, but by his methods, what he takes for granted, his unconscious presence, the foundations of his certainty laid in years of hard work. For a similar reason the authority of Miss Jane Addams springs less from what she says than from what she has done, from the unconscious influence of her character previously known to her audiences, and to the whole country.

Tschaikowsky's [1] method of *musical composition* illustrates the point, but here the unconscious radiations of work illumine first of all the worker himself, his better self, — lost to sight for the time being till the radiations search him out. Tschaikowsky found that his inspired self, the creator in him, often got lost and could be found only through the lantern of hard work, — a lantern so constructed that it threw no light behind it, no light on the plodding working self. He found that inspiration for composition often failed him wholly. For weeks at a time he could force out nothing that he valued. Yet if he waited patiently or impatiently for the inspiration, it did not come, for the kingdom of heaven and the inspirations of genius come not with

[1] M. I. Tchaikowsky, *Life and Letters of Peter I. Tchaikowsky.* John Lane, 1908.

observation. He found that he must go to his desk each day and do something, the best he could, to get out some music. Then, in time, and quite unexpectedly, rich musical ideas would come pouring into his head (whence, God only knows) faster than he could write them down. They were the unconscious radiations of his uninspired daily toil.

Competent *business* men have told me that the best new ideas about their work come to them quite unexpectedly, often on a holiday when their minds were not trying to evolve anything of the kind. Yet, if they take a permanent holiday no such inspirations come. In business or anywhere else the best fruit of work is, of course, originality. That is what brings money, fame, lasting usefulness, and it is what every worker wants to get out of his efforts. But all originality, all new ideas are miracles and come through us rather than of our own making.

So it is that ideas come to us in *science*. "Any one who works hard," says Ostwald, the world-renowned physical chemist in his *Natur philosophie*, "will find something new." But this "something" is usually found, accidentally as we say, while we are looking for something else. It is in this sense that genius results from taking infinite pains. It produces something never looked for, yet something which without the infinite pains could never have come to light.

The heretical Scylla is to suppose that we are "justified" by our works themselves, achieved with our own naked "self-made" hands. The heretical Charybdis is to suppose that because action is greater in its by-products than its intention, therefore action is useless. Religious tradition, artistic experience, the history of scientific discoveries, the natural history of personal influence in families, friendship, school-teaching, public life, the "best ideas" of the man of action, — all these lines of evidence converge to show that the flower of a man's work is that which he does not directly intend or deserve. His flashes of genius spring, — he knows not how, — like a flower from the deep root of his faithful labor. He labors in faith that some good not now seen or certain will somehow, somewhere come, if only he does his best.

We are accustomed to think of "genius" mostly in the field of the fine arts, but I believe that all the unconscious by-products of faithful work are fashioned from the stuff of genius. Genius has its part in industrial invention, in scientific discoveries, in good jokes, in the happy grace of a skillful hostess. It plays through our disciplined natures to express the higher purposes of the race. Conscientious effort to win virtue or success by direct attack, is for most men the necessary precursor of genius, yet the effort itself is clumsy and amateurish. For all self-conscious effort to do better than one has hitherto done involves impersonation, as I shall try to explain more fully in "Play" (chapter XVII). We assume the virtue not yet possessed and try to play up to the character which we aspire to attain.

Indeed, from one point of view this is the whole of morality. But in our highest moments, in all genius and heroism, whenever we are swept along by generous or aspiring impulse, impersonation and self-consciousness vanish. Somehow the deed is done, and as we look back we see that it springs out in the direction of our previous and painful efforts to do right. But it astonishes the doer almost as much as the beholder. Who can say that Shelley is wrong if he attributes his moments of genius to a Power who is greater than himself, yet always at hand as answer to the prayer of utter sincerity?

CHAPTER VIII

WORK AND LOYALTY: THE IDEALIZATION OF WORK

I WAS returning some years ago from a medical meeting in Washington, D.C., when I had the good fortune to overhear in the Pullman smoking-compartment a bit of conversation between the best-known doctor and the best-known lawyer in Boston. Both had been taking a bit of vacation at the capital. Both were fierce, hungry workers; each loved his profession and led it.

"I hope," said the doctor to the lawyer, "that you are coming back to your work with fresh enthusiasm."

The lawyer laughed and shrugged his shoulders, then puffed his cigar and looked out of the window with a grim smile.

"Because," went on the doctor, "you ought to set us all a good example and convert us to righteousness. I'm coming back to *my* work with *loathing*."

"What!" says the novice, "don't they like their work after all; if they do, why do they hate to come back to it?" Yes, that's just the paradox which we must get used to, because it is a true reading of the facts. These men loved their calling as soon as they were in harness, yet when out of harness they sometimes sank into moods of revolt.

"Out of harness!" There's a deal of significance in that trivial phrase. For all work is a yoke and a harness.

We slip it off every night (or ought to) and many times we hate to slip it on again in the morning. We slip it off (or try to) when we get round to our Sundays and vacations. It is often hard to put it on again, all the harder sometimes if the vacation, the opera, the base-ball game, has relaxed our muscles and made us forget how to carry the burdens and responsibilities of our trade.

This paradox, loving a task on the whole and yet hating it when we are "out of harness," must be a per-sonal experience to many of us as it is to me. I have loved my work intensely and for many years, yet I often feel an absolute repulsion for it when I've been "out of harness" a little while. I have all the anarchic caprices, irrational freaks, and dispirited morning lan-guors pictured by William James: "I know a person, for example, who will poke the fire, set chairs straight, pick dust-specks from the floor, arrange his table, snatch up the newspaper, take down any book which catches his eyes, trim his nails, waste the morning *anyhow*, in short, and all without premeditation, simply because the only thing he *ought* to attend to is the prep-aration of a lesson in formal logic which he detests. *Anything but that!*"[1]

Such a mood is not wholly devilish. If we look coolly at it, even while we are shaking it off, we shall see some sense in our revolt. Although a man ought to make a harness for himself and wear it, although only

[1] William James, *The Principles of Psychology*, vol. I, p. 421.

that harness will enable him to support the responsibilities which I've been celebrating, yet he should be able to see himself, sometimes, as a tiny ant, hurrying about to accomplish an ant's proportion of the world's work, but no more. Then his harness looks cheap and mean.

And though our work and our science are symbolic, as I believe, of an eternal and glorious destiny, they are literally very inglorious and insignificant. Only their intention, only the vision that creates and sustains them, is great. Our work is the best we know, and in it as in a ship we have embarked with our treasures; but still it is human-made, and bears the impress of our limitations. Work seen literally is a misfit, and now and then our tired eyes see it so; then it looks like a curse. We should spurn it but for a voice within us which rebukes literalism and calls it a lie. That voice is loyalty.

Loyalty is a force that holds a man to his job even in the moments when he hates it and sees no great significance in it. When this kind of blindness falls upon us, loyalty supplies a new method of guidance towards the substance of things not seen. Like all faith, it holds to the visible framework of daily labor by grim or by smiling determination. It bids us to be prompt at the office, to answer all letters at once, to look as brisk and interested as we can, till the mood passes and the familiar objects and occupations resume their halos.

The modern world is so out of sympathy with the language and atmosphere of religion that it is hard for most people to recognize religion in work. Yet I am convinced that into our prosaic and practical details of business life we often unconsciously transfer that ancient power to "invest the world with its own divinity" which is the essence of faith, though not of prayer. The faith with which we hold to the routine of our calling through moods of discontent and disillusionment, is not altogether different from the faith that makes heroes, saints, and martyrs, and gives them vision of God and of immortality.

William James has reminded us that we cannot fix attention on a point, because attention won't stay there: —

"Try to attend steadfastly to a dot on the paper or on the wall. You presently find that one or the other of two things has happened: either your vision has become blurred, so that you can see nothing distinct at all, or else you have involuntarily ceased to look at the dot in question and are looking at something else. But if you ask yourself successive questions about the dot, — how big it is, how far, of what shape, what shade of color, etc., — in other words if you turn it over, if you think of it in various ways and along with various kinds of associates, — you can keep your mind on it for a comparatively long time." [1]

Your mind circles round the point, connects it with

[1] *Talks to Teachers.* 1909, p. 104.

other points (distant, past, or future, hypothetical
and ideal variations, imaginary extensions or dimin-
utions). As soon as ever you begin to think about
anything, you begin to encircle it with a network of
context. This context may be due to very arbitrary
associations, sometimes harmless and neutral, sometimes vicious and destructive. The wolfish old Tartar
in Tolstoy's "Prisoner in the Caucasus" sees around
the head of every innocent Russian the malignant faces
of the Russian soldiers who once killed six of his seven
sons and forced him to kill the seventh with his own
hand. Though the face of a Russian may beam with
kindness and childlike purity, that is lost to sight in the
hovering cloud of memories which the old Tartar sees
round any Russian. Just because he is a Russian
the old Tartar bristles and snarls at him in fury. Hate
at first sight is thus as possible as love at first sight,
if one sees about a personality so intense a cloud of
hellish witnesses.

Emotional life, whether of enthusiasm or intense disgust, depends largely upon clouds or penumbræ, which
to a bystander may be quite invisible. Now and then
a man gets down to Peter Bell's level, where

> "A primrose by the river's brim
> A yellow primrose was to him ;
> And it was nothing more."

But most of us see above the primrose a cloud of associations of some sort. The momentous question is "What
sort, and how far does it reach?".

The best grade of penumbra is native, not imported. It belongs on him that wears it and is there discovered as well as created by the onlooker's faith. Its colors blend with the wearer's and are not in violent and unnatural contrast. When George Meredith's sentimental English youth fell out of love with Vittoria, the heroic Italian singer, because he detected a whiff of tobacco-smoke in her hair, he did what the old Tartar did, — forced down a wholly unnatural and unfit shadow upon an innocent creature's head.

When, on the other hand, a man sees in his towering factory chimney the promise and potency of all the business that is coming to him with its help, when he sees rising from that chimney a vision of the position he is to hold, the influence he is to wield, the improvements he will make in the customs of his trade and in the politics of his town, — that sort of penumbra really fits.

Such a net of associations clustering around a personality is made up of the things he stands for. Round a President's head we see the glories and the perils, the policies and war-cries of the United States. Round a baby's head his mother sees the promise of his future. Crowned with this halo of future glory, the baby represents far more than he literally is. For the principle of halos is the principle of symbolism and of representation, whereby everything means more than it shows on the surface.

There is nothing unusual or meritorious about halo making. Everybody goes beyond surfaces to some extent. But one of the most important of the differences between man and man is in the extent and quality of this halo-making faculty. Three artists before the same landscape will paint it quite differently, not so much because their eyes are different as because their interests are different. Each of a group of financiers facing the same opportunity will see different possibilities in it. But how far do we go, how wide, how accessible is the field of opportunity which we see in any business venture, any bit of untamed nature, any personal or political situation? If you know that, you can measure the essential differences between great capacity and moderate or small capacity.

The halo of origins, suggestions, and possibilities, about a person has, like all halos, a misty edge, growing dimmer as it recedes from its owner. More or less clearly we recognize that the halo has no definite end or margin. If we are busy and "practical" (as we usually are) we are not much interested in this misty fact; we are soon engrossed in putting through the plans which are the most obvious hints from the halo. At any time, however, our chatter may be struck dumb, our sleepy heads may be shocked broad awake by a sudden consciousness of what this mistiness means. It means that if we could follow the whole of anybody's halo we should grasp the whole universe and its meaning. For everybody stands for the universe, and is a small edition of it, not in what he achieves but in what he means. Everybody's halo really stretches to infinity, though our eyesight does not. Hence we are always staring and blinking at the whole, though we can distinguish only a tiny fragment of it.

No man who loves his work sees it without its halo; and because that halo really has no end, the love of work may at any moment take on a religious tinge. But whether or not we see this divinity in work, it is there, and we all live on its surface, upborne by it as by the solid earth.

CHAPTER IX

THE REWARDS OF WORK

PAYMENT can be given a workingman only for what some other man might have done, because the pay is fixed by estimate of "what the work is worth," i.e., what you can get other people to do it for. Hence you never pay any one for what he individually does, but for what "a man like him," — that wholly fictitious being, that supposedly fair specimen of his type and trade, — can be expected to do.

The man himself you cannot pay. Yet any one who does his work well, or gets satisfaction out of it, puts himself into it. Moreover, he does things that he cannot be given credit for, finishes parts that no one else will notice. Even a mediocre amateur musician knows that the best parts of his playing, his personal tributes to the genius of the composer whom he plays, are heard by no one but himself and "the God of things as they are." There might be bitterness in the thought that in our work we get paid or praised only for what is not particularly ours, while the work that we put our hearts into is not recognized or rewarded. But in the struggle for spiritual existence we adapt ourselves to the unappreciative features of our environment and learn to look elsewhere for recognition. We do not expect people to pay us for our best. We look to the approval of conscience, to the light of our ideal seen more clearly when our work is good, or to the judgment of God. Our terms differ more than our tendencies. The essential point is that for appreciation of our best work we look to a Judge more just and keen-sighted than our paymaster.

Nevertheless there is a spiritual value in being paid in hard cash. For though money is no measure of the individual value in work, it gives precious assurance of *some* value, some usefulness to people out of the worker's sight. Workers who do not need a money wage for the sake of anything that they can buy with it, still need it for its spiritual value. Doctors find this out when they try to get invalids or neurasthenics to work for the good of their health. Exercise done for exercise' sake is of very little value, even to the body, for half its purpose is to stimulate the will, and most wills refuse to rise at chest-weights and treadmills, however disguised. But our minds are still harder to fool with hygienic exercises done for the sake of keeping busy. To get any health or satisfaction out of work it must seem to the worker to be of some use. If he knows the market for raffia baskets is *nil*, and that he is merely being enticed into using his hands for the good of his muscles or of his soul, he soon gets a moral nausea at the whole attempt.

This is the flaw in ideals of studiousness and self-culture. It is not enough that the self-culture shall seem good to President A. Lawrence Lowell or to some kind

neurologist. The college boy himself, the psychoneu-
rotic herself, must feel some zest along with the labor
if it is to do any good. And this zest comes because
they believe that by this bit of work they are "getting somewhere," winning some standing among those
whose approval they desire, serving something or somebody besides the hired teacher or trainer.[1]

I once set a neurasthenic patient, formerly a stenog-
rapher, to helping me with the clerical work in my office.
She began to improve at once, because the rapid return
of her former technical skill made her believe (after
many months of idleness and gnawing worry about
money) that some day she might get back to work. But
what did her far more good was the check which I
sent her at the end of her first week's work. She had
not expected it, for she did not think her work good
enough. But she knew me well enough to know that
I had sworn off lying in all forms (even the most
philanthropic and hygienic) and would not deceive her
by pretending to value her work. The money was
good for what it would buy; it was even better because
it proved to her the world's need for what she could do,
and thus gave her a right to space and time upon the
earth.

[1] At Arequipa, Dr. Philip King Brown's sanitarium for the tuberculous, near Fairfax, California, this principle is recognized and embodied.
Dr. Brown has succeeded in curing patients because the pottery which
his patients make is salable, as well as good in style and workmanship.
Some of the patients need the money which their work earns, but they
also need to feel their touch with the world outside. To make something
which will sell gives them courage, self-respect.

This is the spiritual value of pay. So far no one has thought of so convenient and convincing a way to wrap up and deliver at each citizen's door a parcel of courage for the future, and a morsel of self-respect which is food for the soul.

Gratitude, given or received, is one of the best things in the world. We need far more of it and of far better quality. Yet I have never read any satisfactory account of what it so gloriously means. Its value begins just where the value of pay ends. Thanks are personal, and attempt to fit an adequate response to the particular service performed. Pay is an impersonal coin which has been handed out to many before it reaches you, and will go to many others when it leaves you. It is your right and you are not grateful for it. But thanks are a free gift and enrich the giver. There is no nobler art than the art of expressing one's gratitude in fresh, unhackneyed, unexaggerated terms which answer devotion with fresh devotion, fancy with new fancy, clarity with sincerity. Artists who get their reward only in money and in the stale plaudits of clapping hands are restless for something more individual. They want to be intimately understood and beautifully answered. For such gratitude they look to brother artists, to the few who really understand. There they find their best reward; but even this leaves something wanting.

Why is it so notoriously difficult to accept thanks? Most things that I am thanked for I am not conscious of having done at all. Obviously the thanks are mis-directed. Or, if I am conscious of having done what the thanker is grateful for, I am likewise conscious that I only handed on to a third person what had previously been given to me. I learned from Smith and then en-lightened Jones. Smith is the man to thank. Or again, one is thanked for simply carrying out a contract; but one could not honorably do less. Thanks for going along the usual and necessary road seem gratuitous and undeserved. Or, finally, one receives gratitude for what one did with joy; that seems as queer as being thanked for eating one's dinner.

But suppose that the deed one is thanked for was not an act of passing along what came originally from another, as you pass money in a street-car. Suppose a man has really originated something, an invention, a poem, a statue. He hardly claims it as his, for he does not know where it came from. He did not "make it up." It sprang into his mind, given to him as much as if he had received it from a friend. He does not feel that he is the one to receive thanks. The thanks should pass through him, as the gift did, to some one else, — to his parents who gave him and taught him so much, to his race, his nation, his health, his friends, his oppor-tunities. That is where it all came from; that is where thanks are due. But each of these influences is itself the recipient of countless other influences. Every fact in the universe depends on every other fact. Ulti-mately, then, not he but the universe must be thanked.

He deals with firms and employees, but he looks behind them, over their shoulders, and re-directs their
thanks elsewhere, — ultimately, if he but knew it, to
the World Spirit. One may not remember that Spirit.
One often does not bother about the world's work.
Thinking exhausts some people and fatally confuses
others. But if one thinks at all, he runs up hard against
the world plan, and finds it the bulkiest object in sight.

The unsentimental male American as I have described him is almost morbidly apt to deride anything
like gratitude, sentiment, or moralizing in relation to
himself and his work. "No joy is mine!" he would say;
"what do you take me for anyway, — a holy roller?"

He is just as quick to reject the idea that he cares
about *serving* anybody or anything. He may admit
that he wants to "make good" in a fair and square
way, according to the rules of the game. But "service,"
like "joy," sounds too "stuck up" and Pharisaical
for him.

Nevertheless I firmly believe that his derision is
only a ruse to conceal his morbid bashfulness and
oafish sensitiveness. For in point of fact service is one
of the things that pretty much everybody wants,
however much he may disguise it and conceal it from
himself. I have never seen any more unsentimental
and raw-boned being than the American medical student; yet he is simply hankering for service. Medical
teachers spread before him banquets of tempting

"opportunities," rare "cases," "beautiful" specimens, easy chances to distinguish himself in research and to absorb his medical food in predigested mouthfuls. He often remains indifferent. But the moment you give him a place to work in a clinic, to serve as Dr. Blank's fourteenth assistant in a hospital where good work is done, he will jump at the chance. The work is much harder and more monotonous than his regular studies. Much of it is not teaching him medicine. He has to go on doing Fehling's test for sugar and trying knee jerks long after he has learned the trick. He has to measure stomach contents, to weigh patients, to bandage legs, and to write down names and addresses in monotonous routine day after day. Yet he loves the work, and despite all the drudgery, he learns far more medicine by holding down an actual job of this kind than by lectures and classes. If you separate out the instructive portion of his day's work and present it to him without assigning him any regular position and duties, he does not like the work so well or learn so much.

He is hungry for reality. Service as an assistant is reality. He knows that something genuine is occurring and that he plays a real part in it. He knows that he would be missed and that things would go wrong if he were not there. He senses a real need for him and feels it drawing him like a magnet. At the medical school his classes do not need him, though he is supposed to need them. Nothing would happen if he were not there. He feels ghostly and unreal like the lesson. For the lesson is a copy of reality; constantly it portrays an imaginary state of things:—

"If you find a man unconscious, if you examine a tuberculous lung after death, if you give one half-grain of strychnin, if you wash out the stomach, such and such results will follow." Almost all medical teaching is thus blighted with unreality, mildewed with time. Laboratory work seems more real, but even laboratory work is usually artificial, a make-believe. You are not really analyzing medicines in search of possible adulterants. Nobody wants your work. There is no tug of the world's need to which you respond. It is true that in laboratory instruction we give the student something more or less like the real conditions of life. We try to set him to work as if he were holding down a real job. But he knows that in fact he is only practicing for self-improvement, one of the flimsiest of the pretexts by which we try to call out a man's energies.

Extraordinarily sound, those students' instincts! They are bored when we offer them opportunities to do what is easy and self-centered, but outside the current of reality. It is only when we give them hard, dry work like an assistantship in a clinic, a place where they can accomplish something that has a real value in the actual world, that they fall to with real appetite.

The sense of somebody's need is, I believe, the most powerful motive in the world, one that appeals to the largest number of people of every age, race, and kind. It wakes up the whole nature, the powers that learn as well as those that perform; it generates the vigor of interest that submerges selfishness and cowardice; it rouses the inventiveness and ingenuity that slumber so soundly in students' classrooms. For many of us, for more every time the world takes a step in the right direction, work that is service taps a great reservoir of power, sets free some of our caged and leashed energy.

Pay, gratitude, and service, as ends of work, have each a value, though not of exactly the sort one might expect. How about *success?* Financial rewards are nowadays less talked about than the general prosperity which they express. Civic ideals are kept in the foreground alike by "boosters," real estate men, and chambers of commerce. According to these authorities business success means a flourishing city and a contented community. To help build up a fine city is what we are asked to do in case we take the investment offered us. A fine city is an efficiently-managed, well-lighted community, with plenty of schools, parks, and churches. But stop a moment. What is the use of such a place? When we have built and finished this perfect city, with its smooth-running government, then at last its crime-freed, sanitary streets will be swept and garnished all ready to begin, — what?

It is hard to hear any answer. Few are interested enough even to attempt one. For the interest of civic reform is mainly in the process — far less in the result.

Boys who build a boat or a play-house usually find that
there is far more fun in the process of building than in
using the finished product. So it is with the reform of
a slum or a municipal government. The best of it is in
the reforming. We shall hardly stop to notice it when
it is perfect. We shall take it for granted, as we do the
safe delivery of the letters which we post, and be off on
another campaign. Our civic goals are like the scented
rushes in "Wool and Water." The most beautiful
ones Alice found were always those just beyond her
reach. Perfect adaptation to environment, which
seems to be what the sanitary and civic reformers aim
at, would mean absolute stagnation, — attainment
that buds no more. For what should stir us further?

"Well, anyway, to reform our city is the best thing
in sight. It is certainly in the right direction." Ah,
then we know what the right direction is! *That* is something far more significant than any single step in civic
progress. If we know the true direction, we can point
beyond the civic models to something towards which
they are on the road and get our satisfaction all along
its course.

The worship of "the right direction" is a fundamental
motive in art and play as well as in work. Every noble
game and work of art calls for others, incites to pil-
grimages, reforms, and nobler arts. Art is not meant
to give us something final; everything in it is pointing
ahead and getting its justification because it is "in the
right direction." Everything in art, as in civics, gets

the courage to exist and to push on because of its readiness to be corrected by experience to a truer version of its own purpose. Sincere people want the true in their work as well as in their thinking. But the truth is an Infinite, and the will to approach it is an infinite intention. The fruit of this infinite intention would be our utter prostration of self before the vision. "Do with me as thou wilt." "Thy will not mine be done."

I cannot see the end of all this. I see reform after reform of character and of civilization, progress after progress in science and art, rising like mountain ranges one behind the other. But there is no conceivable sense in all these upheavals if they are mere changes, mere uneasy shifts in the position of a dreaming world-spirit. To make sense they must be moving in a single direction fulfilling a single plan.

It is obvious enough that all work is supposed to fulfill some one's plan, — the worker's plan or his master's. It is good for something. But every one of the goods we buy with our work is itself a means to something else, a coin with which to purchase something more. The goods we supply, the clothes, food, transportation, medicine, knowledge, inspiration which we give, are themselves means to something else, perhaps to comfort, health, education, courage. These again are means to better work, to civic perfection, to family happiness. But these once more are in themselves as worthless as fiat money or dolls stuffed with sawdust unless there is absolute value behind them. Happiness, civic perfection, love, are sometimes named as the ultimate ends towards which the activities of busy men and women are means, but anybody who experiences any of these states and is not a Buddhist wallowing in vague bliss finds that they incite us to new deeds. If they are not soporific drugs, they are spurs to fresh action.

Taken literally, the ideals of utility and civic reform are like the old myth which explained the world's support as the broad back of an elephant. Who supports the elephant? He rests on a gigantic tortoise; and who supports the tortoise? No answer is audible in the business sections of our cities or in the schoolrooms or in the colleges. The church's answer is derided or ignored by a large fraction of us. But it is the right one; and we shall learn to listen to it or pay the penalty. Government does not rest ultimately on the consent of the governed, but on their conformity to the will of the world-spirit which makes and unmakes civilizations.

"Success" in industry, in art, or in love is saved from bitterness and disappointment because we regard our achievements far more symbolically than we know, and rest far more than we are aware upon the backing of God.

Assuming that in every one there is an infinite and restless desire to get into the life of the world, — to share any and all life that is hot and urgent or cool and clear, — we can tackle this infinite task in two ways: —
` By trying to understand the universe in the samples

of it which come into our ken and to draw from these bits a knowledge which typifies and represents the whole. That is science.

By trying to serve. When we try to serve the world (or to understand it), we touch what is divine. We get our dignity, our courage, our joy in work because of the greatness of the far-off end. always in sight, always attainable, never at any moment attained. Service is one of the ways by which a tiny insect like one of us can get a purchase on the whole universe. If we find the job where we can be of use, we are hitched to the star of the world, and move with it.

PART II : PLAY

CHAPTER X

WHY is it that everybody is taking play so seriously to-day? Our fathers considered it permissible within limits, something which we might indulge in, something necessary, even, for young people in order that they might be the better prepared for work. "All work and no play," they used to say, "makes Jack a dull boy,"—dull, of course, at his lessons which were supposedly the real object of his existence. But despite these admissions no one would have dreamed, a generation ago, of a National Playground Association, or of groups of sober adults taking counsel together in prayerful spirit and with missionary zeal, to the end that they might spread abroad the gospel of play! To our fathers that would have sounded as blasphemous as a gospel of laxity, as absurd as a gospel of sweetmeats.

Jack has been permitted (for motives of economy and of hygiene) to play, but this indulgent proverb was framed to excuse only the young. There is no hint that married women and professors, clergymen and bankers in business suits, are also prone to dullness, or worse, if they fail to frisk and gambol on the green. Yet here we are to-day, first broadening our idea of play till it spells recreation, then dreaming of public recreation as the birthright of all men, women, and children, — finally venturing, since Miss Addams's great book, "The Spirit of Youth and the City Streets," to think of recreation as something holy.

What is it that has come over us so swiftly and so silently? Can we deliberate about play, devote time, money, and brains to working it up, without losing our sense of humor and of proportion, — without stultifying ourselves? I hope to answer these questions with a "Yes" that has some ring to it. Would it might echo and pass on to you a deep and rallying note from the spirit of youth and from the city streets, both of which I love!

Take first the question of playfulness in its relation to seriousness. Are they opposites? Need they suppress each other? Shall we become a less serious people, a more flippant and trifling people, if we grow more playful?

The answer is this: Seriousness is so fundamental a trend of the soul that it can accompany any of the soul's efforts. One can play seriously, as children, baseball experts, and chess-players do. One can be both serious and funny: witness G. B. Shaw (*passim*), Lowell in the "Biglow Papers," and the fool in "Lear." Work, love, and even prayer can be either flippant or serious.

But just because seriousness is universally acceptable as an ingredient, it tastes harsh and crude when we get it alone. Bare and unadorned seriousness is indistinguishable from dullness. Like the sky, we always want it as a background. But put it in the foreground, take away all else, and seriousness becomes a void or a mist quenching animation, vivacity, and effort.

This should not surprise us, for seriousness is only one of many things which are essential as backgrounds, but disastrous as foregrounds. Any bodily function, breathing, for example, is another such background. It should rarely be suspended, but it should never obtrude itself. Apoplectic old persons, whose breathing has become a serious and noisy business, try at least to conceal the fact as best they can. They do not pride themselves on their puffing and wheezing. Only when a man is near to death and has left behind him the powers and beauties which make him human, do we say, "Yes, he is still breathing."

Seriousness simon-pure is a residual state into which one relapses when one has nothing better to do or say. The preacher who cannot kindle us for righteousness, or summon us to repentance, or re-create in us some vision of the living Christ, falls back on pure seriousness, that is on dullness. No impassioned speaker or skillful fighter is ever thought of as "serious." We take his seriousness for granted like his good intentions, because it has flowered into something more vital. Seriousness at the funeral of a stranger may be all that is left us, if we can feel no poignancy of grief, or triumphant love, but see only the blackness of it all. For to be merely serious is to be as colorless as those somber trappings, which are so often a libel of the glorious dead.

No less somber is the "serious" editorial, sermon, or essay written by one who cannot be crisp nor richly ornate nor smooth and musical, nor sarcastic nor prophetic nor minatory. Of course seriousness may and usually does underlie all these moods, but if we get down to the threadbare and colorless solemnity of the merely serious we reach the soporific.

Sleep, indeed, is the blood brother and dearest friend of seriousness.

"Yes, we are always serious at breakfast," said a charming Canadian girl at an uproarious Californian breakfast-table in the summer of 1904. "I don't see how you can laugh so much in the morning. Grandmamma sometimes smiles at breakfast, but then you see she gets up at half-past five."

Seriousness is in itself no crime. Most of us pass through two zones of it daily, on our way to sleep at night and back again in the morning. It is a natural phenomenon when the machinery of the mind is running down, or not yet in full play. But in Heaven's name let us make no virtue of it. Let us decently conceal it, like our yawns, for (with apologies to John Milton) it is only a kind of "linked yawning long drawn out."

Unfortunately for all such good resolutions, this form of sleepiness, unabashed and chronic, is apt to

invade every corner of the day. It will not be confined
to the breakfast hour, nor to the mysterious and silent
watches of the night, when the editorials of morning
papers are written. What is this melancholy and crest-
fallen line of persons, whom I see moving along Beacon
Street or Commonwealth Avenue, towards the heart
of the city, a little before nine, in the crisp and frosty
morning? So mechanical and spiritless is their gait
as they plod along that one might fancy them members of the sad, exploited proletariat, crushed by over-
work, exhausted by want of sleep. In fact they are
prosperous bankers and lawyers on their way to business, and the only trouble with them is that they have
just lapsed into being serious and serious only. It has
never occurred to them that walking can be anything
better than a means of sober progression. Poetry in
walking? Don't suggest that to practical men. They'll
think you a dangerous character.

Well; demonstration is better than argument. Look
at that four-year-old walking to *his* business at the
same hour in the morning, and improvising rhythms
not only with his legs, but with every animated
muscle. His themes are suggested by the curbstone,
the granolithic pavement, or the morning itself. He
is not merely fooling. The serious intention of getting
somewhere underlies all his skips and dances; he has
on the whole a direction, but he is not merely progress-
ing like most of us "serious" walkers. The rhythm of
his steps is not like his elder's, a stern barbaric tom-tom,

bare and monotonous. It is flexible and various; it
becomes hopping *staccato* or sliding *legato*, as his mood
demands. It is not bound to a single *tempo*, but, like
the winds of the spirit, it is slow and lingering, or fast
and furious. Could any picture be more moving, and
yet more humiliating, to heavy adults? Surely some
future "Golden Treasury of Moving Pictures" will
contain a reproduction of that exquisite rhapsody
called "Steps Taken While Crossing Harvard Bridge
at School Time," by Lyve Chylde, Esq., — a truly
moving lyric composed in his fifth year!

But why is it that almost all the best pictures in
that Golden Treasury of lyric motions, which each of
us is compiling in his memory, are composed before the
thirteenth year? Simply because the child is still alive
and trailing clouds of poetry as he walks, while we
"serious" adult walkers are half dead or half asleep.
Our creative energies are domiciled elsewhere, like ab-
sentee landlords, far from the tenements of our clay.
Yet it is not always so. I have seen a man who, even
under the responsibilities of the highest office in the
Commonwealth of Massachusetts, kept his soul fresh
and alive in his moving body. One of the pictures that
I treasure in memory is the figure of Governor Roger
Wolcott walking to the State House in the morning.
He was magnificently alive and therefore creative.
With every step he was composing triumphant martial
music. I could almost hear the themes as I walked
behind him. He little knew "what argument his *gait*

to his neighbor's creed had lent." Many others must be thanking him to-day, if not with their lips yet certainly in their lives. For in his established maturity he radiated vigor and abundance like a happy child.

I wonder how many of us now living can bear such a comparison? One I know who can: a doctor in Chicago whose American lineage stretches far back of the Mayflower, back of any pale-faced newcomer to this continent. I do not forget that as doctor and as civic leader he has put Chicago and the whole country deeply in his debt. But my memory picture of him (and yours if you know him, as you probably do) will live to inspire and rebuke us even when we forget Chicago and civics and medical ideals. For they are only part of life, while our friend F. is the very incarnation of life as he moves in the city streets. He brings the open country with him and the untarnished freedom of mountain air. You can learn both "the cause and the cure of civilization" if you will walk with him on Michigan Avenue; for nothing in modern civilization has cramped him, not even its "serious" clothes.

What an incubus we (males) carry with us in the dull and solemn monotony of our clothes! They are serious as the school history of England used in "Alice in Wonderland," to dry the wet company about the pool of tears. "It's the dryest thing I know," said the Dodo. Our garments, we boast, are quiet, staid, and unobtrusive; yes, like the mien of the drooping horse in the treadmill! But not because any one really likes them. It is simply because we are too stupefied by custom, too much cowed by the threat of fashion, to do otherwise than as our neighbors do. Who can blame us? To put a feather in our cap might lose us our job, and there are many better causes for self-sacrifice than dress reform. But let us never again insult children or childlike races by inviting them to *step up* to our level and become as dull and ugly as we are in our gait, our dress, and our behavior. Let us clearly recognize that we stepped down to a lower level when we gave up playfulness and adopted the merely serious carriage and the "quiet" clothes of the modern civilized adult.

Let us cease to blaspheme against the spirit of eternal youth by supposing (as Karl Groos [1] does) that Play means chiefly a preparation for the "serious" work of life. Whatever has seriousness as its dominant note is a senile degeneration, a sad relapse from the healthy, adventurous playfulness of childhood.

Worst of all, perhaps, is our habit of associating morality with a drab and bleak solemnity. Why should we confuse morality, the stuff of which heroes are made, with the dead-and-alive tissues of seriousness? Perhaps it may be as Joseph Lee surmises that the grim "practical" determination, which we have come to associate with Puritanism and "morality," was originally an armor-of-proof which we put on temporarily for battle against the Cavaliers, and then in a fit of absent-mindedness forgot to take off, like a tired man who

[1] *The Play of Man*, pp. 2, 168, and *passim*. D. Appleton & Co., 1908.

drops asleep with his boots on. Perhaps there was once real use in the stiff, ugly armor miscalled seriousness. Perhaps it served to scare the enemy or to diminish the appetite for everything but battle, and so save costly supplies.

Our present business, in any case, is to divorce morality from dullness. God never put them together. If in the past, for temporary and specific purposes, man has brought them together, it is now man's duty in the service of eternal ends to keep them apart. Would to Heaven this book might sever them once for all!

We have begun to make the separation, else we never could have initiated to-day's revival of interest in play. In this interest we have come to recognize that morality need not be dull, and what is more, that it must be sometimes playful. We are beginning to take play seriously as all children do, yet without forgetting that it is play and not work or worship. This brings us back to our starting-point both in this chapter and in life. We need not be afraid of taking play seriously so long as we distinguish seriousness from dullness. What is more enchanting than the seriousness of child's play, — the "top-heavy solemnity" with which he applies himself to piling sand into a bucket and emptying it out again. Yet he is never dull, no matter how impressive his seriousness. It is the tired adult who is always prone to relapse into dullness in his gait, his talk, and his dress.

CHAPTER XI

WITH the decline of the mistaken respect for mere "seriousness" (which is either congenital dullness or simple sleepiness exposed in public view) we are to-day cultivating play instead of merely permitting it. We want it recognized in schools (and ultimately in colleges) as an essential part of the curriculum. Why should it be allowed to grow up like a weed outside the garden of childhood? Froebel knew better; he put play in the very center of that garden. To-day we see a long procession of educators, social workers, municipalities, and churches tardily trailing behind Froebel, quite ignorant of the fact that he is their leader. But their direction is right. At last they are on the move, determined to put play where it belongs because they believe, with Stevenson, in the duty of happiness and in the destiny of man while serving his God "to enjoy Him forever." We want to diminish the amount of submerged "busy" work and to expunge all desperate and hopeless work; we want to see fun and games playing through it, as heat lightning plays through heavy clouds.

I will not be entangled at this point in any *liaison* with fascinating definitions. I know that one can defend a definition of work which will include all that I mean by play; but I think that it is more convenient to distinguish the two. I know a few rare people who can touch any dull job with a magic which turns it into sparkling play. I am quite aware that it is the spirit which we bring with us, not the necessities or laws of nature, which labels certain things "Work" and others "Play." Along comes a blithe and bird-like spirit, picks off all the work-labels from monotonous tasks (such as typewriting, book-keeping, and chart-making), sticks play-labels upon them all and proceeds to make their new titles good. With such an example daily before my eyes, I am not likely to forget that radiant souls can change the gray of work to the golden-green of play.

Mindful of this exhilarating fact, I nevertheless recognize that, for most of us, work and play often split apart and call for separate names. Fiddling is good, but not while Rome burns. Why not? Because fiddling, just at that juncture, may result in the abolition of all future fiddling through the combustion of fiddles, fiddlers, and their audiences. Nero, I suppose, retired to a safe distance before he began his historic performance, but not all fiddlers can get away in time. Somebody must stay and put out the fire, which is work. We work in part because we must, in part because we have not got what we want and are divided into a restless or unsatisfied present and a yearned-for goal in the future. But in play we possess what we want. The tension of present against future is released. Definitions, educators, and all of us, then, must recognize that play has a soul of its own and that Jesus played in the streets of his native town.[1]

We have ceased to think of play chiefly as an indulgence, as a loosening of bonds, or even as a pleasure. We have begun to admire it not only as recreation, but as re-creation. That idea makes us open our eyes, for anything that can make us over anew calls out the respect even of a utility-ridden age like ours. Even our Puritan ancestors would have hastened to a healing spring if they had believed in it, and so we go tumbling over each other to learn recreation when we hear that it can renew our power to *work*. Great is the power of a hyphen! If play is not only recreation but re-creation, why then it is to be born again (a wholly orthodox procedure) and better born. It becomes a form of applied eugenics. Perhaps after rebirth we may go back to our work with deeper-seeing eyes. We may even be less "stupid in the affections." Play recommends itself more highly when we see it from this point of view. We begin to think there may be something in it besides fooling.

That mighty engine, the hyphen, which like some giant telescope has helped us to see new worlds, new freedom, spring-time and rejuvenation in the familiar word "recreation," can give it yet another glory. For

[1] "We have piped unto you, and ye have not danced; we have mourned unto you and ye have not lamented." Matthew XI, 17.

what is it that art, music, literature, drama do for us? Is it not the re-creating of jaded, humdrum lives? Art carries us off into a far country, more beautiful, more poignant, more tragic, perhaps more humorous and sparkling, perhaps nobler and more heroic, than is shown us in the workshop or the home. We emerge refreshed by this intense experience, and for a few precious minutes we look upon the world as if our eyes had never been dulled and stupefied by repetition and inattention, never lost the child's divine power of surprise.

Art and play, then, fulfill the same function, provide us the same refreshment. Moreover, they are both their own excuse for being. In work, and to some extent in love, we are building for the future; we are content to save, to sacrifice, and to repress, for the sake of a "far-off divine event." But in all art, including the variety called play, we anticipate heaven and attain immediate fruition: we give full rein to what strains against the leash. Subject to the rules of the game, or the rules of the art, we let our energies go at full gallop. We utter ourselves, like a schoolhouse turned inside out for recess. You know the sound!

Play and art, I believe, are essentially one; beauty lives in each, and though the beauty of athletics or of whist is not always quite obvious, it is no more obscure than the beauty of tragedy or of rhyme. Artificial they all are; an outlet for the cramped human spirit they all furnish.

Luckily for my present thesis, dancing has lately
come so much to the fore that our minds are prepared
for the transition from art to athletics and play. Anybody can see without an opera-glass that dancing is at
once play, art, and athletics. So is baseball, though I
fear that some of my readers have not been regular
enough in their attendance upon the exhibitions of our
greatest national art to thrill with recollection as I mention the exquisite beauty of the line-drive over short
stop, and the noble dignity of the curved throw from
third to first. Nothing in the art of dancers like Isa-
dora Duncan is more beautiful than the habitual motions of ball-players as they throw, strike, catch, or
slide. Of course beauty is not the whole of baseball nor
of any art. There are also significance, heroism, suspense, response. Also there are serviceable materials,
such as catgut, pigskin, horsehair, oil-paint, grease-
paint, printer's ink, voices, muscles, whereby spiritual
meanings are expressed and conveyed from the artists
who create to us the "creative listeners" in the
audience.

We get fun and sometimes health from play and from
some other arts; but if any reader thinks that athletic
games exist chiefly for the sake of fun, let him turn for
a moment to another field of art and look over my
shoulder at the face of the painter or musician while
I inflict upon him that ancient painful congratulation:
"What a pleasure it must be to you, Mr. Genius, to
produce so much beauty." Now watch his effort to

cover with a smile his pitying contempt for your green-horn's ignorance. "Pleasure? Yes, but at what a cost!" Art is grinding hard work, much of the time; so is football; and but for this arduous element, half its attraction to the youth would be gone. He wants what is hard, adventurous, and therefore exhilarating. Things soft and easy, like listening to lectures, or passing college examinations, do not attract him.

My thesis, then, is this: Play is at least one quarter of life and love another quarter, hence "conduct" in Matthew Arnold's sense cannot be three quarters of life. But play, the quarter which concerns us now, means recreation, and this is also the essential function of art. Play is one type or aspect of art, a fleeting, fragile improvisation in children oftentimes, a sternly disciplined construction in games like chess, football, or aviation. But like other arts it is at all times relatively complete in itself. It is not, like washing, gymnastics, or telephones, a means to life. It is life itself, striving quixotically for immediate perfection, breaking for a moment into perishable blossoms.

It must be admitted that some of the noblest and wisest men in America still think of athletics chiefly as a means to health and morality. College presidents are wont to praise the sound body chiefly because they consider it a means to mental soundness. They think of athletics, and even of dancing, as a good method to build up the body and divert sexual energy from vicious outlets. That athletics and dancing may be means to these ends is true. It is also true that cows are a valuable means to leather boots and (I believe) to gum-drops; but I doubt if that is the end and aim of the cow's existence. Dancing strengthens the calves. "Nothing like dissection," said Bob Sawyer (you remember), "to give one an appetite."

Violin-playing strengthens the fingers. But it is hardly worth while to remark that we don't play the violin for our health or for our finger-ends. Violin-playing also flattens, deforms, and callouses the finger-ends, but there are easier ways of obtaining these results. The art is good despite these drawbacks. So football is good despite many injuries, not because it always improves health, but because it is a magnificent expression of the human spirit, a fine example of popular art.

We make a ridiculous fetish of health nowadays. Three of the very best things in life — heroism, artistic creation, and child-bearing — are often bad for the health. To avoid heroism, creative work, and child-bearing because they may injure the health, would show a conception of life no more warped and distorted than that which bids us dance and be merry because forsooth it is healthy to do so! As a rule, and in the long run, athletics and games probably promote that total enhancement of life, one aspect of which is health. But temporarily, and in some cases permanently, they leave their scars upon the body, though not such scars as are ploughed into mortals by the more strenuous and dangerous activities of helping to create a new machine, a new symphony, or a new child.

Let us, therefore, give play, recreation, and the other popular arts their proper place beside the fine arts, and avoid the common error which degrades play to a medical instrument. Thus we shall help to preserve the "fine arts" from dying of isolation. That is a real danger to-day. Chilled by our formal respect, discouraged by our practical neglect, mortified by our sentimental petting, the musician, sculptor, and painter are dangerously out of the current of vigorous American life. Or, to put it from the other side, American life is dangerously neglectful of some forms of art as well as of most forms of scholarship. The drama, baseball, and dancing are now the only popular arts of America to-day. Let us realize that *they are nevertheless genuine arts*, and plant them close beside music, literature, painting, and sculpture. Such a realization will help to keep vulgarity out of popular art, and to save the fine arts from degenerating into fastidiousness or dying of super-refinement.

CHAPTER XII

THE POPULAR ARTS, THE MINOR ARTS, AND THEIR BIG BROTHERS

In the name of informality the guests at a large club dinner (with a presiding officer and speeches to follow) are sometimes left to seat themselves. Some sad and embarrassing moments follow. The presiding officer finds his chair of honor and there he stands alone, gazing wistfully at the rest of the company, as they place themselves at so respectful a distance from him that empty chairs, half a dozen or more on each side, are his only support. Respect for greatness turns out to mean the painful isolation of greatness, until at last some one takes pity on the unfortunate great or is ruefully begged to move up and be neighborly.

So it is with the "fine arts." A society should be formed to alleviate their cruel isolation. In the first place, more amateurs are needed. What would not our painters and sculptors give for such unfeigned interest, such discriminating approval and criticism as is daily shouted out by thousands of spectators to those happy and unconscious artists, the "Red Sox," the "Cubs," and the "Giants." A baseball audience is made up of enthusiastic amateurs, a considerable fraction of whom are confident that they "could have made that play far better." To get such audiences for ordinary artists every one should be brought up to paint and to play some musical instrument, as all boys are brought up to play baseball. We know that very few of the children who learn writing in our schools will ever reach any greater literary distinction than the composition of a good letter. But we do not, therefore, give up teaching them to write. Neither should we fail to teach children painting merely because we know that only one or two in a million will ever get beyond the pleasures and appreciations of the amateur.

The Fine Arts are now treated as an aristocratic affair, an occupation for fastidious and delicate souls. So we think of them, so we treat them. Are we not brutally imposing these misconceptions upon the unfortunate and struggling artist? Are we not forcing him to play a part that is utterly foreign to his nature? I think so. For art, I think, is as full-blooded and dashing a pursuit as fox-hunting or football. The artist differs from you and me chiefly because he is more alive. He burns; we smoulder. Everybody is slowly burning up in the fire of physiological metabolism. What we call "fire" is simply a bit of creation where the forces of life burn a little faster, a little hotter, and more beautifully than in human tissues. Were there more realization of this among us there would be less "patronizing" and more love of the fine arts, less listening and gazing, more practice.

But there are many to plead the cause of Fine Arts, and the Popular Arts (baseball, dancing, and drama) need no amateur eulogist, since the magazines began to do them justice. My chief concern is with *the minor arts*, such as humor and good humor, and especially with some of the simplest among them, — speaking, gesticulating, letter-writing, seeing beauty in common things or putting it there, anticipating another's wish, threading one's way deftly in a crowded street, steering a discussion into profitable channels.

The major games and the finer arts are arranged to fill up any space that may be left in or after a working day. They come at stated hours; we leave our jobs and our homes to attend them. Doubtless this must always be so with the more heroic and permanent forms of art. We cannot play a football game on the hearthrug. We cannot carve statues while waiting on customers. But some of the humbler and less celebrated forms of art can penetrate every place and irradiate every hour.

I mentioned just now a couple of the most important minor arts: *humor;* and *good-humor*, a form of good manners. Shining examples of both these arts are close round us in daily work, though we often ignore them. In 1910, I knew a butcher dying of lingering disease who by his fun and radiant good humor kept at bay the specter of death, and in "the pleasant land of counterpane" maintained to the last a successful and happy life. When on my morning visit I would ask him to turn upon his side that I might examine his back, you would fancy from his expression that I had invited a hungry man to eat. He could have answered with no more engaging alacrity if I had proffered him the chance to step back into health. He took pleasure and gave it in each of the trifling services rendered him in the hospital routine. He beamed and thanked me for shifting a pillow as if I had given him a diamond. He chuckled over my clumsy attempt to tilt the glass feeding-tube into his mouth without forcing him to raise his head; and each morning he smoothed and folded the flap of the top sheet like one performing an act of ritual.

As we exchanged the most unpoetic information about his daily routine, the dull framework of question and answer was spangled over with a profusion of delicate, brilliant, meaningful looks that rose and flowered silently over his listening face, or leaped out of dull sentences like morning-glories on a trellis. So step by step as he went down the last gray week of his life, he taught me all unconsciously as many lessons about art, beauty, and playfulness as about heroism.

One of his greatest and most naïve arts, one of the best of all his good manners, was that million-hued miracle called a smile. I can recall but a tithe of the unspoken verses, the soundless improvisations of his smile, — serene, wistful, mischievous, deprecating, tender, joyful, welcoming. Not a moment of his ebbing life seemed prosaic or joyless, for each had in it the fore-taste or the aftertaste of a smile, born without effort and dying without pain; birth, fruition, and end, all equally beautiful. Sometimes at the beginning of our talk his face and eyes were silent, and only the lines of his eloquent hand spoke to me. Then, at some rousing recollection, there would break from his face a perfect chorus of meanings, each feature carrying its own strand of harmonious but varied melody.

Well, I must stop talking about him and try to explain what he has to do with play and art. He exemplifies two of the minor arts through which life may be enhanced and refreshed from moment to moment, whether marching up hill or down dale. It is said that the best crew is the one which gets its rest between every two strokes. So between every two strokes of effort we need the games and the arts to re-create us from moment to moment so that our souls shall never be prosaic or discouraged. Play and beauty, running like a gold thread through the warp and woof of our life-fabric, are surely as needful as the more concentrated and exclusive recreations. To sing (or whistle) at one's work, to carry melodies and verses in our heads, to do things with a swing and a rhythm as some Japanese and all sailors do, is to preserve our souls from drouth. The games that we play with vocal intonations, the dramas we carry on with smile and glance and grimace, need not interrupt work. They call for no apparatus and no stage. Best of all, each of us "makes the team" in these games; in these dramas each of us has "a speaking part."

All these arts, major and minor, need, as I have already intimated, more intimacy with one another. In them all there is beauty and renewal of the soul. There are fun and play in them all. A material basis is presupposed for them all. Health is an uncertain by-product in them all. Being thus congenial, they need one another. Popular arts and minor arts can win dignity and strength from closer association with fine arts. The latter will gain inspiration, dash, and effectiveness when they are freed from solitary confinement and allowed to mingle about town with their less self-conscious fellow arts.

Our generation ought to introduce these long-estranged brothers, each to each. We have made a beginning in the revival of pageantry and "folk-dancing." The pageant and the folk-dance have beauty, form, and technique like a fine art. Yet they are done in a playful spirit and by the general public, unversed in the fine arts, unconscious as ball-players. The special, secluded class of "artists" is suddenly merged in a crowd of delighted performers, who have all the better right to be called artists because they do not call themselves so. This is a good beginning. Further progress can be better charted out when we have considered in the coming chapters another group of minor arts.

CHAPTER XIII

JEWELS

I HAVE a prejudice against precious stones because they cost so much and can be enjoyed by so few. But suppose we strip away the coarser husks of people's enjoyment of them, especially the element of exclusive possession and the suggestion that their wearer is richer and therefore better than the rest of us. Suppose we isolate the peculiar beauty and power which jewels possess, do we not find that all can have it? What jewel sparkles like the glint of a low sun on the windows of a distant house, or like dewdrops on the grass, or like the opalescent snow-crystals seen when you look towards an afternoon sun across a fresh snow-field? Shift your position one inch and the whole amazing cluster of lights has changed to a new set. You see not one jewel, but hundreds; not one color only, but rose, green, and violet sown across the white snow in tiny globes of fiery light which make the "precious" stones seem dull by comparison.

What more would you get if you could pick them off the snow, keep them, and call them yours? Do the jewels that you buy ever again look so marvelous to you as they did when first you handled them on the jeweler's velvet? One may clench his teeth and shut his fists and swear that he will not let himself "get so used"

to the beauty of things that he hardly notices them.
To some extent one may succeed by various devices in
postponing or diminishing the depreciation of his own
pleasure in his property. But nothing can prevent it.

One need not try to prove that possession is pure evil
or that familiarity steals *all* that we care for. Doubtless possession has its counterbalancing advantages.
But, on the other hand, I cannot doubt that there are
great and certain advantages in the jewels which we
cannot keep. "*Verweile doch; du bist so schön,*" is always a risky thing to say to one's experiences. The very
brevity and fugitiveness of their flash may be needed
to "stab our spirits broad awake"; a longer, slower
illumination may not arouse us at all. Slow down a
sparkling *scherzo* by Tschaikowsky or Chopin till each
note stays with us a minute instead of a tenth of a
second. It is ruined, of course, but its ruin is not more
complete than the dilapidation of our possessions, stone
by stone, as appreciation is undermined by the stealthy
seeping waters of time.

Of course we can and must fight against this ineradi-
cable, original sin of satiety,—original sin because it
is one in which even the most saintly and heroic share.
Great souls keep it under, but no one wipes it out. Yet
it is not "original" in the sense of being inborn. Children are marvelously free from it.

Because we cannot preserve intact, as children do,
this virgin freshness of the often repeated, we need
especially to cultivate the minor art of seeing jewels, of

expecting the unexpected and absorbing its full impression, so that on the canvas of later memory it will shine like a high light.

Perhaps I should here explain more concretely what I mean by the jewels of daily life. Here are some: the flash of a moving violin bow (as well as of the note it invokes), the shock of cool water on your heated face, a thrush note at dawn, a *cadenza* of swift laughter, the crash and foam of a breaking wave, the silver needle of a fife note, the rocket flight of a piccolo flute, all fireworks and brilliant lights in city streets, the light of speaking or laughing eyes, the first glimpse of an hepatica in spring with the white ends of its stamens shining against its deep purple cup like stars in a summer night, — all these brilliant points of delight have this in common that, like an electric spark, they set off trains of thought and action which of ourselves we are powerless to ignite.

Down through the stratified layers of our inheritance deep into the geologic ages of our souls the jewel's flash can penetrate, and from those black depths come up tiny but precious specimens of what were otherwise inaccessible. Ancient, fragmentary perceptions which no other power can exhume, leap to the surface of consciousness when I hear a thrush sing, and though I forget them, they have had "their moment" and have acted on the whole texture and surface of my thoughts.

Brief and limited though it is, — this game which we play with the jewel-like elements of perception, —

yet it possesses one of the typical merits of fine art: its intense and far-reaching suggestiveness. The concentrated and profound significance of a jewel-like moment can sustain and nourish us through long stretches of Matthew Arnold's "conduct" and give edge and point to the dullest thinking. A shining moment may center the meaning of a whole month, as a single cadence dominates the development of a whole symphony.

Why should we not prize these ubiquitous jewels the more because they are accessible to all? They are more brilliant than rubies, less subject to the depreciation of familiarity, or fashion, and infinitely more various, since they can appeal to us through sound, touch, odor, and taste as well as through the vibrations of light. That possession of them costs nothing and excludes no one is surely a reason for valuing them still more highly. No one wants to be selfish. It is hard for any one to appropriate money or delight for the lack of which we know that others may be hungry. On the other hand, the homage we pay to the neglected jewels of light, water, sound and fire, so far from dispossessing other people may enrich them; for it may become contagious. Others may catch such enthusiasms without diminishing our stock. Our abundance cannot mean another's lack.

They are democratic, then, these jewel-like experiences, — free to all, shareable by all, the privilege of each. Yet to those who prize (as I do) the virtues of

the monarchical state and want to see them *somehow*
persist in the amber of democracy, it is comforting to
observe that in its own kingdom every jewel is an absolute monarch. A high light is annulled if copies of it
are peppered across a picture. Like every climax, it
makes our pulses throb and our imaginations leap just
because it is a monarch on its throne, honored by de-
pendents and subordinates around it. Its virtues, like
those of monarchy, are communicated to all parts of
the picture, but the less luminous tones have no equal-
ity or fraternity in relation to the high light. Their
virtue is in their subordination.

This monarchical quality of jewel-like moments
gives them power over long spaces of time. They live
in their afterglow and in the thought and action which
they touch off. We mourn their brevity, their intense
but fugitive energy, as mothers repine because their
children will not stay young; but in truth we do not
want them prolonged any more than we want quick
music slowed down, or a smile that is put on to stay.

What is the peculiar value of the minor art of finding
jewels? In the first place, any one can practice it.
There is no lack of such sparkling bits in any one's
environment. Next, they are extraordinarily dynamic;
like high power explosives they can open up deep hidden
strata of consciousness and unlock the springs of lasting happiness. For they are in fact little bits of heaven
which we see by anticipation, as children peek at the
Christmas tree through the curtains.

CHAPTER XIV

GIVE–AND–TAKE IN THE MINOR ARTS AND ELSEWHERE

OVERLOOKED, ridden down, and left by the roadside, there lies a host of divinely simple arts and games. But though we must try to pick up and take home with us as many as we can, we need not crowd out thereby any of the regular occupants of our home. We can play these games and do our "useful" work (good luck to it!) at the same time. They may serve to brighten and tone up whole chapters of otherwise prosaic existence, and even when they are scarcely noticed they often give a sparkling surface to the world we are living in. They are various in a hundred ways, yet in essentials they are much the same.

One of the essentials in the minor arts and games (as well as in the fine arts, in work, in love, and in worship) is "give-and-take," or initiative and response. In the major arts this fundamental may be so overlaid with technique and æstheticism that it needs to be specially pointed out, but in the minor arts it stands out clear. Take, for example, one of the unnamed sports which I will christen as the game of "Getting a Meaning Across."

We can easily learn to recover the child's delight in getting a meaning across and in receiving a return. All

boys, and some undegenerate elders, are fascinated
by the technique of giving and taking a message by
wig-wagging or with a Morse telegraphic key. The
precise nature of the message is a minor point. For until
we grow dulled and rusted we enjoy the art of getting
any message to or from another. It is good fun to wig-
wag any command, to send any words, no matter how
dull or familiar, through the ticking key.

Two things only we demand: there must be somebody
watching at the other end, and the words which we send
must mean something. No art for art's sake will do
here. We are down to fundamentals. We are recognizing and being recognized, ever sacred and mystic arts.

So my dying patient, the butcher, turned with a hom-
ing instinct in his last days to some of the least of these
arts, and found happiness in the elemental, — yes, the
sacramental, — "give-and-take" of speech. He still
possessed that privilege which we hope is not withheld
from any part of creation. If the soils, the flowers, and
the animals get meaning across to each other, doubtless
they enjoy the art as deeply as children do, or as adults
who learn a new language by practicing it upon every
foreigner. My dying friend enjoyed the miracle of communication no matter how simple and unoriginal was
the matter conveyed. He spoke with a smile and answered with a smile, not only for politeness' sake, but
because he enjoyed the give-and-take.

Recognition — no matter of what — is always a
surprise and an adventure, until our appreciation has

died down into dull, senile gazing. Some one holds up his fingers and we delight to see a rabbit's head in the shadow on the wall. We were not told beforehand what we were to see. From among the shadows we plucked out that bit of clear meaning afresh and for ourselves. Therefore it has all the zest of a "find." It was not isolated, framed, labeled, or double-starred in a Baedeker. We are given the same privilege of discovery whenever we listen to the simplest word that falls from another's lips. Till it actually issues, any meaning is possible. The prophetic, the illuminating, word for which the world is hungering may leap forth.

And it is not only from a noble soul, like my butcher's, that the miracle may be expected. "We may be talking with a peevish and garrulous sneak. We are watching the play of his paltry features, his evasive eyes and babbling lips. Suddenly the face begins to change and harden, the eyes glare like the eyes of a mask, the whole face of clay becomes a common mouthpiece and the voice that comes forth is the voice of God uttering His everlasting soliloquy."[1]

So in the midst of a madman's chatter I have heard the awful word of Truth sounding through. I have heard a maniac expound a scheme to save my soul and yours, a scheme saner, more practicable, and far-seeing than most that I have yet heard. He is well now and venturing forth to put that plan in practice. It holds good now that the madness has left him, yet he never

[1] G. K. Chesterton, *Life of Browning*, p. 202.

conceived it or uttered it till he was in the grip of in-sanity.

But I am still more interested that we should recog-nize and cultivate the very primitive game of Recog-nition (called "see the point" or "catch the idea"), when nothing great or beautiful is specially to be looked for. You *give* a look, throw out an idea, hazard a guess. You *take back* an impression, a surprise, a delight. Tennis is a great game, even when it is played by duf-fers, and when you play the game of Recognition with any person, there need be no heroic wisdom on the one side nor impressive beauty on the other. You do not even need another person. You can play the game alone. For instance: —

The hour is seven in the morning and, though it is summer and bright sunshine, you are still sleepy. But though your mind is not yet fully awake, something unexpectedly fires you into the ancient game of Recog-nition.

"What is that thing over there?"

With your ocular and pupillary muscles, with retina, brain and mind, you aim and fire.

"Just there," you send your bullet. "I'll bet I know what it is." There is a moment of suspense. Yes, you have got it. It is as you thought; that wonderful and beneficent object *is* a toothbrush! But in your new posi-tion the toothbrush sends something back to you. You have given; now you take the return. You are forced to recognize something that you did not pursue or expect.

"What's this that I find upon my retina, left here like a foundling, just as I am starting upon another errand? Why, it is as beautiful as the rainbows over the Niagara mist and far more brightly colored. Surely no one has put an opal into the handle of that toothbrush."

Then naming begins and the first flush of miracle fades, as we recognize that "this" is the "light of common day" striking the glass handle of the toothbrush and broken into rainbow colors on the towel beneath. It is only the "hygienic glass-handled toothbrush" which you have recently purchased. But it has given you a glorious hunt, and though the quarry is now bagged and lifeless compared to what it was before you fired a leaden conclusion into it, you have still the hunter's golden memories to look back to.

To take a message or send a message by the telegraphic system which we call sight or speech, is a pleasant game to many children, many Italians, Negroes, French, in fact I suppose to pretty much all the nations except the sober "Anglo-Saxons," — a game endlessly flexible and variable, a sport of which one never tires. The "give-and-take" of sight (never "take" alone if intelligence is awake) has the excitement of battledore and shuttlecock. Nay, rather battledore and shuttlecock is fun because it apes language in the fullness and neatness of its give-and-take.

Here I believe is one of the most searching tests of any game or art: Is it so various, so flexible, and yet so artistically limited, that there is room in it for many kinds of give-and-take, such as improvisation, surprise, adventure, clear success, and obvious failure? If so, it is a good game, a fine art. If not, it is sure to degenerate into gambling, into technique and æstheticism, into nirvanesque vagueness, or into a simple bore. Let us follow this clue somewhat further.

With each ball sent in, the baseball pitcher "gives" and the batter "takes," or leaves, an opportunity. Never before in the history of the world has precisely this chance been given or taken. Hence freedom and the stamp of individuality is in every play. But more than that, the rôles are perpetually changing. If the batter hits the ball, it is his turn to give and the fielder's to take a chance. The peculiar greatness of baseball, compared with other games, is in the endless variety of opportunities given, taken, refused, or missed, and the innumerable ways in which one can give, take, or miss. Success and failure are clean-cut. There is no limbo between.

In football, tennis, billiards, leap-frog, shooting, fishing, boxing, wrestling, fencing, chess, whist, hide-and-seek, — the fascinating variety of "gives" and "takes" is clear. But this is not so true of rowing, bicycling, sailing, swimming, skating, coasting, and track athletics, for it is now with inanimate antagonists that we engage. Oar and water hit or miss each other as we row, but it is not a very vital sort of conversation. Ice is still less various and responsive. When we come to track athletics, we must confess that the running-track and the ground from which the jumper "takes off" as he rises, can hardly be said to respond at all. It is because these sports are lacking in give-and-take that men rarely sprint or jump merely for the fun of it. Hence competition is left as the heart and soul of all track athletics and marks them thereby as inferior to games like baseball and whist, which contain a back-and-forth element. There is mighty little fun in a mile run or a hammer-throw unless you win. It is hard work and soon grows monotonous. In other words, it is not the best sort of play.

Oratory, if the audience and the orator are at their best, is a fine example of an art built up and adorned by give-and-take. The true orator does not merely spout a piece previously learned by heart. He answers the mood of his audience as dancers answer one another in their dance. Back and forth goes the impulse and the idea, — perhaps through spoken question or comment from the audience, oftener through responses swiftly written in the faces of the hearers and deftly read by the speaker. Ordinary lectures and sermons, on the other hand, suffer because of the passivity of the audience. It is all give and no take, all batting and no return of the ball.

Not so is it with adventure. The give-and-take between man and nature becomes a lively game of "question and answer" when we explore an old clock, a new

country, an animal tissue, or a gas. Our search is no
passive observation and record of what happens; it
is a voyage of discovery. Sometimes we put a loose,
open-minded question as in roaming, browsing, tramp-
ing, "gypsying"; sometimes we plan a tight, narrow
search for one thing only: "Is arsenic present or ab-
sent in this wall-paper?" But the essentials of give-and-
take are always the same. First we shape a searching
question which we cast out like bait or serve like a tennis-ball. Then comes the answer from nature, something caught by the bait of your question, some return
of your service. If we get no definite answer the search
is a failure; it was not sufficiently well planned. Good
exploring knows what it is after and shapes its plan so
that it is sure to get an answer telling whether it has
succeeded or failed. The explorer who seeks the Pole
must know when he gets there; if not he should stay at
home.

If there is a long interval between service and return,
between question asked and answer received, we call
this investigation "work," not "play." For example,
it is bent and painful toil to count the red corpuscles of
the blood; for during the lengthy operation, the mind is
suspended between the question: "Any anæmia here?"
and the answer, "Yes" or "No." We touch no firm
ground of interest on either side. The count is an adventure of the mind, but, as in many adventures, there
is a stretch of desert to be plodded through. Much
scientific work has this arduous, laborious character;

it is far more work than play. But if the answers to our questions come in thick and fast, as they do when we explore a new acquaintance, a virgin forest, or an old house, then science becomes one of the best forms of the Great Game of Give-and-Take.

Contrast the lack of this vital response in the passive music-guzzling of languid matinée audiences. Art is there debased. Consider M. Des Esseintes of Huysman's romance, with his concert of smells.[1] "By means of his vaporizer the room was filled with an essence skillfully compounded by an artist's hand and well deserving its name — 'Extract of the Flowering Plain.' ... Having completed his background he breathed over it all a light spray of essences ... such as powdered and painted ladies use and added a suspicion of lilac."

But what can he do about it all? What answer can he toss back? What thanks? No "inner imitative creation," no creative attention is possible. Unless he has the senses of a Helen Keller, he is more powerless and passive before his chorus of smells than before any other vivid experience. As hand answers hand in touch, so we can answer sound with sound, look with look, dance with dance, landscape with picture or poem. But before a concert of smells we can only breathe and nod. It is pleasure, but nothing more. It is no game, no art.

No art, I say, for the best of art is never in looking

---

[1] Quoted from Groos, *The Play of Man*, pp. 19-20.

on; always in getting into the game. So in watching a jumper I have seen a dozen spectators, at the moment of his leap, quite unconsciously jerk up a leg till the foot was in position to enter a horse's stirrup. Each spectator was giving his mite of aid, and a very substantial aid it is, seeing that practically all the best jumping records are made with the help of an audience. In the cold, alone, men hardly ever jump or run their best.

In listening to music or looking at pictures the same sort of aid and response must be given by audience to artist, if the art is to be fine art. This active aid is what Mr. Schauffler has called so finely the art of "creative listening." [1] We follow the movement of music as spectators follow the flight of the tennis-ball in a match game, craning heads rhythmically to right and left, as if they had but a single neck. "Tone movement glides, turns, twists, hops, leaps, dances, bows, sways, climbs, quivers, blusters and storms — all with equal ease. To reproduce this in the physical world, a man would have to dash himself to pieces, or become imponderable." [2] Yet when we listen to music we seem to perform all these impossible feats (as we do in dreams) and thus give back to the player the response which he needs. We play up to his playing as subordinates support a star. — "Look! I show you a hazy, level horizon over a hot desert," says the music. — "Aye, aye, sir," says the audience, and sees it. — "Now, it's rearing

[1] Robert H. Schauffler, *The Musical Amateur, and Other Essays.* Houghton Mifflin Co., 1912.

[2] Köstlin, quoted by Groos, *The Play of Man*, p. 28.

up against the sky like a drawbridge. — Fly up with it
and over it. — Swoop down on the other side," comes
the order, and with surprised alacrity we obey.

Such a maneuver, initiated by music, carried out
with free improvisations by the audience, is to be dis-
tinguished from the simpler movements suggested by
rhythm. To rhythm, the response of the audience,
with nodding heads and tapping feet, is much easier
and much more obvious. What is our response to the
pitch and quality and intensity of musical tones? I do
not know. It is one of the problems that I hope to see
worked out. But we may rest assured, I think, that we
respond in some way to all that we appreciate in art.
We play over within us what is given us, reshaping
and continuing the idea as we do in talk. This is the
"inner imitative creation" of Souriot.

To "play the game" of life is a phrase that is often
on our lips. I think it should always include both serving and taking the return whatever matter it may be,
grave or trifling, that is sent over the net. Again and
again in this chapter I have said or implied that play
and art find something very fundamental or even sacred in the practice of "give-and-take." In "Work" I
tried to suggest the same thing. Labor without return,
abundance passively gulped down without labor, are
degrading. To make labor worthy, service and return
must occur within such a span as the imagination
can bridge, else we have not work, but drudgery. I
shall try to bring out the same vital responsiveness

in every form of love and of worship which deserves respect.

I suppose any one may be misled into quoting Scripture in support of his fads and fancies. I hope I shall not do so, but I intend to take the risk, for I have long been impressed by the importance of the passages in which Christ emphasized the elemental and universal significance of response: —

"Ask and it shall be given you; Seek and ye shall find; Knock and it shall be opened unto you."

"Take, eat, this is my body."

"He that loseth his life for my sake shall find it."

In the crude ideals of justice ("an eye for an eye and a tooth for a tooth"), in the Christian idea of returning good for evil, in the marriage ceremony when vows and rings are given and received, in the communion service, in the funeral service, even in the service of baptism when the child is offered by its parents and received into the church and state as a gift of God, we find give-and-take wrought into some of our most sacred and time-honored institutions. If this is so in fundamentals, it seems to me only what we might expect that responsiveness should be the keynote of good play and the criterion for distinguishing it from bad.

Summing up my sketch of the minor arts I will mention some of their most characteristic advantages: —

 ✦ (1) Anybody can learn one or more of them and most

people do so. They require no musical ear, no expensive training in Paris. They can be practiced at any time, even in the midst of work and love.

(2) While the service of major arts may drain the artist dry and leave him no vitality for human intercourse, the minor arts (especially humor and good humor) are not so exacting. They exhaust no one; they ease and sweeten our daily life with our fellows. This refreshment is all the more constant because the minor artist seldom finds his audience cold. He has a hundred appreciators (in America, at least) for every one who supports the major arts by his sympathy. Give-and-take flies fast and furious between every minor artist and his audience.

(3) "Good nature" is a singularly rich and pregnant art. Did you ever think of its literal meaning, its headlong plunge to the sweet, sound core of a man? The "good-natured" man is easy to please and hard to sour, because of his supple readiness to play any minor art or game that is going on and to suggest one if nobody else offers to do so. Any minor art and any minor part suits him. He demands no leading rôles, no monument of permanence. His ready smile is the symbol of all this; it is the flag which he flies whenever a game is begun, an adventure launched, or a return taken.

TRANCE IN PLAY

AT the height of our appreciation of beauty and play there is a tendency to dreamy states of mind, and finally to trance. For Ecstasy is the goal and climax to which musician, painter, dancer, poet are leading us, and if we cling to that climax and try to prolong it, we may easily slide over into a sort of Nirvana where life is quenched. The beauty overpowers us. "*Vedi Napoli e poi mori.*"

Oriental music and dancing are directed straight at this goal. They are meant to produce an anticipation of Nirvana by quenching desire, thought, and all awareness of self. In Occidental art there is also much of this semi-hypnotic quality. Strongly marked and monotonous rhythms, with very little melody woven upon them, approach the confines of trance. One favors the hypnotic state or true sleep by listening to any monotonous regularly repeated sound: a ticking clock, a buzzing bell-hammer, a humming insect, the rhythmic clank of sleeping-car wheels.

Music, dancing, and verse make use of this thought-quenching power, whenever a simple rhythm is allowed to become the dominating element, as in barbaric music it always is. In a drum corps, on the other hand, the rhythm is broken; its staccato quality is in itself arousing. It wakes us up, as irregular noises always tend to do.

Now sleep is one thing and play another. Any play which tends to put us to sleep is a poor play, especially if it puts us partially asleep, drugging our intelligence like alcohol and leaving the rest of us awake but ungoverned. Swinging, rocking, chewing gum, and any formless type of music, dance, or verse exemplify what I mean. Such plays are essentially formless. They have no beginning, middle, or end. They minimize variety. They are as circular as worry, returning again and again to the same point, and soon approach the mechanical "running on" of the machine. They leave us passive as the clay of the potter spinning upon its wheel after his shaping hand is withdrawn.

At any moment one can break the trance and relieve the monotony of pure rhythm by weaving an improvisation upon it. Boys seldom stay long in a swing without contriving "stunts" to put variety and adventure into the drowsy motion; but I have seen girls swing indefinitely without variation or check. Such formless plays are meant to kill time, — the Oriental ambition. They are like the endless rhythmic rocking of idiots, or the restless to-and-fro of caged animals. Human prisoners also have such spasms of aimless walking up and down their cells. It quiets the frantic mind.

But in any life-giving play or art these shapeless and narcotizing waves of sound or motion meet their own type of control. There are rules of the game, conventions of the art, a climax, opportunities for originality and courage. Even the loosest nonsense-book, the roughest horse-play, obeys some unwritten code of laws. Despite the groping, sprawling outbursts of energy, it is still pointed towards a vaguely defined end.

It is to be admitted that the utterly loose and form-less plays, like rocking, swinging, and gum-chewing, bring with them a fascination of their own. If we surrender ourselves to them we may succeed in loosing ourselves. Then our finite sorrows as well as our hot ambitions are swallowed up. But such an empty infinity devoid of meaning and activity is, for Christian people, and for any one not poisoned by opium or by the idea of Nirvana, a hell, not a heaven.

We must admit, then, that every game has in it the seeds of degeneration. Like any fine art it can easily slide over into sensualism and fooling. There is truth in the reproach directed against art by the "practical" men and against play by the anti-kindergartners. The soft, pleasure-seeking, enervating effeminacy of the mere æsthete is a danger always threatening us both in the fine arts and in play. But any one who realizes this danger can give the alarm and call the police when he finds that a game, a song, or a dance is beginning to be dominated by the Infinite Void in the shape of slow rhythm. We must clearly recognize that every intense delight is a trap unless treated lightly, symbolically, or as a climax. Crystals are refreshing and rejuvenating if we glance at them and pass on. But crystal-gazing is a disease which splits apart the united soul.

> "He who bends to himself a Joy
> Doth the wingèd life destroy.
> But he who kisses a Joy as it flies
> Lives in Eternity's sunrise."
>
> (*Blake*.)

To bend the Joy to one's self, to cling to it, prolong it, imagine it extended to eternity, crushes out its life in satiety or in the coma of somnolent ease.

"Move on" is the watchword of the Lord, obeyed in every live play and art, as it is in every animal tissue that holds off death by reincarnation. But this eternal and ever valid command meets in play and art an obstacle.

"Got what I want," says Play.

"Bound for death in trance if you stick there," is the answer.

For what decent human being is so smug that he wants to remain as he is? Your vision of beauty and delight is a call to action. Intense emotion calls for intense and far-reaching action in response to the call note of beauty. In work we know this well enough. In art and play we are tempted to forget it, and try to snatch at heaven. For play is a little heaven, a symbol and foretaste of that closer hold on God which in worship is still more nearly attained.

To kill time and personality instead of using them is the defect of the trance-like types of arts and play.

There is no proper response, novelty, and adventure in them, — no moving on from life to greater life, as there ought to be in work, play, love, and worship alike. Lacking response, any one of these four blessings will soothe us into passivity, and become at last a curse. When work deadens and enslaves us by its monotony, it is because it lacks either initiative or response. Slavery is all give, no take; but the slave of business habits or office routine, the drudge who never sees the product of his own labor, gets no more response from earth or soul than the beast of burden. Pay is, indeed, a symbol of response; we take it in answer to our effort. But this symbol, like a dead religious rite, may become a mere form unless there is life or substance behind it.

Play and art, then, like commerce, live by the interchange of value. Barter is native to all games and all creative work. By the swapping of values, beauty as well as wealth is distributed. But if one tries to maintain converse with the empty air or passively to breathe in the spirit of beauty, sleep or lethargy results. "You bet they do," said a "practical" man to me the other day; "and that's why artists are such a lot of sensual loafers. They howl against us commercial people, but in the clubs and wherever the fleshpots are, you'll find the artists congregated like flies and not paying their debts either."

To escape such reproaches the devotee of art or of sport must prove to us that he can recognize and escape the dangers of trance and lethargy which lurk near his road. For his efforts must always aspire to be crowned with a moment of ecstasy and in ecstasy he will linger till it becomes lethargy, unless he has something of the Puritan or of the ascetic in him, some Brünhilde who beckons him on like Siegfried from present victory "*zu neuen Thaten.*"

CHAPTER XVI

MUCH of our physiological need for recreation is in truth not a need for rest, but for freer activity. We must bend and huddle over our work to get it done without mistakes; but the stoop leaves us cramped. We want to stretch. Self-control, which is essential in good work, results not merely in the guidance of some energies but the suspension of many more. The collegian at his studies is far more conscious of a general repression than of any particular guidance. Some one is sitting on the lid of him; that is his chief impression.

Now, in play, somebody gets off the lid and whatever is beneath flies up, with all the stored energy of repression, — provided the cramp has not been too long continued. In time repression may produce such atrophy and flaccidity of our mental muscles that we are incapable of play. But if the great muscles of the soul, unused in ordinary work, have not degenerated, one of the greatest blessings of play is to unleash our straining energies.

Watch a dog that has been tied up, yapping and springing to the limit of his chain, while his master is getting ready for a walk. This is what work means to many. Then watch him when the chain is snapped off; how he rushes away *ventre à terre*, every particle of his energy flung into each bark and leap, as he tears hither and thither. He does not know or care what he is after. He knows only that he is free and that the whole of him is in action. Children just out of school explode with the same whole-hearted and formless glee. We say that the holiday spirit is in them. But anxious householders (with orchards or gardens near by) say that the devil is in them. For like the dog just unleashed, they will run over anything and anybody that happens to stand in the path of their rush. Respectable elderly people ruefully tolerate the destructive explosions of youthful energy, or lament the lack of application and diligence in the young people of to-day. It is hard for "grown-ups" to realize that application and diligence bring with them necessary evils, which it is one of the tasks of play to undo; hard to appreciate the wild onrush of youth's torrents. Spring torrents they certainly are, for they issue in destruction as well as beauty.

Play has in it some of this torrential energy demanding relief. It wants to get out and it ought to get out. It is unhealthy and destructive for the human spirit to issue forth always in parsimonious driblets, as it must in work, never letting out its full force. Play balances work because for children and childlike adults it is one of the most wholehearted things that they ever do, — almost as enfranchising as a sneeze. Birds sing and puppies bark not merely with their throats, but with their tails and with every intermediate bit of themselves. More of this freedom we all need; more totality flung into our days. Athletics provides glimpses of such an outlet to one, music to another, drunkenness, I suppose (for lack of a better), to a third; but no play can satisfy our hunger for total and sincere expression. Worship is the outlet which we really need. Play is a useful safety-valve, but the safety-valve is hardly more beautiful than the steam whistle. It lets off energy; but that is the best we can say of it.

"Expense regardless of pleasure" is the formula for some of the worst forms of architecture, interior decoration, and dress. Expenditure of energy, careless of form, goal, or skill, is the formula for a good deal of bad play, — bad if it continues long enough to be called play at all. An occasional "barbaric yawp," a brief "fit of the giggles," may give harmless relief; yet it is neither play nor sin. So moderate doses of horse-play in the right place and time do no harm; but prolonged, premeditated horse-play soon becomes as tiresome to the players as to the spectators. It is chaotic, and only the degenerate can take chaos in large doses, without a desire to force order into it.

Besides the trance-like plays and the chaotic plays there is another low-grade variety which we may call the "scrappy" or "flashy" plays. Most of these games provide their own funerals, for they dissipate desire without satisfying it; but some of them linger on in deserted corners because they are not challenged and killed out by better sports. If boys can think of nothing better to do, they will wander about, stare in an aimless and vacant way at the doings of their elders, or tear things to bits, not from curiosity to know what is inside them, but from mere restlessness. Adults in the same mood twiddle their fingers, tap with their feet, and read miscellaneous newspaper items. Picking up cigarette stubs and teasing the "cop" are also scrappy games, yet redeemed to some extent because they contain a leaven of adventure which raises them above mere lumpishness. They soon lose their fascination, however, when boys get the chance and the brains for baseball, for scouting, or any play which calls for more originality, more accumulation of skill, and more teamwork.

Gambling, the king of bad plays, is both scrappy, — because no one can carry out a plan, — and passive or lethargic. You get your result, for gain or loss, without any proportionate effort. You open your mouth, shut your eyes, and take what comes. But what you give has no relation to what you take. There is no response and no progress.

Just here, threatening to smash the thesis which I meant to maintain, comes the thought: But God treats us just this way now and then! He gives us friends, powers, delights, and also black losses that we have done nothing to deserve, and when we fail to live up to them he still gives and forgives again and again. The gambler, then, is the man who tries to play God's part, to scale the walls of heaven and act as Providence to himself. He disintegrates morally because it is not for us to decide when we are to have a perfectly unmerited gift or an unearned sorrow.

A summary of the good and bad elements in play may help to pull this chapter together. In bad play we may find rhythm dominant and all other form sacrificed. Rules, limits, and finish are at the minimum. Dash, risks, construction, and originality are not encouraged. Everything is bound, with the fetters of perfect safety or of perfect fatalism. People can keep up a bad game indefinitely or fitfully without a tendency to rebound into work or constructive thought. Passivity and receptivity are so completely in possession of us that there is little for the "actor" to do but to sit still until he becomes a mere spectator. Gambling, listening to lectures, gossip, swinging, rocking, chewing tobacco or gum, opium-smoking, and, in some people, cigarette-smoking, are amusements of the vicious type. They have no end or form. They leave you as passionless and passive as the suburbanite reading his after-breakfast newspaper on the train to town.

Good play is subject to rules; it has a clear-cut form and organization. It may use rhythm and repetition, but subordinates them to improvisation and adventure. It gives intense and varied delight, but in

such dynamic form that pleasure is ever quickly lost
and found again. It is full of give-and-take, dramati-
cally loses its life to find it, and ever seeks, asks, knocks
at the door of the unexplored. Its house is full of symbols and empty of idols.

CHAPTER XVII

THE GAME, OR ART, OF IMPERSONATION IN WORK, PLAY, AND LOVE

PLAY is drenched with symbolism and ritual. Think of the mystical significance of being "it" in tag, or in hide-and-seek! A unique and invisible crown of distinction descends suddenly upon a boy and he is "it." Just the tag, just the mystical laying-on of a hand, has transformed your harmless and undistinguished fellow into a bearer of destiny and danger. The responsibility may fall upon any one, regardless of color, creed, or previous condition of servitude; but how swiftly it transforms one's every feature and movement! Uniform and insignia of office are unnecessary because every one sees them in imagination.

All play begins with such an impersonation. Every player assumes a part and if time permitted should be costumed. The lowly second hand at whist should certainly have a costume to distinguish him from the dashing and original first hand, and the lordly, judicial third hand. But in whist, rôles are exchanged so swiftly that no quartette of lightning-change artists could keep pace with them. The musician who throws himself into his music assumes in each piece a new character. An actor of extraordinary versatility he thus assumes himself to be, and he fails if he cannot prevent us from recognizing his familiar personality sticking out through the monkish cowl of Bach, the Byronic cloak of Chopin, and the goat-skin mantle of Debussy.

To paint, one must put off the spectacles of every day through which one perceives the literal and utilitarian aspects of nature, and put on a mask which shuts away one's ordinary features and senses. For to front nature as a painter is to be blind to the interests of the landowner, farmer, miner, or woodsman.

This ever-present need of impersonation in play and art is closely bound up with their symbolism. For to use symbolism is to put a new personality into an object, while impersonation puts a new personality into one's self. A football loose in a broken field of players is the very incarnation of desire; it is only when the whistle blows for an intermission that the ball becomes as dead as the dirt beneath it.

Moreover, though impersonation is perhaps more complete and successful in play than anywhere else, play enjoys no monopoly. Play-acting turns up in almost every department of life. We put on a character in work, in love, and in every moral effort. In medical work, for instance, we assume at the start the rôle of medical student and try to play that sardonic part with success. Underneath the mask we still recognize ourselves as scatter-brained boys, but we do our best to forget this and to maintain the disguise. Next, in our hospital service, we don the white coat and the lofty airs of the house-officer, while still unused to being addressed as "doctor" and feeling a bit of humbug in the title. Finally we graduate as full-fledged doctors and sit in an office waiting for patients. But there we are more than ever conscious of impersonating some one woefully different from ourselves. We are cast for the part of the wise old physician. We who have been in scrapes half our lives! We, who are in terror that our ignorance may any day be unmasked, are set here to inspire others with confidence in our wisdom! For did not the professor tell us that the first essential for success is to "gain the confidence of your patient"? My! what a fool that patient will be if he gives any such confidence!

I know that there is need of the art of impersonation in medical work, and I see no reason to believe that the budding lawyer, legislator, or plumber feels any more at home in his rôle. After many years the costume comes to fit better, and when our growth stops altogether we are wholly reconciled to our part and begin to take ourselves "seriously." In time we may even be persuaded (if we are dull and credulous) that we fill our parts well. But as long as there is any fresh sap flowing in us, we shall recognize the humor and the pathos of our attempt to be what our professional title proclaims us to be. A game it will always be, a game to play the best we can, to practice as hard and learn as thoroughly as our nature allows; but still a game.

Thus art, play, and impersonation seep into every crack and crevice of the structure called work. Is it any different in love and friendship? What man has not suffered from stage fright when set to impersonate that most august, yet most versatile and accomplished character, the husband? Nor is the rôle of a "friend" a much easier one to play. No friend feels friendly all the time; yet he cannot tear off his wig and let out his raucous natural voice every time that he happens to feel less than amicable. Nor can he throw up his job whenever he feels sulky and envious of those who play the leading rôles, such as lover, boss, or professor!

What more exciting game, what more difficult art! It is not all play. Mighty hard work sometimes. But the spirit of play has come to aid the spirit of work. Effort and fruition, work and play, are interwoven as tightly as the strands in a carpet.

One more word about the art of impersonation in relation to knowledge and to love. Sympathy is admittedly a long step towards love. Sympathy with every product of creation is the desire of every one who wants to live intelligently in the world and not monkishly outside it. There is no comprehension without sympathy, and sympathy means impersonation. Therefore, to be able to impersonate like an actor every scoundrel and simpleton, every wind of prejudice and current of politics, brings us to the limit of pure intelligence and to the threshold of love. How can we deal wisely with the simpleton, justly with the scoundrel, unless we learn to put ourselves, like an actor, in their places?

This involves no danger of adopting permanently the characters that we impersonate. We can choose good from bad all the more clearly if we know them intimately, by true sympathy. To cultivate love sounds mawkish and unnatural, but to cultivate sympathy is a large part of liberal education. I can see no limit to the benefit of impersonative sympathy in a well-balanced mind. I have a friend who likes to impersonate a wave or a barn swallow. I am sure he gets closer than the rest of us to the life of waves and swallows because he loves to shape himself into their image. It is hard, I admit, for swift, locomotive Americans to impersonate (as Oriental mystics do) the rigid immobility of the tree or the smiling passivity of sunshine, but we must acknowledge our limitation. Only the narrowly anthropomorphic can be content to say, "I count nothing human as foreign to me." What about the non-human world? No doubt our nearest kith and kin should come first. Charity begins at home and impersonation, the servant and forerunner of charity, should naturally begin with the imitation of Christ. But when he told us to consider the lilies of the field, he did not invite us to look down upon them patronizingly nor, at the other extreme, to worship their beauty. He meant us to divest ourselves of human prejudices and to recognize their superiority to us in certain traits, — worthy our respectful and sympathetic imitation.

Impersonation, then, is an art much needed in order

to prepare and discipline our stiff-necked individuality
for the love and the knowledge of all created beings.

Impersonation includes the whole field of morality:
"Be a brave girl and don't cry"; "Behave like a gentleman"; "Take a man's part in this fight." Such ex-
hortations bid us assume a virtue if we have it not, and
in assuming it to impersonate a better self. So long as
we are growing, so long as we are divided within ourselves, striving to be or to become what as yet we are
not (but ought to be), there is impersonation in our
effort.

Why, then, is a school of acting not the only school
of morality? Because in learning to act we are trained
to suppleness of impersonation; we are taught to sym-
pathize with any character so deeply that it becomes
for the time ours. An actor should be able to impersonate a mean sneak or a cruel liar as sympathetically
as he dons the hero's mantle. Carry this process to
the limit and a man's native character could be dis-
solved not developed, his moral vision dazzled not
clarified, and his progress towards his own personal
ideals *nil*. But of course the actor, even of the Salvini
tradition, does not carry acting to the limit. He leads
his own life and minds his own business both on the
stage and off. In so doing he chooses, as we all do, the
sort of personality (which means a mask) that shall be
his. He is no longer impartial and pliant. He is himself.
   The sort of impersonation which is the whole of

morality, and constitutes a large part of work, play, and love, differs from theatricality, first because each actor chooses the part which he thinks will best suit him and tries to stick to it (more or less successfully) until he sees a better. He is not at all ready to play the heavy old gentleman, the dastardly villain, or the disappointed lover. He claps the lid upon his sympathies when they run to self-pity. The professional actor must welcome the opportunity sympathetically to impersonate self-pity like any other characteristic. In life one does not practice the art of losing one's temper or beating one's wife, but on the stage these accomplishments are strictly in the line of business.

I have said that impersonation is the whole of morality. The growing sapwood of our nature, all that is struggling against itself towards perfection, advancement, or skill, is perpetually passing in and out of the art of impersonation. All this? What, then, is left? Very little, it appears; for are we not to be ever pressing forward towards the mark of our high calling? Does not all that is decent in us want to be up and growing more decent? Shall we not perpetually aspire, or at any rate "climb"?

No. For the morality of impersonation and self-conquest is not the whole of life. At our worst we sink below impersonation; but at our best we rise above it. There is no impersonation in heroism. A self-conscious, theatrical hero is a contradiction in terms.

Either he is carried away by his impulse or he is no more heroic than you or I. Art, when it rises beyond talent to genius, is the product of a present self-surrender, though perhaps of a past self-conquest. Overwhelming grief is no impersonation. It is elementally sincere.

On the other hand, innocence is not impersonation. Children pass through a period when there is no perceptible division of better against worse, no straining towards a future, no attempt to be other than they are. In this *Blüthezeit* they attain perfections which their elders never reach. Or, quite uncorrupted, they may commit acts which in an adult would be sin.

Adults, I believe, occasionally lapse or escape into this innocence. "I never hear the word escape," says Emily Dickinson, "without a quicker blood, a sudden expectation, a flying attitude." In the vast majority of us, such passion to escape is simply a blunder or a bit of selfishness, and corrupts when it conquers. But it may be a flash of genius; it may rush into musical or metrical composition. It may also be an irruption of the animal in us which wrecks lives around us, yet leaves us ourselves unscathed because there has been no yielding, nor any informing consciousness of what we are about. In one's self it is safe to assume that such passivity is always bad. But let us sometimes give others the benefit of the doubt. They may be feeble-minded. They may be innocent.

Impersonation, then, is essentially playful. Yet it penetrates into every part of active life, plays its part

in work, in love, and even in worship, which must
be learned like everything else by throwing ourselves
whole-heartedly into what seems at first strange.
This means that the divisions named in the title of
this book are not mutually independent. Like key,
time, shading, and timbre in music, the four energies
of which I am writing cannot be torn apart without
wounds or death for all. In a book one can fix attention on one at a time, but in life they constantly inter-
act. The better the life, the more perfectly they answer
one another, as I shall try to show in the final chapter.

CHAPTER XVIII

THE PENETRATION OF WORK BY PLAY AND THE MINOR ARTS

I WAS watching the engineer of the train which I left at the terminus the other day, as he climbed down from his cab for a word or two with the conductor. In their talk you could see "work" and "play" swiftly alternating and interweaving as they do so often in American life. First there was a moment of work, — the exchange of serious professional information. Then I heard a reference to "the old man" (whoever he was), and instantly fun began to roll about in their cheeks like a quid of tobacco. Feet and legs began to twitch, sketching suggestions of a cake-walk or a double-shuffle, while words were jerked out in snatches over their shoulders. Business flashed in again when a passing brakeman hooked his hand into the conductor's elbow and emitted a brief message. Their faces fell and stiffened for an instant, but relaxed again as the engineer pulled himself up the perpendicular cab-steps with a parting witticism.

In America this leaven of humor is, I suppose, the commonest of the interpenetrating minor arts. As it plays through and around the dullest tasks, one wonders whether the solution of the problem of drudgery may not come in part through learning to get our work done as automatically and unconsciously as we perform the huge labor of breathing. Consciousness might meantime be occupied with something better worth while. Many people whistle or sing as they work, and I think it is especially in the dullest jobs like housework and coal-heaving that I have heard them sing.

The engineer and conductor whose skillful interweaving of work and play I tried just now to sketch, remind me of another dull job, irradiated by the beauty of art. To take tickets as one walks down the aisle of a railway car is ordinarily a very serious and mechanical process, dull work if not drudgery. I have occasionally seen it done with pleasure and grace by a chatty and amusing conductor, but the greatest triumph of art that I remember was the performance of M. on a suburban branch of the Boston and Albany Railroad. For though he lacked the facilities of gossip and humor, he succeeded in making the dry act of surrendering one's ticket a pleasure to every suburbanite who rode on that branch.

The exquisite, deferential, and courtly was his line. He wore the regular conductor's uniform of dark-blue cloth and brass buttons, but he contrived to keep the blue so glossy and the brass so resplendent that his entrance quite lighted up the car. He had, as I have said, no conversational powers. Perhaps it was this lack which led him to the quaint but pleasant habit of carrying a rosebud, or some other flower, in his lips. It sounds expensive; perhaps he was a disguised millionaire and gathered the blossoms in his own greenhouse each day. Anyway, he carried the perfume and fresh beauty of *somebody's* greenhouse into those dingy cars every day throughout the winter that I rode with him.

He took each ticket with a slight bow and just the ghost of a smile, but most characteristic of all was the reverential care with which he received the ticket, as if to express his sense of the great favor that you did him in surrendering it at all. He reminded me of the minister's gracious tenderness as he takes a baby from its mother to baptize it.

With the reception of the ticket M.'s art ceased abruptly. He punched it like any other machine. Could he have done otherwise, I wonder? Could Cyrano de Bergerac have punched each ticket with spirit and originality? Is there an irreducible residue of pure, eternal drudgery? Surely not. You and I reach our limit. We are checked by something we cannot mould to the purpose of art, — something that remains hard work and nothing else. But then you and I cannot take tickets like M., nor make rhymes while we fence like Cyrano. We are still too serious and self-conscious; but there are hopes for us yet with the Jews, Irish, and Italians pouring in to leaven our lump of Anglo-Saxondom.

CHAPTER XIX

BY-PRODUCTS OF PLAY: CONSECRATION OF PLAY

THE central value of play is apt to be obscured by over-emphasis upon its minor issues. Among these are health and disease, pleasure and honor, education and victory.

Health as I have already said, sometimes results from some games and arts. Thus well-to-do girls on the whole probably get physical benefit from dancing parties, though the late hours and bad air go far to neutralize any benefit. Whist and chess, painting and music probably do us more harm than good physically, but no one abandons them, or ought to abandon them on that account. The net hygienic results of college football have been calculated differently by different observers. I believe that they are good on the whole, though not in every team or in every member of any team. But even if the bad hygienic results overbalanced the good (as I think they do in music), I should believe in the game just the same. Many a player looks back upon his football career and is glad of it for the sake of the game itself, though he bear the honorable scars of contest.

Pleasure certainly bears an organic relation to play. Unless for money or some other extraneous reason, no' one, I suppose, pursues an art or game which is painful on the whole. On the other hand, many pleasurable acts — sucking candy, for instance — are not games or arts. Pleasure is the sense of getting what we want, and play is one of the things which we want. Pleasure, therefore, accompanies it as it also accompanies worship, the receipt of money, the process of going to sleep, and many other non-playful acts. It is a natural accompaniment of play, but not a mark by which to characterize it.

The *education* of minds and muscles by play is of great value. It also helps to educate us towards self-control, originality, and many other good qualities. But education, like pleasure, must usually be forgotten if you are to attain it in play. If you think of your feet while dancing, you cannot dance. If you think of your educational gain or your pleasure-income while you are in the heat of play, you will miss both. For mental integrity — knitting up the divided mind — is essential to play. To throw one's self into a game, as good players do, is to forget one's self and all one's possible earnings.

Victory is the part of play most often abnormally prominent in popular games. Of course nobody wants to fail in a game or anything else; but when one loses one wants to be a good loser, and this art of being a good loser is half the battle both in good play and in good living. If it is a pure misery to lose (as it is in gambling), then the game or the player is debased. Furthermore, if the only satisfaction is in winning, all close games are misery until the result is known, and then they are over. This predominance of what we don't want would soon drive us into disgust with any game, if winning were its only point. That most boys like to play games, such as football and baseball, which are often close, that boys dislike one-sided games and weak opponents, proves that the desire to win is not the only motive nor the chief one. Yet the desire to win must be a factor, else the game is tasteless.

In all good sport, then, we are in a paradoxical state of mind. We want to win, but we want still more to play the game according to the rules and against a tough antagonist. We want to win fairly and in a contest that puts us on our mettle. To win easily is not much fun. To win by cheating leaves us aware that, in fact, we did not win at all. Cheating is rife especially among two groups of players; first, those who are playing for money (salaries, bets, or bribes) or who have lost their interest in the game itself; secondly, among beginners who have never acquired much fondness for it. Cheating is also common in all games with ill-defined rules, games such as horse-dealing and the manipulation of investments.

Education towards good sport consists in the proper placing of the desire to win, a desire which is essentially the same in athletics, professional life, and moral aspiration. Walking, talking, eating, running after one's hat, — every conceivable act wants to win its goal. The presence of a visible competitor is not essential. Winning and losing feel much the same whether there is a human competitor or not. For when you win you always defeat something (if not somebody). To be beaten by the waves when you are trying to swim the English Channel must feel very much the same as being beaten in the race with a man. The worst of the disaster is in losing, not in losing to somebody else. Unless you happen to hate your competitor, you do not care who gets the trade or the game which you lose. It is your own loss that hurts, because it is a blow to pride and self-respect, rather than because it deprives you of any tangible prize. In amateur athletics this point is usually obvious, though the social honors naturally paid to winners somewhat obscure the issue. Even these honors, however, show that the heart of the desire to win is a hunger for increased self-respect. The praise of others feeds our fundamental desire "to make good."

Moral aspiration is nothing else but this "desire to win" generalized. The moral aspirant, like the athlete, has to learn the spirit of fair play and good sport. His desire to win must be disciplined till it is a desire either to win under the rules of life's game or to take defeat in good part. You want an education, a chance to put your powers at the service of the public, an opportunity to know the people who will show you your limitations and tempt you beyond them. But you do not want these prizes unconditionally. You do not want education if you have to steal the money to get it. You will not take the money if that acceptance means crushing the life out of your family, draining their resources dry in order to push you ahead. If another member of your family can obviously do better with that education than you can, family affection will make you want your own defeat. That is only fair play. The popular prayer, "May the best man win," is as appropriate for educational aspiration as it is for athletics.

This prayer is the absolute and unconditional wish behind all the renunciations of good sport. When both teams before a football game heartily and unconditionally wish that the best team may win, they can both be sure (barring flukes) that they will get that wish fulfilled. So in a sense they all win, whatever happens. If accidents seriously interfere with the game, it ought to be played over, as in some cases it is. At any rate, fair play and the honest desire to prove which team is best, demand that the game shall be played over.

Is it a bodiless abstraction, — this desire for a fair game, this chastened but mighty desire which can always win its end? On the contrary, with mature players (who are the best players) the desire for good sport may become as whole-hearted and natural as any bodily appetite. They get their satisfaction, as singers do, in the game itself, and they get it all the way along, not simply in the triumphant termination of the games which they happen to win. Moreover, they are always thinking of other games and in this sense "never know when they are beaten." They try to learn from each game (successful or unsuccessful) what will serve to win the next. Thus contests, like years or tennis games, get linked up in sets, and our losses in one guide us to the next. In view of what went wrong in the last, one plans for better success, or at any rate a game fight in the next.

To lose a game or a political fight, without losing one's courage, is to feed on the invisible when visible food is taken away. Beaten in every obvious and literal sense, the undiscouraged loser falls back upon the inner life. He takes to his inner line of defenses, there to maintain the fight unbeaten and undismayed. The "lost cause" becomes idealized into something which no one can lose until he loses the courage to fight for it. No sensualist, no one who has not some sort of faith in the ultimate victory of the invisible right which he serves, can keep his courage in any defeat, great or small.

On the other hand, no winner can avoid conceit and the pride which traditionally precedes a fall, if he takes his victory at its face value. The sympathy and applause of the bystanders are rank poison to a winner who has not learned to discount them, to look away from them, and point his admirers to the value of comrades, the wisdom of trainers, the good luck and good teamwork on which he has ridden to victory. Standing as the product, the representative, the symbol of all these great forces, he can take his victory without inner disaster.

The good winner is apt to take victory lightly for still another reason. Like the good loser, he is always looking forward to another and greater contest. Now that he has topped a foothill, he sees the steeper ranges ahead. The very moment of victory over the last hill spreads out before him for the first time the arduous prospect of the one ahead. Victory, literal and un-abashed, means looking backward. The good winner looks backward too; he is not blind to what he has won; for one ecstatic moment he tastes its full sweetness, but next instant he looks ahead and prepares for the harder contest.

The consecration of play, the element of spiritual nobility which utilitarians and the unplayful cannot see in it, is the necessary result of faithfulness to an invisible ideal of good sport. To be a good winner and a good loser is a wholly spiritual desire. In the political battles of some Spanish-American republics, the winning party guzzles and tyrannizes; the losing party revolts and tries to kill or banish the winning team. This means simply that there is no loyalty to the rules of the game. The desire to win is unconditional; the spoils of office are the only moving power and the only reward of the winner. The loser cherishes no hopes for his lost "cause," but sulks or storms.

But in good sport or good politics there emerges the paradox of self-government, the subordination of a self to a Self (good citizenship, lawful government, fair play) which lives on and deserves our best service whether we win or lose. In good sport neither success nor failure is taken at its face value. Victory is not purely sweet; defeat has its compensations. The cause which you work for in athletics is rarely recognized, I suppose, as part of the service of God. But in honest politics (for which "good sport" is certainly the best training) most sincere enthusiasts believe themselves to be servants of "the people," and many aspire to find, through them, the will of God. Ask any one who has worked to uphold the standard of good sport and later has labored for good government, whether the two efforts do not call for the same spirit and exercise the same spiritual muscles. Not only leaders and prophets of sport, but all subordinate players who obey the rules of the game and learn to be good winners and good losers, are working to uphold the standards of good sport. They are practicing the art of taking victory and defeat symbolically; they are living the spiritual life.

I must digress at this point to explain more clearly what I mean by *symbolism* both in play and outside it. Most of us hear of symbols in algebra or in religion, but have no idea of meeting them in play. Yet to my mind play without symbolism is like music without notes or verse without words.

· A symbol is a representative, standing for something greater than itself. The golden balls stand for the pawn-broker, the striped suit for the convict, the cross for Christianity. Increasingly civilization rests on symbol-ism, as commerce rests on credit. Yet to the unin-formed, all symbols are meaningless. The savage may value an old newspaper more than a thousand-dollar bill, because the newspaper is larger. He takes the bill as literally as some people take death or birth, recog-nizing no larger value behind it. The bill is a bit of paper. To the savage it is nothing more, while to most of us it is hard to recall the time when we saw it merely as paper.

The great value of symbols is that they enable us to handle or to express what would otherwise be too great for us. To carry a thousand dollars in silver or gold would make swift or nimble motions impossible and fatigue always imminent. To carry about and barter the goods which this thousand will purchase is quite impracticable. Hence money-symbols are short cuts and labor-saving devices. When word-symbols replace our earlier picture language, we save the time needed to draw and to understand the pictures. Further, people are enabled, by symbols as by the switching-towers in a railway yard, to plan and to execute much more complex, far-reaching, and accurate results.

Whether in play, in speech, in currency, in religion, or in politics, symbols are precious because they con-vey a wealth of meaning in compact form. Despite their convenience they are quite arbitrary and ridiculous to those who do not grasp them. So are the rules of a game, which limit the players' freedom and unite them despite their rivalry. These rules are as arbitrary as the designs on currency, and incapable, like currency, of giving us an immediate reward or tangible utility. "Hang the rules," we are all of us prone to say when they balk us of victory. Shall a few sentences, perhaps not even printed but only handed down by tradition, — shall these bodiless ideas stand in the way of our getting what we hotly want? Yes, they shall do just that, and we shall learn to submit to them as we submit to greater laws, national, moral, and divine. For every business man is tempted to "hang the rules" when they interfere with his profits, and every one of us longs to hang the moral law when it interferes with what we want to do.

Respect for vital but intangible meaning behind a reasonable law, which baffles or defeats our will, is a training in the use of great symbols and so in the exercise of spiritual muscles. Respect for the same law when it brings us profit and success, means triumph in a yet more searching test, and exercises another set of spiritual muscles.

Our moments of success or of defeat are not merely what they seem on the face of them. They stand as symbolic representatives of what the law and the invisible powers of the world have put up to us. They are interpreted like words or coins by remembering what stands behind them, out of sight. For in success we recognize (or ought to) that without the protection of the law we should not have won. Chance or the crude strength of those opposed to us would have rolled us in the dust but for the law. In almost every sport there are moments when it is only by the rules that our opponents are prevented from running away with the game. In some of our great cities there are criminal gangs which, but for the law and its enforcement, would break over us like a tidal wave. It is not by our own personal merits, but by the force of law and by the help of our fellows that we win free space for happiness and creation. Elemental nature, too, is kept at bay, not by what you and I do, but by the police protection of science which keeps us safe because we obey the laws of that great game.

Play, then, is consecrated by its symbolism and the ideals of good sport which it embodies. But the essence of good sport, — obedience to rules, ability to be a modest winner and cheerful loser, — is also the essence of self-government, good service, and spiritual growth.

PART III : LOVE

CHAPTER XX

THE ALLIES OF LOVE

IT seems hardly decent to discuss so sacred a matter in the publicity of print. Dimly aware of this, we try to approach the subject delicately through such phrases as "The Spirit of Youth" (Jane Addams) or "The Life Force" (G. Bernard Shaw in "Man and Superman"). To free the word "love" from its association with boudoirs and morbid novels, we try to identify it with something genial and all-pervasive, to ally it with the great, sane forces of nature. For we believe that if these allies stimulate and reinforce personality, if they awaken and intensify our feeble energies, then they tend to ennoble our affections.

Elemental nature is one such ally. A group of people who start on a camping trip tolerably indifferent to each other, will usually come home bubbling over with friendliness. There may have been very little talking during the entire trip. What has drawn them together? Is it not the close contact with elemental conditions in paddling, carrying, cooking, and sleeping by the camp-fire? To share fatigue, disappointment, surprise, hunger, and good appetite, gives people a common life. Facing nature they join hands, reinvigorated. Friends who went through the horrors of the San

Francisco earthquake in 1906, and kept their spiritual
senses alert, tell me that their most poignant experience
was not one of horror or of pity, but of the almost
miraculous attainment of human brotherhood. During the days just after the disaster, when rich and poor
waited in line together for their allowance of bread and
milk, "I saw," says a friend, "a rich woman from the
St. Francis Hotel lying asleep on a doorstep with her
head on a muff. A long sable coat was thrown over
her and under one corner of it a young Japanese boy
was curled up asleep. . . . Everybody was everybody's
friend, and though we were all dog-tired, there was not
a word of complaint or ill-nature." To bivouac together
in the park and take care of each other's babies around
fires of driftwood gathered from the beach, made men
and women once more defenseless children of the earth,
revealed each to each in their innate and genuine love-
ableness. Common danger and mutual helpfulness,
common misfortune, common work, common confront-
ation with the elemental, brought a swift achievement
of almost ideal brotherhood. A crushing blow made
all the world for a time kin.

Within a few weeks, it is true, the San Franciscans
forgot this beneficent revelation and slid back into their
old animosities. Any other set of people would have
done likewise. But even that pitiful relapse serves to
make my present point the clearer. Affection, this time
in the form of comradeship, was for a day reinforced,
almost consecrated, by contact with hostile nature;

then lost its sacredness again, when the bond of contact was broken and "civilization" once more got the upper hand.

In hospital work patients, doctors, and nurses, who face terror and disease together, are often knit into comradeship, like soldiers on a campaign. The "new patient" just entering a hospital is often forlorn and terror-stricken as a child lost in a forest or landed friendless in a strange country. The menace of illness, the hospital's dark and fearful suggestions, its sights and sounds and smells, make him hunger for friendly guidance. Hence it is marvelously easy to serve him as a friend in need. Through the simplest physical helpfulness or decent sympathy, one gains a foothold in friendship which could not be won in months of acquaintance outside of the hospital. Why? Because disaster and sickness renew our instinctive alliance with any human being against the assaults of the non-human world.

I have been speaking so far of strangers made friendly by working together against elemental nature. But nature can bring new strength not only to the most general and vague affections, but to *all* affections, even to the most sacred of human ties. On one of our rare country outings last spring, my wife and I wandered away from the violets and the apple blossoms and came all at once upon a place where the grass was afire. Some stumps and one small cedar were also burning. It was a bit of country precious to us both; so as soon as we had explored a little and mapped out our task, we started to choke out the remnants of the fire.

Some parts we could beat out with a stick, others we smothered with damp earth. Before long each of us was possessed by that passion of accomplishment which so often carries one far beyond the original plan. We quite forgot each other, and when at last I straightened up and looked over the stump which I had been pounding, I could just see my wife far off on the brow of a hill. Her back was towards me, but I could see that she was stamping and beating out the patches of smouldering fire, quite as engrossed in her work as I had been in mine. When I joined her, her shoes were white with dust. There were flakes of ashes on her black hair. Her skirt was pinned up, and she was on the warpath, so intent on her task that when she raised her head her eyes scanned me for an instant almost as if I had been a stranger. But what I felt most vividly was that we had both been down into a bath in the elemental — "the healthy underworld where things slumber and grow," — and that in our very forgetfulness of each other, our love had taken up into itself some of the sweetness and patience of the earth.

We are apt to think that our contact with nature, in work or play, is good chiefly because it benefits our health or increases our knowledge. But I think we should remember and cultivate nature's beneficent influence upon our affections. On them, as well as on our muscles, nature bestows new spring, tone, and control.

Art no less than nature can enrich and reinforce the springs of our affection. How warmly we sometimes feel toward those with whom we have just sung a stirring chorus or a noble hymn! Have not all of us come away from some deeply moving music, aware of something curiously familiar and endearing in those previously indifferent to us? Any lover of Wagner will recall, for instance, the wonderful passage in the second act of "Lohengrin," after the marriage of the hero and heroine. Their love for each other rises to a higher power when Lohengrin goes to the window and throws it open. A flood of spring moonlight and spring fragrance pours in. Permeated by the beauty of the night, spring's creative forces in their veins, they are more deeply united to each other, and every spectator who has ears to hear is also united more sacredly with whosoever is dear to him.

We must agree with Tolstoy that lawless art stirs up lawless love. On the other hand, to read of Stevenson's affection for Walter Ferrier [1] or Dante's exalted passion for Beatrice, surely increases our capacity for the nobler types of love; for to appreciate is always in some measure to appropriate.

Each of love's neighbors contributes something precious towards the richness of its chords. Nature gives them a new timbre, art adds an ampler vibration. Playfulness, patriotism, loyalty to truth and to honor but-

[1] As suggested in the essay called "Old Mortality."

tress and strengthen them like contrapuntal melodies.
Like a symphony without its mischievous *scherzo,*
love is maimed and darkened if it cannot express itself in "jest and sport and quip and crank." We laugh
for love as well as for joy or triumph, and smiles carry
the messages of affection as often as those of fun.

By nature and art, by playfulness, patriotism, truth-
fulness, and all the greatest forces in our nature, love
is penetrated, nourished, and supported. I marvel
sometimes when I see two people marry, and then try
to feed their love simply on each other. It is inconceivable that any love can live and grow unless it draws
sustenance, as every soul and body must, from the
world around us, from work, from play, and from all
the higher loyalties that we serve.

Another ally of love comes to light when we answer
the question: Should one ever force or impersonate
affection? Surely not, yet love, like a musical ear, can
be cultivated to some extent through *knowledge.*
There must be something to build on, some basis of
respect, or at least of compassion. But given that,
we may confidently call to our aid that great master-
builder of affection, knowledge. If we give a man every
chance, he is almost sure to disclose some lovable
quality. Knowledge joined with faith is the way to
give him these chances. For example, you know
people better in their own homes; you have there a
promising opportunity to catch a liking for them.
You find out some people's strength by seeing them

at play, others' by learning the structure and history of their past, others' by watching them as they build up plans for the future.

Of course such fuller acquaintance may reveal not strength but weakness; we may be repelled where we hoped to be attracted through close intimacy. Yet there is no other path. We are taking the only chance, and if we persevere there are few personalities so repellent as to foil us altogether. I speak with confidence upon this point because some of the strongest and most inspiring friendships that I have known were raised from very near the zero point of attraction to the pleasantest warmth simply by taking every opportunity for better knowledge, and by hunting for favorable points of view. The affection which gradually developed was from the first genuine and unforced, but it would never have come to anything had it not been cultivated and reinforced through every available avenue of knowledge. And after all, is it not quite natural that human affection should come to us, in part at least, through intimacy of acquaintance? One gets fond of many a city, many a landscape, many an art or science in just the same way, and most of our antipathies — though not all — are to be explained like Charles Lamb's by our ignorance.

A friend said to Lamb: "Come here. I want to introduce you to Mr. A."

Lamb replied with his characteristic stammer and drawl: "No, thank you."

"Why not?"

"I don't *like* him."

"Don't like him? But you don't *know* him!"

"That's the *reason* I don't like him."

I do not mean to suggest that we can often win a friend merely by scraping together a fund of knowledge about him. I mean that if you are once convinced that you ought to conquer a certain dislike or acquire a certain friendliness, knowledge is one way to go at it.

The influence of elemental nature, of knowledge, beauty, playfulness, patriotism, truth-seeking,—all the reinforcements which I have been describing, are for the most part a consecration of love, often a blessing, rarely a curse. For most of the perversions and diseases of love, which are just now so much in the public mind under the false title of "sex," are due, as I believe, less to an excess than to a deficiency of vitality, — less to lack of control than to lack of depth.

But not all! Swift-running streams drop out some impurities, but there are intrinsic qualities in the chemistry of the water-borne molecules which cannot be changed from bad to good by any increase of power in the stream which surrounds them. We want a swift-flowing stream but the internal structure of the water — its chemistry — must also be right, else the water is bad. Love also may still remain a vague, impersonal life-force unless its internal structure is right. That structure is my next topic.

CHAPTER XXI

LOVE'S HOUSE OF MANY MANSIONS

In a happy marriage the wife's affection for her husband is often maternal as well as conjugal. She treats him like a grown-up son, looks after him and mothers him like one of her own boys. We all know this habit and love it. We should recognize that something was missing if there were nothing *but* the maternal in a wife's attitude. But we should also recognize something missing if there were nothing but the conjugal. Moreover the pair should be good comrades as well as husband-and-wife and mother-and-son. Together these three affections make a richer love than any one of them alone.

The filial and maternal may also be united in a single relation. I knew a little girl of ten, devotedly attached to her mother and fond of sleeping near her on the porch of their house. One night a storm blew in; the mother was awakened not by the storm, but by the touches and whispered words of her little daughter who was at her bedside covering her with a rainproof blanket, and (as soon as she saw that her mother had waked) pouring out a stream of such endearments as a mother uses to her child. She was mothering her own mother; yet the next morning she was as much her mother's child as any one could wish.

Extend to their limit the possibilities suggested in

these examples: then all possible human affections are united in the richness of a single love. I have a brother who is good enough to make his home with me and to share with me the privilege of affectionate intimacy with his children. As I read or play with his eight-year-old daughter I find in my love for her, elements of every type of affection that I can conceive. The touch of her hand thrills me. I am equally conscious of the impulse to protect and guide her, to fight for her, to foresee and prevent the dangers that will meet her at play and in school, — in short, to be a father to her. I also want her comradeship; I want to work and to play with her as an equal and not merely as a hopeless "grown-up." And when I see how much clearer than mine is her sight for the new, how much fresher her enthusiasm, how much more beauty of speech, gesture, and mood her life contains than mine, how much more wisdom there is in her unconsciousness than in most of my thinking, I look up to her with veneration. Around and beyond all this I see that she belongs to the larger life of the world and to that Personality which envelops us all.

If I am right in the interpretation of these examples, we must learn to think of personal love not so much as a single quality or impulse, but as a house of many rooms. Each room represents some type of affection, — conjugal, paternal, filial, or friendly. Each room opens into those next it, so that an impulse originating in one must pass freely through all. Moreover, the house is open outwardly. Through its windows there is a perpetual give-and-take between our affections and the infinite love of God. The currents of infinite love as they sweep through the universe rush through all the chambers of love's house, giving to all, receiving from each, mingling them with each other and with the divine.

What are the practical results? If each member of the family of affections possess some traits of each of the others, then each is enriched without surrendering its central characteristics. We find, then, in each affection a structure something like the present elective system at Harvard and at Yale, where each student must so choose his courses that he studies a great deal of one branch and a little of all the other main branches of knowledge. His scholarship is mainly of one type, but includes a dash of the other types for better sympathy with their aims. So a father will be mainly a father to his son, but will also be something of a comrade and a brother to him, and will even look up to him in some respects as he would to a father.

A physical element should enter into all affection. Even to clasp hands should always be a pleasure. But if we feel no physical attraction for a person, the contact of hands is boresome or distasteful. In exuberant and affectionate families, especially Europeans, it is natural for men to kiss men now and then, as women so generally kiss women. This is the normal. When those of the same sex fall in love with each other, it means simply an exaggeration of the normal physical attraction which should play a part in all human relationships. This is no more shocking than masculinity in women, effeminacy or "old-womanishness" in men. The child prematurely old, the tomboy, the "sissy" have each of them too large a share of sympathy with types other than their own. But *some* such sympathy there ought to be as a basis for affection and mutual understanding. Why should a man be all strength and no tenderness, or a woman all tenderness and no strength? Why should we not preserve as we grow up some of the child's playfulness, some of the boy's independence, and the girl's swift intuition?

As character is the richer for a mixture of many sympathies and interests under control of a single purpose, so I think love is ennobled when all types of affection are united within it, under the leadership of one. A mother's love for her son becomes too clinging and sentimental if she is only his mother and not also his comrade. As comrades respect each other, every mother must learn to respect something in her son, and to recognize somewhere in their relation his authority over her as well as hers over him. He will come to treat her paternally as he grows up. Very early in boyhood he will have the instinct to protect her if she recognizes and responds to it.

When a man is tempted to be base in his treatment of a woman, one can sometimes appeal to him with success in the name of her weakness. Because she is weak she needs his brotherly or fatherly protection; his guidance, not his pursuit. He would not treat his own sister so; but she is in part his sister, because he has in him at least the germ of brotherly love for her.

All the unworthy or unhappy affections that I know of could be set right, I believe, by a greater infusion of some other type of affection. By the appeal to chivalry we can call out a romantic element latent in most men's love for women just as we call on a boy to "be a man" when he is babyish. He is not a man, but there are germs of manliness in him and to these we appeal.

So far, I have been maintaining that love is true and right when all its varieties (physical, paternal or maternal feeling, filial respect, comradeship, and the rest) are duly mingled with each other or open into each other like the rooms of a house. Disasters here threaten us when we shut the outer doors and windows of our affection, shutting out the love of truth, the love of country, of art, of nature, and of God.

Jealousy is a consumption bred within the structured house of love when all its windows are sealed. When we are jealous we try to shut ourselves up in shadowed privacy or timid miserliness. We want someone all to ourselves; we fear that if we open the doors and let in the currents of others' affection or the winds of impersonal interest, our own share of love may be swept away. A woman may be jealous not only of her husband's friends but of his work, and even of his religion. This means that she has kept her windows closed and shuttered, so that she looks always at the walls of her house of love, never through and beyond them.

Personal love is enhanced and purified by the contact with elemental nature, by the inspiration of art, play, truth-seeking, or patriotism. Floating in through the windows of love's house, these interests sweep out impurities and cleanse the air in stagnant corners. They may be imperious and insistent, but unless they are allowed to break down the partitions and monopolize the whole house, they leave it brighter and richer, never dimmer or poorer. They kill nothing but the germs of disease. Yet, if we are to persuade a conservative and timid love to open its windows, we must first convince it that a friendly and beneficent Spirit is always touching our spirits as the infinite space touches our bodies, a Spirit which pursues us like the "Hound of Heaven."[1]

A vague and traditional awareness of this infinite spirit is preserved in the familiar idea of the "divine spark" within every man. But we know a great deal more about this divinity than our ordinary habits betray.

[1] In Francis Thompson's poem.

CHAPTER XXII

OUR AWARENESS OF INFINITE LOVE

A COLLEGE friend of mine, devotedly fond of his friends, was also devoted to his diary. On a certain page of this he inscribed their names and arranged them in the order of his preference. Here he listed his (1) best friend; (2) next best; (3) third best, etc., though he reserved the right to shift this order now and then. He thought this an admirably clear arrangement, and was much surprised when he found that all to whom he confided his list were moved straightway to inextinguishable laughter!

But why this joyful noise over my friend's pet scheme? Why do we look with mingled pity and amusement at that diary and at all attempts to arrange our friends in an order of preference? Order, we are told, is Heaven's first law, and certainly everything under the sun can (and sometimes ought to be) put in order and arranged in just such a hierarchy as we indignantly reject when applied to our friends. I believe that you will find it true that all finite facts can be arranged in a series and sometimes should be so arranged. The population of cities, the prices of pictures, the weights of children, the chemical ingredients of foods, the magnitude of the stars,—one could go on indefinitely with the catalogue of finite things which can be reduced to a common denominator and arranged in a row, often with profit. But you run against a snag the instant you begin to deal with things or thoughts which are infinite. Try to answer, or even seriously to ask the question, "Which is longer, past time or future time?" and you attempt the absurd. Try to state which is longer, the distance which you might travel through the space to your right or that which you might go to your left, and how either of these compares with the distances which you might go in any one of the infinite number of other directions. You are involved at once in absurdity.[1]

The same absurdity results when you attempt to rank your friends. They cannot be arranged in a row and numbered as first, second, and third because each of them is infinitely lovable, infinitely valuable in his own unique service to the rest of the world. No good mother will admit that she loves one of her children more than another. She loves each with all her strength. There is no limit to her power of loving each of them, no limit to the amount of loveliness which she can find in each. With scrupulous and sacred sincerity she can write to each of her children a letter beginning "My Dearest."

What does this prove? It seems to me to show that our love is traversed by the current of an infinite af-

[1] I know that some infinites are greater than others; but I see no such difference in the size of the particular infinites which we call persons.

fection which sweeps through us and off to whomever we love, — a current which cannot be compared with any other, because it is an infinite love, and if infinite, divine.

Another familiar example may make this idea more credible. "How often shall I forgive my brother? Unto seven times?" Christ's answer: "Yea, I say unto you unto seventy times seven," does not mean four hundred and ninety. One limit is just as vicious as another. Christ meant that our forgiveness of any one whom we love is infinite, — that in true love there is literally no end to forgiveness so long as it means not condoning or forgetting, but the ampler understanding which is pardon.

Not all forgiveness can be thus infinite. Forgiveness must be definitely limited, for example, in the official relation of employer and employee. There is an end to the number of mistakes which an employer can rightly forgive in an employee. But it makes all the difference to that employee if, when he comes to lose his job, he sees that, though as an employee he cannot be further forgiven, as a friend he still holds his place. I remember that to my mother, after fifteen years of service on a school committee, was assigned the task of telling superannuated teachers that it was time for them to go. Why this was always my mother's job is clear enough, I think, when I say that many of these poor teachers came away from the fateful interview loving my mother as a friend. They could not help seeing that, although in her official capacity forgiveness must be limited, she never forgot the warmer and more human tie, limited by no official duties.

We can make it hard for the gigantic forces about us to do their proper work within us. We can plaster up all the chinks of our nature for a time, but we cannot long escape the "majestic instancy" of God. I believe that the idea of a structural continuity of human and divine love was contained as a part in the meaning of Christ's words: "For I was an hungered, and ye gave me meat: I was thirsty, and ye gave me drink: I was a stranger, and ye took me in: naked, and ye clothed me: I was sick, and ye visited me: I was in prison, and ye came unto me.

"Then shall the" (literal-minded) "righteous answer him, saying, Lord, when saw we thee an hungered, and fed thee? or athirst, and gave thee drink? and when saw we thee a stranger and took thee in? or naked, and clothed thee? And when saw we thee sick, or in prison, and came unto thee?

"Verily I say unto you, Inasmuch as ye did it unto one of these my brethren, even these least, ye did it unto me."

Christ's word "inasmuch" implies the sort of continuity which we know in physics. As I write I am pressing (not merely leaning) with an appreciable weight on my table. But inasmuch, or just as much, as I press on this table, I press upon the whole earth. Precisely

as much power as I exert at this point is transmitted
to the entire globe because of the continuity of matter
and the indestructibility of energy. Inasmuch as I
do anything to this table I do it to all that is in continuity with this table. Inasmuch as I vote and influence
others to vote right, I influence the whole country, because my vote and my influence are part of a practically continuous spiritual whole.

Because Christ is in a relation of spiritual continuity
with "the least of these" and with each of us who feeds
him or gives him drink, all the good will which we
put out is transmitted to Christ and to the Father of
us all.

I do not see how we can make sense of Christ's words
and believe them true unless we have, at least vaguely,
in our minds the permeable structure by which I picture our love in its relation to God, a structure such
that love freely given to any of the children of men must
at the same time pass through him to his Maker. Unless
the whole structure of divine and human love is thus
permeable, I cannot understand how our human love
and our worship, our love of nature and of country, of
work, of play, and of God can mingle and reinforce
each other as they do. Furthermore, unless we think
of our own personality in such a relation to Infinite
Personality as I have hinted, I do not see how any
sociable human being can bear without intolerable
humiliation the volume of affection and gratitude that
is poured out on him. In practice one explains it, one

makes it sweet and sane only by passing it on. No human being can support the full weight and impact of another human being's love. It turns to absurdities and blasphemies, unless it can pass through us to God.

CHAPTER XXIII

SYMBOLISM IN LOVE

SYMBOLISM is a late and meager growth in many of us New Englanders showing itself considerably more in play than in love or worship. As a boy I saw no sacredness in the national flag nor in the symbols of religion. What others called "enthusiasm about the flag" seemed to me a false and painful attempt to pump up emotions which could not spontaneously arise. One set of symbols, namely, words, I was even then accustomed to use. Literally a word is nothing but a grunt or a cough, a vibrating current of air in the larynx, or a series of black marks on white paper. Yet by almost every one these literal facts are symbolically interpreted. Indeed the force of this habit is so imperious that when we wish to divest ourselves of it in reading proof-sheets, so that we can see precisely what the black scratches are, it is almost impossible. In this field of symbolism, then, we are almost all of us expert; but our proficiency is very limited. Our own home or our own fireside has usually a symbolic sacredness and value. We do not stare at its walls with cold literalness. We love them, and there are a few other symbols, such as bowing, mourning, Christmas ceremonies, patriotic songs, which most of us love.

Nevertheless, the average American is stiff and awkward, when he tries to use symbols. Current thought and life discourage the use of such imagination and penetrative intelligence as symbolism demands: for a symbol which does its work must awaken us to the invisible. If we love the flag, it is not merely because its image falls on the retina, but because we see in it much that is invisible. We see the history of our country as we know and love it, the beauty which we believe is characteristic of America, the national energy and inventiveness of which we are proud. In moments of enthusiasm for the flag these hopes and memories surge up and rush across the surface of consciousness like the picture in a cinematograph. It is because we see invisible facts that any symbol becomes for us pregnant with meaning.

The marriage vow is a great symbol because it calls up with marvelous swiftness and vividness great realms of the past and future, moments which have led up to the consummation of this union, happiness which we look to in the future. In this vow we call the future before us as a witness; "for better, for worse, for richer, for poorer, in sickness and in health." Before these invisible witnesses called to range themselves around a man and woman at the altar, the pledge to faithfulness is taken.

Any symbolic act or phrase points beyond itself. The most sacred symbols point to the widest and most precious reaches of invisible life. The most durable and universally solid symbols are actually part of the larger life which they call up. They serve us not merely by chance association, as a post-box calls up in our mind as we pass it the thoughts with which we last posted a letter there. The best symbol gives us a sample of what it symbolizes. Being married is part of marriage. Words like "thunder" and "zigzag" portray in miniature what they symbolize. An autograph stands for its signer: but not arbitrarily, for something of his character is given you visibly in the shape and arrangement of his letters. Unless the symbol is a piece of the reality which it symbolizes, and recalls that reality as a face recalls a character, it cannot serve the needs of many persons or extend its influence through the centuries.

There are symbols that mean abnormality and weakness, not power. People who are clumsy in the use of spoken language try to make good their deficiencies by more or less grotesque gestures, emphases, and attitudes. The symbolic act is then evidence partly of ineptitude. But, on the other hand, a man's acts may beautifully convey what words are too poor to express. There are feelings so elemental yet so intense that action seems to express them more naturally than speech. When the dead are borne past us in the street, we uncover our heads because that silent act conveys our reverence better than words. The act of bowing can be a trivial or ludicrous thing, but those of us who have seen President Eliot bow as he presents the

degree of LL.D. will agree that only poetry could express in words so much of dignity and significance.
What splendid fitness and fullness of expression there
may be in the act of kneeling, when soldiers kneel
about the grave of a dead comrade, or when a woman
kneels by her child's bed!

The physical symbolism of affection expresses another deep human need. The clasp of two hands is literally a physical contact of two pieces of human flesh.
Woefully secular and lifeless it can be! We all know the
flabby, the clinging, the nervous, the icy hand-grasp.
Yet who has not sometimes rejoiced in the grasp of a
hand that conveys life and love? Two souls are here
united by a physical contact that gives birth to new
aspirations and new certainties. Two human beings
are here linked hand to hand, in mutual respect,
mutual trust, and mutual encouragement.

Part of the richness and value of such experiences
comes from the cloud of unseen witnesses who cluster
about them. When I said good-bye to my father in 1898,
going into what turned out to be a ludicrously slight
danger in the Spanish War, the farewell clasp of hands
joined me also to many memories. I faced uncertainties and possibilities that gave me, I suppose, the same
experience that I should have had, if the war had
proved serious. My mind traveled back to the evenings
when my father used to read to us from Emerson's "Essays" the passages that meant most to him, recalled the
long mornings in his study among the pine woods at

Beverly where he was patient with my struggle to learn German, the afternoons by his side under a sketching umbrella, — my first lessons in drawing. At partings such memories flash through one's mind and one sees as from a hilltop, in a single panoramic glance, the high points of the past. There are pledges, too, in such a hand-grasp, unspoken but no less binding, that may reach across the grave, pledges of mutual faith, trust, and backing: "My faith in your fidelity till you come back to us": "My love with you always." The parting words of Pandora to Prometheus in W. V. Moody's "Fire-Bringer," express incomparably the spirit of such a parting, and of all parting.

> "Whither thou goest I am; there even now
> I stand and cry thee to me."

Because we thus envisage the invisible past, the incalculable future, somewhat as God must see the whole life of the world, the physical symbols of farewell contain in their union a myriad of meanings, hopes, memories, and pledges to the unborn. Like the most intimate physical union of man and woman, the hand-grasp should set creative forces working through us and be consecrated in them. Live and ardent people always strike fire out of each other like flint and steel. Your best friend strikes thoughts and deeds out of you that you never knew were in you, and that truly were not full formed in you till your friend woke them to life. The need of them, the whisper of their coming, was there, but it took both of you fully to create them.

It is through the symbolism of the physical acts such as meeting, parting, or waiting upon one another's physical wants that one understands the deeper significance of conjugal affection. Many resent the physical intimacies of love, because they take them literally, not symbolically; looking straight at them instead of through them. Nothing can bear that direct, passive stare and retain its sacredness. Viewed in hard literalness what is more ludicrous than the ceremony of raising one's hat to a lady, what is more worthless than a dirty greenback? Yet without a moment's hesitation we go behind the surface appearance of these symbols. In them, matter and its meaning, body and spirit, are fused into harmony as they should be, and as they are in the following words written by one of my dearest friends to one of hers: —

"I want to tell you very boisterously and worshipfully how much I love you. I also want not to tell you at all, but to do something for you with my hands and feet, to make your bed, to pick lavender pine-cones for you, to do something you would never know that I had done. For of the many ways of love, one of the dearest is to serve in silence, to celebrate and not be found out. Mothering is a great business on these lines. The babies never guess or care how many myriad thoughts of love go into bed-making, or hair-brushing."

In this letter the joy of giving expression to love in physical service is mingled with the exultant awareness of a purifying secrecy, which banishes the thought of reward. But her joy in the expression of love "with my hands and feet" is just now my special interest, because it is an example of that "unity of soul and sense" in love which symbolism makes possible.

Though soul and sense belong together, they have a constant tendency to split apart, in work, play, and worship as well as in love. Work splits into physical drudgery on the one side and unpractical scheming on the other. Thus we breed anæmic "thinkers" who accomplish nothing, and submerged laborers who put no soul into their work because they get no freedom out of it.

Play and art are always in danger of suffering a similar schism; music without expression, pictures that are all technique, exemplify the fate of sense divorced from spirit in the field of art. When shapeless "Spirit" tries to live without body, we are afflicted by the performance of amateurs who neither learn nor inherit their art, — but try to sing without breathing and to draw without outlines.

In love the same split produces, as we know so well, a blind and destructive passion which burns itself out without vision of individuality. But on the other side of the chasm we find a corresponding monstrosity often mistaken for virtue, a sterile and frigid aloofness that shudders at loud-voiced enthusiasm and is insusceptible to physical charm. It is as bad to be dried up as to be burned up, but worse still is to live in perpetual winter because we were born withered. Such desolation is no ground for blame; like any other inborn deformity, it deserves only our pity. But it never deserves praise or helps us to defend a standard of noble love. For love, like all that mirrors divinity, must be incarnate.

The "puritanical" reticence about the body is right enough if we are equally reticent about the disembodied soul, and refuse to describe or cultivate either body or soul save in terms of the other. We are often told that we should "teach" the sacredness of the body. Yes, but the body is most sacred when most forgotten in the absorption of hard work or keen sport, in the enthusiasm of dancing, painting, singing, oratory, love, or worship. So it is with the soul. Taken literally "mental culture" seems to me as bad as "physical culture" wherewith the devilish split of body and soul has invaded the domain of education. To think about one's body or one's soul, to love with one's body or one's soul, is to paralyze the best activities of both. The foreground of consciousness should never be littered up with such fragments of a dismembered self. We want to devote the whole of ourselves to our job, to our family and friends, to nature, to play, to beauty, and to God.

In the industrial world the division of labor and the necessity of doing one thing at a time splits us up into woefully small and centrifugal units. This we cannot altogether avoid, but we must fiercely insist that each of these units shall be a fragment of *soul incarnate*, never an arid wisp of disembodied soul or a shapeless lump of flesh. If we can prevent that diabolic schism we shall never be crushed by the dead weight of drudgery, or enervated by fruitless and unchristian attempts to disembody our meanings or to realize them without the travail of incarnation.

So far as we succeed in this attempt we keep symbolism alive in every action. When we build our houses and sweep our offices, clothe and feed our children, we look through these acts to a deeper significance behind them. We do them in the name of the Highest that we know,—be it business, family, nation, or God. We feel a deeper respect for the material, greater willingness to study its texture and detail, because we believe that it stands for infinitely more than appears.

If I have conveyed anything of the sacredness of the physical expression of love, it will now be obvious why we shudder at its desecration. The greater the symbol the more horrible is its perversion. In "The Ring and the Book" Browning makes us feel the snaky loathsomeness of Guido's crime because it concealed itself beneath a priestly robe. The crime was terrible enough in itself, but far more revolting because perpetrated by a priest, who used the great offices of the Church for mercenary and sensual ends. Was not Judas's kiss of betrayal the most awful act in history because it was through this sacred symbol of love that his treachery was consummated? So it is with that greatest disgrace in modern civilization, prostitution.

It is not chiefly because of the physical miseries that may (or may not) follow in its train. It is because of the holiness of that great physical symbol which it drags in the mire, the misdirection of a world-force that ought to mean the creation or re-creation of all that is best in life.

Love is *consecrated* not only by its purity from foreign admixtures, but by taking up into itself the best life of elemental nature, knowledge, art, play, patriotism, and the devoted search for truth. These vivid spirits permeate love, and revive it by the infusion of their own virtues. When, moreover, the whole family of human affections and the Infinite Love which contains them are represented in each of the separate affections, then each of them is consecrated by the strength and tenderness of all. When through symbolism we "hold infinity in the palm of our hand" (or our hand-clasp) and "eternity in an hour," we are at the altar of consecration.

When we make a dead failure of a living affection, we secularize it. Sometimes we begin the day with a disaster of this kind. Our "Good-morning" is as secular as a snore. We come downstairs half awake, our lips so sleepy that they scarcely move, our minds still torpid and vague. We shuffle into the breakfast-room and slide into a chair. Physically, mentally, spiritually, we have scarcely been penetrated by personality. Far within us its fires burn at a point near to extinction.

But there is another and still worse element of secularity in our greeting. We scarcely notice who it is we greet. The personality that should exhilarate us is for the time veiled by familiarity. So often we have greeted just this comrade at breakfast that to-day the greeting has become automatic. The spirit has gone out of it. Were a stranger at the table, perhaps we might be aroused. A new personality might bring us to our senses like a dash of cold water. But as it is, our dull eyes merely record the outlines and colors of the person before us, like a savage who sees only black and white scratches in a piece of manuscript.

When we are at our best, a flood of life pours itself out in the simple old words, "Good-morning," — a flood of meaning which strains to express itself in a thousand ways, but has to be content with verbal symbols. Our physical and vital energies, our love, our playfulness, our stores of gratitude for the world's past gifts, all that is calling us toward the future, comes rushing out in the time-mellowed greeting. The depths of us, the concentrated and imprisoned energy of our inmost life call across the distance to the unseen depths of our fellow.

Through the external and symbolic, the invisible depths of any friend loom up, not only in moments of enthusiasm, but whenever we are clearly aware of his individuality. "Love," G. B. Shaw somewhere says,[1] "is a gross exaggeration of the difference between

[1] Quoted by Ernest Jones, M.D., *Journal of Abnormal Psychology,* 1911, p. 235.

one person and all the rest." Translated from pagan
into Christian terms this means that in love we call
out to what is unique and individual in our friend and
therefore infinitely different from all other beings.
His individuality is always staring us in the face, but
we wake up to it only when we love him. Others may
not see it. That is their misfortune.

In our use of symbols and in our effort to penetrate
through them to what is lovable, we must give every
one credit for his own type of symbol and his own
fashion of consecrating it through affection. The railroad magnate gazing at a mountain-side, blasted and
seared by the clearings which his engines have found
necessary, sees there the vision and symbol of the great
railroad which is to be built. That is his child. He is
blind to the mere external effects that to you and me
are secular and shocking, the scarred and denuded
hillside, the splendid trees and cliffs torn from their
places. For the hopes and visions of the future, his
dreams and plans of service, center in this spot. Their
light illuminates the place for him. He sees it with no
such alien and disillusioned eyes as ours, and we must
put ourselves in his place, even though we may think
that he has chosen the object of his affection strangely.

We should be even more modest when we judge the
historic symbols of the Church. If we can take the
Sacrament of the Lord's Supper as an act of consecration, it is because deep calls unto deep. We bring to it
our best store of thankfulness, of reminiscence, and

communion with the personality of Christ. Through the symbolic elements, and in the service, we feel the light and heat of Christ's personality more vividly than at other times. Yet I remember that, looking on this ceremony as a child, I found it not only devoid of anything to excite my reverence, but prone to drag me below my normal level. Nothing can constrain us to symbolism. We may be bored or amused or even disgusted by it. Nothing can force us to find a thing sacred; nothing can remain secular if we determine to make it sacred.

Any unconsecrated affection, any infatuation, jealousy, or nagging habit, any horror such as prostitution or careless excess within marriage, errs through a low tone of personal energy, a feeble, drifting, slavish attitude, or, on the other hand, through an impersonal gaze. It sees a thing, a case, a machine, where it ought to see an infinitely valuable person.

A symbolic deed of love is mystical, not because it is vague, but because of the richness of meaning packed into one narrow act.

CHAPTER XXIV

LOYALTY IN LOVE

WRITING of love and marriage in " *Virginibus Puerisque*" Stevenson says: "I hate questioners and questions. '*Is it still the same between us?*' Why, how can it be? It is eternally different and yet you are still the friend of my heart. *Do you understand me?* God knows; I should think it highly improbable."

Stevenson hated such questions because he found it impossible to answer them truly. But I wager that he hated them also because of their dearth of venture and generosity. Such a timid questioner, anxiously scanning the weather-gauge of affection, finds it steadily falling toward zero. Under such observation no love can grow or flourish. We need not contribute *all* the warmth without waiting to be invited, but surely we must contribute some of it.

I lived for a time some years ago in a community whose members seemed to me more tempest-tossed and unhappy than any human beings I have ever known. They were so "stupid in the affections" that they had never learned the most elementary lesson about human relationships, — that a passive attitude never works. Two of them happened to notice that they felt fond of each other; they married. Shortly afterward they observed no particular fondness for each other, and therefore separated. The winds of feeling blew them now together, now apart. Mated or severed, they were quite helpless and apparently quite unaware that they could do anything to help themselves or to maintain any single direction among the veering currents of feeling.

Probably every one of them knew that if he consulted his feelings each morning as to whether he should wash his face or not, he would find the forces of desire often at the zero point or on the negative side of the scale. But being moderns they probably pay no attention to their feelings as regards so important a matter as cleanliness! In all practical affairs (among which the average American does not include affection) we know that loyal adherence to one's original intention, however one happens to feel, is one of the greatest forces that make for success. Passivity, reliance on the moment's whim, literalism in reading the face of the future or of the present, is fatal to happiness and to success. No business venture and no human creature can bear the passive stare of the utterly disengaged soul.

Chesterton reminds us that if we face man with the cold and fishy eye of science, we cannot overlook the ludicrous and damning fact that he has two legs. To see him waddling over the ground between these two points of support is more than any one could bear with composure did he not view the apparition with a gaze tempered by affection, good nature, and faith.

Yet, as he tells us, there is one still more unforgivable fact about man when we view him with the literal eye. How can one ever again view with favor, still less with love, a being whom one has actually caught in the act of making an opening in his face into which he then puts portions of the outer world?

The point of these illustrations is this. Without commitment, faith, the power to distinguish and disregard what is unessential, there is no stability in any human relation. It takes but little experience to show us that no human being is merely what he is seen to be at any one moment. He can no more display himself in a single act or a single year than a musical theme can be expressed in one of its notes. A musical theme is all that it can become before the desire which launched it is slaked. So a human being is in truth all that he has been and can become, not because he now embodies it, but because that vast arc is the only sufficient explanation of his behavior, the only working basis for affection.

But this attainable personality he certainly will not attain without your help. His fate is determined in part by what you do about it, and the most important thing that you can do is to expect of him always a little more than you can see, projecting your vision toward the unseen depths of his soul, not arbitrarily, but in the direction suggested by what he has already done.

This creative act of loyalty as it overcomes another's diffidence is not unlike a football team "getting the jump on" its opponents. The opposing teams face each other in the rush line. The game, pausing after one of its "downs," is renewed. Each side tries to push the other backward. But it is not chiefly a predominance in weight or in strength that determines which line shall make an advance, which shall yield. It is rather a question of alertness. One of the teams will "get the jump on" the other by being the first to lunge forward. Whoever succeeds in preëmpting this initial *ictus* takes the other slightly at a disadvantage and puts himself into a correspondingly stronger position. The opponent's disadvantage still further weakens his opposition and lets the successful team advance with increased momentum.

You can "get the jump on" another's diffidence if you shoot into his soul a message of welcome, of encouragement, of faith in his power to do something better than he has yet done. You do not wait for him to show his best. Your impulse of welcome breaks down his reserve, melts his shyness, and brings him nearer to the thing that you expect of him. This is mirrored in his face. You see it, and your original faith is reinforced. You follow up the trail of sparks which you have spied within him; the spirit and exuberance of your quest redoubling in him the fire which you seek.

No one can set a limit to this wonderful give-and-take, as the lightning of two souls leaps back and forth. Yet it is no mystical or unusual affair. Emerson referred to something of the kind when he said: "I have heard with admiring submission the experience of the lady who declared that the sense of being well-dressed gives a feeling of inward tranquillity which religion is powerless to bestow!"[1]

Mr. Slack, a timid citizen, emerges from his door unusually well-dressed and thereby "gets the jump on" his passing friend Bouncer. The good impression made upon Bouncer is written in his face and instantly makes him more attractive and stimulating to Slack who brightens and responds by giving something better than his ordinary pale gruel of talk; a delightful exchange is set in oscillation; the day becomes brighter and the two march downtown to business in a path of glory.

This process of "getting the jump on" any one is an expression in modern slang of a spiritual truth which sustains the life of industry, invigorates science as well as religion, and is the essence of psycho-therapeutic "suggestion."

A fine example of this occurs in Shakespeare's "Henry V." The king is before Harfleur. His soldiers lean on their scaling-ladders, taking breath in a pause of the fight. By all they hold sacred in home and country Henry urges them once more to the attack. Then his creative faith breaks loose: —

> "I see you stand like greyhounds in the slips,
> Straining upon the start. The game's afoot;
> Follow your spirit: and, upon this charge,
> Cry — God for Harry! England! and Saint George!"

[1] R. W. Emerson, *Letters and Social Aims*. Essay on "Social Aims."

He saw them straining, — yes, with the eye of faith. They tugged like greyhounds in the slips, — especially after he had recognized their eagerness. He brought to birth in them more spirit than had otherwise been born, and they in turn brought to his lips, as he faced them, the very nobility of his words. A disloyal or uninterested spectator would have seen merely a crowd of dirty, sweaty soldiers. King Henry saw that, too. But *within the gross total of what he saw he selected and summoned forth what most belonged to him and to them:* — their germinating souls, their destiny, the courage which they had when he believed in it, not otherwise.

Thus the best of one's loyalties, those to vocation and to one's mate, begin with a choice. With this profession, with this person we determine to unite our forces. But if we are to keep these pledges and preserve the spirit of youth, the initial choice must be renewed again and again. After choosing the physician's calling, I have still to determine what sort of physician and finally what particular physician I shall be. Within the broad field of medical service I must select the kind of work (research, teaching, public health, surgery, midwifery, general practice) which is best suited to me and seems most needed at the present time. Then within that field I must find some particular path, some combination of methods and manners which are individual and progressive. Year by year our initial choice is thus revived and made more sharply distinctive. Success and happiness demand that it shall be so.

It is the same in marriage or in friendship. Again and again we repeat and re-form our original choice. Within the domain of our friend's life we find a certain corner (his recreation, perhaps) where we can contribute something to enrich the friendship. There are other parts — say his family life — where with our present ignorance we are in the way. We choose and cultivate the parts that we are fit for, leaving the rest for the present undisturbed. Next year, when we come to choose again, we may be able to direct our efforts more effectively. Here we can learn; there we are baffled. Here we are in full sympathy; there we are in the dark. We select and select again, as often as a wave of enlightenment strikes us.

But selection goes further still. There are double and triple meanings in many of your friend's remarks. You can make a sentence or a person mean different things by the emphasis you put on selected bits. Then, if you are tactful, you pick out and answer the meaning most in harmony with the whole texture of your friendship; the other meanings you ignore. I do not mean anything subtle. A woman hears in her husband's greeting at night fatigue, anxiety, a shade of irritability, and a touch of playfulness. She ignores all but the playfulness, and by encouraging that healing element helps him to recover his balance. Just so she starves out some of her child's faults by choosing to ignore them and to cultivate his best.

You can be willful and cruel instead of beneficial in

this selection, or in all innocence you may go clean
astray, but you cannot escape the necessity of choice
by remaining passive, for even passivity is never neutral. It reinforces some element in your friend's character. If you decline to choose, the wheel of chance
makes the selection for you.

An old Scotch phrase describes a lively companion
as "good at the uptake." He is responsive, always
ready to help out, always keen for the game. If he
pauses it is but to make sure what game it is. On
such responsiveness friendship thrives. When we ask
a friend for the loan of his cloak, he is swift to strip off
his coat also. When we ask for advice he gives us also
sympathy and his purse. Later as an historian he may
place and judge us, but now and as a man of action
your friend takes his chances and contributes to fate
his best strength.

To meet our opportunity as Newton met the falling
apple, to greet our friend as the "wasteful woman"
greeted Jesus when she poured out the box of precious
ointment (and was chidden by the onlookers for doing
so much more than was demanded) — this is the way
not only to friendship, success, and health, but to originality and creative power. It is when we "greet the
unseen with a cheer," then, that we and our opportunity enter into each other and of our union something
new is born.

In love, as in work and in play, give-and-take is *the*

great source of novelty, of creativeness, and so of miracle. Therefore between friends there should grow up a child, a new truth and vision sprung from both. This miracle of sprouting friendship and truth is not best described as "giving" or "getting." It buds while we talk or merely sit together, fruit of our lives like other children, common delight to all, gift of God to all. Each of us contributes something; God over our shoulders contributes far more, which neither of us is conscious of giving but each of receiving.

Friends always face the unseen child of their friendship, if they are faithful to their unspoken oath. Faithfulness to this new child should guide every moment, every sentence. In every hearty hand-clasp, in every flash of eye to eye, something new is created. As you speak to a responsive friend you feel him speaking through your surprised lips. Then your words live and fit the occasion. You try eagerly to thank your friend for giving you such thoughts to utter. But it is rather God's bounty — his perpetual miracle of new life sprung up between two lives — that deserves our gratitude.

For our "child" and in his name we can accept laudation without shame or self-consciousness just as we welcome money for precious ends. For the work, or the new insight which we create together, we can take — nay, demand — "favors" which modesty would prevent our taking for our naked self, unclothed by the loyalties which dignify our clay. We can accept money, time, love in quite an amazing way, provided it is for the palace we are building. For this palace is one not built with hands, — eternal in the heavens.

CHAPTER XXV

IMPERSONALITY IN LOVE

ONE of the most sacred things about human ties is
this, that in any intimate and sincere affection you
discover what is unique and, choosing it out of all the
world, unite yourself with it. To you if you love your
father there is literally no one else like him on earth.
To outsiders he looks much like the rest of mankind;
not so to you. It is true that you did not choose your
parents, yet much that is most precious in your family
tie is of your own making. Your own family life you
have helped to build up; the family jokes and customs,
the pet words, tones, and gestures, are sacred to you
in part because you have helped to create them, by
what you have encouraged and what you have discouraged.

The more durable relationships are moulded and
perfected by a multitude of distinctions. If these distinctions are blurred, the love within us that should go
to build up a family life, a center for our other activities, may burst its proper channels as electricity darts
from the overcharged wire, destroying itself and other
lives outside. When marriage is late or unhappy, because of poverty, because people cannot find their
mates, or for less worthy reasons, love becomes impersonal, a blind, gigantic world-energy, hardly a blessing,

easily a curse. When it fails to build up a home or a happiness, it may ennoble us like any other lost cause; failing that, it may drag us lower than the beast.

In perverted forms love falls from the spiritual heights of choice and mutual understanding, and is swept into a current where there are no distinctions between right and wrong, between higher and lower, between person and person, or between person and thing. The essential shame of perverted affection is its impersonality. It is so impartial that almost anything will serve its purpose. Losing the miraculous clear-sightedness of loyal love, we follow the blind vague urgings of a force that stupefies and debases us until we bump up against a human being as though he were a post. Persons are treated like machines. Indeed, a clever machine might do as well.

If I am right in charging up the sins of the flesh to the score of *impersonality*, the scope of our campaigns against them must be widened and the tone of our just condemnations must be changed. In a recent book called "Hygiene and Morality" (though it deals almost wholly with disease and immorality), the great power of the truth is weakened by a bitterness which stimulates that most disastrous of all class antagonisms, the antagonism of all women against all men.

Such bitterness would be impossible if we realized that the essence of the sin against which we fight is impersonality, the sin of treating a person as less than a person. For is not that a sin of which we all are guilty?

Is there one of us who does not sometimes treat a person like a machine? Do we always think of the railroad conductor as more than a machine for taking tickets? Do we not often treat our fellow-creatures like masks or flat cards without substance and personality? I have been striving for years to overcome in myself and in my medical fellows the stupid professional habit of treating a person as a "case," or a walking disease. But the habit of impersonality persists like original sin in myriad forms and unexpected ways. In law courts we treat a human being as a "prisoner at the bar," as the "plaintiff" or "defendant," to the exclusion of the fact that he is as real and sensitive as ourselves.

I often hear my faculty colleagues talk with similar impersonality about "the student," his failings and malefactions. But few of the teachers who speak in this way know their students even by name. They are further still from grasping the personalities which make up their classes. Yet merely from the point of view of success in teaching, it is folly not to know those whom we are trying to teach. I have often found that after a man has given me the opportunity to learn something of his personal life, his home and family, his hopes and forebodings, he begins to do better work in class. Such improvement goes to show that we never get the best out of people so long as we treat them as a class, ignoring the unique interest and value of each individual. Love at its best is a command as well as a desire and an intimacy. Its law reads, "Find and create a new personality in so far as loyalty to your previous pledges and insights allows you."

If your love is pledged to one God, it is sacrilege to worship others. If you have sworn fealty to one country, it is treason to work against it in the interests of another. If you commit yourself to the faith of Christ, you cannot experiment with teachings which contradict it, unless you first renounce your faith. You hate to see a dilettante meander from flower to flower of literature, or friendship, because you know that such a life is full of broken pledges and is falling apart from the rottenness of its own structure.

But in many of our most poignant experiences we seem to love what is impersonal, and to make no pledges of loyalty. When a man drinks his wine or jumps into a mountain stream for pleasure, we do not reproach him with unfaithfulness or brutality. Some people certainly love animals as much as they do human beings. I think Emerson preferred companionship with trees, flowers, brooks, and skies to the company of men and women. Many a musician loves music, many a poet loves "inanimate" nature as passionately as he is capable of loving any being. Yet these affections seem to involve no loyalty. We turn from one to another in a way that would be villainous if we were dealing with persons.

Love of food and warmth, of reading and sewing, adventure and research, love of beauty,—these may be very impersonal and lukewarm emotions in some of us, yet no cooler than our love of persons. From birth to death, tepid may be the hottest one knows in human relation, and there is no standard of normal temperature in affection. Neither is there any standard for the degree of personality which we should recognize in our fellow men. Most of us can be justly blamed, when we stumble over a fellow creature as if he (or she) were a chair — most of us, but not all. Age makes a difference.

On a crowded sidewalk of the tenement district have you never felt a baby wandering between your legs and fending you off with its hands precisely as if you were a tree? A few years later he will duck and dodge around your person in the heat of an exciting pursuit with just as little realization of your august and delicate soul. Such impersonality is normal enough in babyhood. But some of us grow long and wide, put on the dress and occupation of adults, and are piloted about the streets without ever ceasing to be babies at heart, — without ever acquiring the heart that recognizes a person as a person. More often we get over the baby's absent-mindedness, but never grow beyond, say, the ten-year-old's or the adolescent's limited sense of individuality.

Swedenborg expresses this by saying that, in its early and elemental forms, our love is attracted by *sex*, not yet by *one of the sex*. Even in babyhood some girls show a decided preference for men. Love of a whole sex is already awake in them, but they are rarely

devoted to one man to the exclusion of all others. A
newcomer is especially welcomed. This means that their
love is at first general and vague, though later it will
attach itself to one individual and cleave to him, forsaking all others. This lesson we sometimes fail to
learn. We then remain impersonal and desire the emotions of love, as many people desire the emotions of
music, without any awareness of an individual, or of
the meaning of the piece. To yield to such a desire is
villainy in case we really know better (as we usually
do), but not otherwise. When we listen to good music
we are actually listening to the outpourings of the
composer's heart. He is speaking to us earnestly and
intensely and we are listening to him, — not to it. And
yet it is often no crime to drink in music merely as
pleasure; indeed, for most people it cannot be a crime
because they know no better. But it is always a ghastly
mistake, for it is treating music, which is a bit of a
person's life, as a means of sensual gratification.

Do not misunderstand me. I condemn the act of
man or woman who, knowing the nature of the act,
uses another as a means of pleasure. But I insist that
there are some who do not know the nature of their
acts, loose livers who have no more idea that they are
dealing with immortal souls than most of us have
when we drink in an artist's music merely for our
pleasure. Ignorance is often their curse. Sin there
may be, but if so, it is the sin of impersonality and of
sentimentalism.

For the rake is a sentimentalist, that is, he loves emotion for its own sake. He will take or buy emotion from many, just as a girl may dissipate her energies in a multitude of suitors or of novels, sucking in the enjoyment for its own sake without answering by word or deed, without learning anything or building anything out of the experience. Her mind is too feeble to recognize individuality and to treat it accordingly. Let us blame her as we blame the ignorant sexual offender. For if we exclude (as in some cases we can) the evils of disease, alcoholism, slavery, secrecy, and violation of marriage vows, the curse of prostitution is this: It involves degradation because it treats life as less than life. That is a grievous error, but one of which every one of us is guilty in some degree.

To recognize the universality of the sin which we are discussing makes us condemn ourselves enough and others enough, but no one too much. It is essentially the same sin which we meet in many forms: in official insolence, in professional blindness to the person behind the medical or legal case, in heartless gossip, flirtation, prostitution.

Have I been justified in using the sacred word "love" so broadly as to include sex-relations outside marriage? It is easier and cheaper to draw a sharp distinction between love and the more elemental sex-relations which we condemn as merely "physical" or brutal. But I believe that the use of these distinctions

often does harm. To condemn even the most impersonal and momentary attraction as "merely physical"
is like calling a man a mere brute or a child a mere
blockhead. The name of the act tends to brand itself
on the person, and to degrade him at a time when he
most needs help.

Call a dog a bad name and hang him. Throw mud
enough and some of it will stick. The more degraded
a man is the more he is hurt by our contempt. But in
their ordinary context "merely physical" or "mere
lust" are words of contempt, not of scientific descrip-
tion. To condemn any conscious human act by calling
it "merely physical" is not only bad psychology; it is
an attempt to push a living act out among the dead,
and the attempt may succeed. It is like cutting an acquaintance or disdaining a poor relation. Just when
an act is most in need of improvement, we damn it
with a phrase. Just when a traveler is most dreadfully
astray from his road, we further dishearten him by
telling him that he has no road.

In the less personal types of love, falsely called "physical," an elemental impulse, almost blind to the sacred
meaning of its trend, is groping its way along. We
should help it to find its goal, instead of branding it as
forever outcast. If I think of my sight and my hearing
as "merely physical," or if I am convinced that I am
tone-deaf and color-blind, in either event no spiritual
comprehension of music and color is possible for me,
I can only give up trying.

Those who are color-blind and tone-deaf in their affections are rare. They include among others the "moral imbeciles" of the courts. If we have accurately named them, they cannot do right or wrong, and cannot be hurt or helped whatever term we apply to them. But in the vast majority of instances we apply these terms with reproach and condemnation. First we separate body and soul by an impassable chasm; then we attempt to spiritualize and subdue the body. A hundred recent books on "sex hygiene" tell us that we should teach the sacredness of the body and of sex. But the instant we have branded love as "body" or as "sex," we have begun to deprive it of sacredness. For the sacredness of love comes from choice, and a "body" cannot choose. The sacredness of love springs from enthusiasm and self-direction such as no "body" possesses.

It is with an *instinct* that we are dealing, and the sacredness of an instinct is developed by showing its profound though vague spirituality. The lower can be rationally governed by the higher only if they share a common nature. Passion can be mastered only by an intenser passion, not by any power that stands aloof and contemptuously denies its kinship. Personality is what we want in love, because personality is always both physical and spiritual. In the impersonal, one of these elements often seems to get lost, though it is *never* gone beyond recovery.

CHAPTER XXVI

INTEGRITY IN LOVE

PERSONAL love begins with a choice and a pledge. It lives on through daily reincarnations of that original choice in finer discriminations. It is debased whenever it becomes impersonal or passive.

I have still two points to enlarge upon: first, the integrity of love; and second, its centralization.

Integrity, whether in love, athletics, or debate, means that one's personality is well knit, cleanly articulated, "all there" when needed.

> "Nur wo du bist sei Alles,
> Immer kindlich.
> So bist du Alles,
> Bist unüberwindlich."
>
> (*Goethe.*)

The opposite of an integrated personality is an impersonal "loose-liver," and his sin is not only in his impersonality (just dwelt upon), but in his looseness. This looseness is like our dawdling days, our shapeless, plagiarizing or windy speech (which hits all around the mark like a drunken carpenter), our slack-minded skimming of newspapers, our vague complaisant purring before a sunset or a symphony. Vagueness and diffuseness in love are bad, among other reasons, because they disintegrate personality. Life literally goes to pieces. The scenes and acts of its drama express no plan, have no unity. The loose-liver drifts into an *amour* and out of it as drunkards drift down a street of theaters, lurching into one playhouse after another, without comprehension of their own lives or of the spectacle before them. The loose-liver wants the emotion for its own sake without relation to any loyal plan of life. This is bad in sexual relations outside marriage. It is just as bad inside marriage. It is shamefully common in our relations to friends and to art.

Personality, as contrasted both with loose-living and with an official and business-like way of behaving, is a fine art. To be a person, not an automaton, and to treat others as persons, not as stuffed images, is a task like that of commanding an army. We need to see what is now and for the first time before our eyes. We want to know exactly what we are about. If our love declines from integrity into infatuation or jealousy, we are drifting in the trough of the sea.

Such a declension takes many forms. A familiar type of it often causes undue alarm. When women lose control of their affections for other women, the life-giving force that makes friendship great, loses its guide and becomes infatuation. The evil of such "crushes" or infatuations is not that some morbid and evil element called "sex" has suddenly entered the relation, but simply that the people have lost their heads. They forget their other interests and duties; they neglect their studies, their friends, and their health. They get morbid and sentimental, self-centered and soft. They are so near one another that they cannot see their way. They can no longer choose at all, for infatuation is idolatry, a form of slavery.

The evil of infatuation or idolatry takes the form of jealousy when we are so near a person that we cannot see his background or our own. If you are infatuated, you want a person all to yourself; then jealousy is inevitable. The world's claim, the claim of other friends, is forgotten. You are so blind, so deaf that you want to own another person. But not even in the closest love of man and woman is there any excuse for forgetting that they belong also to the world and are here to do its work.

Jealousy and idolatry are opposite perversions. In jealousy you want to keep a person wholly to yourself. In idolatry you want to give yourself wholly to a person. These opposites may be combined. Idolatry may take the form of jealousy. But whether simple or complex, the diagnosis of the trouble is essentially the same. Choice, orientation, self-guidance are in abeyance. The personality has become split into conflicting parties and now one of these, now another enslaves the rest. Reason — that greatly maligned habit — is now precisely what we want. Reason cannot cure many of the diseases to which love is subject, but when our integrity is split apart, when we have lost our way and are wandering at random, common sense, the matter-of-fact spirit, the ability to reason things out, is the obvious remedy and in my experience efficient.

CHAPTER XXVII

RETICENCE, MODESTY, CHASTITY

In the attempt to write about love, I am rushing in where angels fear to tread. Some of the most angelic and heroic people whom I have known never would suffer a sentence to be wrung from them on such a subject, and my admiration for them is all the greater because of their silence. For it was their reverence which made them dumb. Love and religion, they thought, are cheapened and besmirched by being discussed in public. I agree that this is often true. I have seen writings which cheapen and debase those great subjects; much which *can* be said about them should never be said. The idea that *anything* can profitably be blurted out in any language and to any audience, the ideal of pure frankness, is babyish and barbaric. Babies and fools have no reserves, because they make no choices. Personality, decency, and all that is human in us grows up through selection. By their choice of work, of play, of companions, of words, people are made what they are.

But every choice is also a multitude of rejections, more numerous and more instructive the further we advance. There is no virtue in emptying out your mind as a boy does his pockets; for minds, like pockets, contain not only valuables, but rubbish of all sorts. Literal frankness is achieved only by maniacs and by village gossips, the doors of whose minds swing free and let out indiscriminatingly whatever happens to have accumulated inside. Such literal frankness conceals nothing, has no more reserve than one of the lower animals. I recently saw an advertisement of a book (typical of many more) boasting that about sex the author "has no reserves and shuns no details."

This is like saying, "Dr. Skinemalive is bold enough to reveal all the details of heaven, together with the anatomy and physiology of angels, the method of tuning harps and the construction of street pavements in the New Jerusalem. He has thrown off all false modesty. He has no reserves; he shuns no details."

Any one who supposes that he knows so much about love and sex that he needs only to open his mouth and frankly emit the truth on these matters is astoundingly, pathetically, ludicrously ignorant of the huge continent whose shore he is touching. Frankness is a virtue only when the subject in hand is perfectly simple. For instance: "Are you or are you not hired by the United Railways to vote in their interest?" "Have you more than one wife?" "Do you like my cooking?" To answer these questions frankly may be a difficult moral act, but there is no need of modesty about our knowledge. We know enough to answer. The only question is, Shall we let it out? But the people who are quite ready to be frank and open about love, forget that their minds do not contain what they are offering, but only a caricature of it, ghostly as the harp and angel pictures of heaven, grotesque as the ideal of married life depicted in comic supplements of Sunday papers. The "virtue" of frankly letting out what we do not possess is a vice or a misfortune.

For a half or quarter truth may be, in result if not in intention, a gross libel. To call a string quartette "the scraping of horses' hairs on cats' bowels" is literally true, but if any one believed it to be the whole truth, it would become a blasphemy. Most of the "frank" statements made or printed about sex within the past decade seem to me as false and misleading as an account of music in terms of gut and horsehair. What we venture to say on so great a subject must attempt to be representative of the vast regions left untouched, as the flag represents the country, — not literally, but symbolically.

But grant (*per impossibile*) that a person might know all that is vitally important about love; would frankness be then the chief quality that he would need in order to enlighten others? Does a great teacher of history or music need chiefly frankness to convey his knowledge to others? Does he not rather need art, painstaking choice of methods, scrupulous avoidance of anything that is misleading? Good teaching of history requires eloquence, penetration, and grasp; it also requires (and this is my present point) rejection, reticence, and reserve.

The limitation of our knowledge and the difficulties of presentation should be enough to make any one aware that frankness will avail but little in speaking or writing upon any great subject. But in dealing with love and sex there is especial need of restraint. One brings up the subject presumably because one hopes to direct some one's attention profitably, to help some one to guide himself toward what is beautiful or heroic in love and away from its baser aspects; in short, to focus some one's consciousness aright. This attempt implies that consciousness can get out of focus, or can get its focus in the wrong place. Indeed it can, and most disastrously! Medical students, while studying saliva, sometimes become so vividly aware of their own mouths (the inside of them, I mean) that a copious and sometimes ludicrously inconvenient salivation results. I have seen a hospital patient drooling night and day as the result of a "fixed idea" about the inside of his mouth. He began to think about it and could not stop! You can try the experiment and verify the result (on a small scale) whenever you like, but I advise you not to. I should not have brought up the unpleasant subject at all but for a desire to reduce to absurdity the statement so often made that there is nothing about sex which cannot harmlessly and profitably be talked about. This belief is false. It is contradicted by the physiology of reflex action. Saliva can be made to flow copiously not only by pepper or any other irritant, but by thinking about the saliva in one's mouth. To be

constantly or imperatively conscious of sex is to be in
a miserable or a dangerous state. Talk about sex may
produce or augment this danger.

There is ample reason, then, for reticence and modesty when we approach anything so sacred as love.
There ought to be a taboo, not about venereal diseases
and their consequences, but about anything that tends
to upset the scenery of consciousness and dislocate the
background into the foreground. There is much that
ought to be kept out of sight and out of consciousness
most of the time, for the same reason that wise people
do not think of their saliva, of their personal beauty,
or of their personal ugliness. Consciousness does harm
whenever it interferes with something meant to be left
out of it, — the heart, the digestion, one's feet while
dancing, one's self while speaking in public.

One of the saving graces of reserve, then, is to preserve consciousness from dislocation. It has other uses.
Reserve is normal and right about anything that is
germinating in consciousness. To talk about such things
is like pulling a young plant up to look at its roots, or
pulling open a closed bud. You can seriously hurt a
germinating aspiration, a nascent perception of beauty,
truth, or love by exhibiting it in public or even in the
full light of consciousness. Such things should grow,
like roots, in quiet and in darkness. Books or talks that
are rightly considered "too old" at any particular
stage of a child's growth, do harm either by withering
what is not yet ready for the light, or by stimulating

premature growth. I have no doubt that some of us adults are still too young for many of the ideas that are floating about to-day. But who is wise enough to act as censor?

Each "grown-up" must decide for himself, and to onlookers his decisions about reserves must often seem arbitrary. The choice of what you will bring into the full light of publicity, what you will reveal to a few, and what you will not fully reveal even to yourself, is as personal, as private a matter as the choice of a profession or of a mate. If each is true to the best he knows, his fundamental reserves and choices must often seem incomprehensible to the rest of us. We should expect and respect such obscurities in each other as we admire the half lights and shadows of a picture. We should deprecate the lack of them.

One night, after reading Swedenborg, and imbibing, I suppose, something of his habits of mind, I dreamed that I heard the sound of many voices, and when I inquired of my spectral guide what their meaning might be, he told me that they were praising the virtues of men.

"Look," said one, "with what an agony of heroic effort that poor athlete is struggling to lift a hen's feather!"

"True," said another. "But can you not pity and praise still more that generous millionaire? See, he is giving his hard-won copper cent in bounteous charity to the newsboy who begs of him to buy the last of the evening papers."

"My admiration," said a third voice, "goes out irresistibly to that high-born Fifth Avenue damsel who from cannibalism so rigidly refrains. In all the unspotted record of her life where can you find one charge of breaking and entering, one moment's yielding to the sweet lure of assault and battery?"

I believe that much which is called chastity is about as virtuous as the people of my dream. Chastity surely means nothing without some temptation to be unchaste. It is as soulless and dead as the "courage" of those who are not aware of danger, or the "temperance" of those who hate the taste of liquor. In frigid people the absence of sexual sin is no more virtuous than the absence of hair on a bald head. Purity, like health or peace, may be an accident or an apathy. It may be the fruit of heroic victories. Only the Eternal knows. No acquaintance with a man's daily doings reveals anything decisive about the matter. Statistics and science, when asked to testify, have other engagements. Hence no one will ever be able justly to indict half the human race till a measure of temptation as well as of temperature is invented. With such an instrument who knows how many zero readings would be registered?

We cannot praise chastity as the abstention from certain acts, for then normal marriage would be unchaste. We cannot praise it as the innocence of evil, for without temptation there can be no virtue. Chastity must mean victory over the enemy, not ignorance of his strength. We must feel the temptation and overcome it. By what power? *By cultivating the highest type of personal relation to which we can attain.* Whatever person, book, game, or art wakes us to admire or to approximate heroism in personal relations, discourages unchastity, for heroism in personal relations is the basis of all genuine chastity.

By the consecration of affection we gain victory over the lower or impersonal affection. We do not eliminate the enemy altogether, but we prevent his dwelling on our territory. For unchastity is domination by the impersonal love of sex rather than by love of an individual. Such domination (inside or outside marriage) disorganizes soul and body even when no visible act of unchastity is committed. A certain type of day-dreaming and novel-reading may disintegrate and ruin character more hopelessly than prostitution.

What is it that is poisoned or deformed by unchastity so defined? No law of the state and no law of health need be broken. In many forms of unchastity no other person need be injured, no utility need be destroyed. What is injured is that for which the state, the laws of hygiene, and all other utilities exist: the integrity and richness of personality. The worth of a personality is not determined altogether by the quality of the ideas or impulses which pass through it. Many of the thoughts and desires of maniacs, criminals, and degenerates have at some time, in sleep or waking, passed through

most people's minds. But normal minds do not welcome such thoughts or give them harborage. They are
pushed out by an instinct of mental integrity which
it is one of the main tasks of education to cultivate.
They are warned to "move on" because they threaten
that integrity.

But in the effort to suppress mental anarchy it is
foolish simply to eject offending thoughts and try to
keep busy in athletics, science, or business. As soon as
our attention is distracted by fatigue or leisure, what
was forcibly (not rationally) thrown out comes creep-
ing in again. An evil or impersonal love must be cherished and made personal, — developed, not crushed.
The saint must become more human than the sinner,
or fall below him because impersonal love (unwisely
called "mere sex attraction") is *less than human*.

I wish to head off two false conclusions which might
be drawn from the foregoing remarks: first, that celibacy is lower than the marriage state; and, second,
that in marriage, love can find its perfection. I see no
reason to believe in either of these popular modern
dogmas. The second depends upon the first. If we
believe that in marriage it is possible to achieve the
highest ideal of love, to reach the goal of perfection in
personal relations, of course celibacy is at best a necessary evil. But if we believe, as I do, that marriage
and every other form of human happiness becomes idolatrous and hollow unless it is conceived and lived out
as a symbolic representation of our union with God,

then in celibacy one may find other (and, for some persons, better) symbols of that union.

The idea that marriage gets its highest significance as a means to the perpetuation of the race is to my mind another shallow one. Marriage is a means to more human life, but what is human life for? It is perfected, we are told, in marriage, wherein again it perpetuates itself in its offspring. This is arguing in a circle. The Christian idea of the sacramental or symbolic purpose of marriage seems to me the true one.

CHAPTER XXVIII

IMPERFECT MUTUALITY IN LOVE: ROMANCE

WE expect and demand mutuality in all sorts of places. We are always striving for it in talk, in the interchange of actors and audience, in the relations of labor and capital, as well as in affection. Doleful and comic are the failures of mutuality in shaking hands. Some hold and pump our hands *ad nauseam*. Others go into a hand-grasp as gingerly as they pick a hot coal from the carpet. Yet for a lover, the touch of a beloved hand is almost a kiss.

What have we to hope for in the attainment of a more perfect response in love? What can we do about it?

Perfect response in any sort of human intercourse is almost as unattainable as literal justice (falsely called "poetic"). Some cherish the hope of a justice which always responds or corresponds with what we deserve. But as no man knows what he deserves or what would repay him, justice can never be more than a clumsy approximation to his desires.

All responses are tainted with the same imperfection. When I laugh at your joke our wits do not precisely meet. Only a practiced tolerance or an unusual dullness can prevent us from seeing that there is more (or less) meaning in the joke than in the laugh; there must be, just because the joke is yours. It has been bred amidst the particular associations, the unsharable memories, the comic failures and abortive aspirations of your life. By these your own appreciation of your joke is tinged; but my appreciation cannot be. Perhaps I see more in it than you do; I cannot see precisely the same. But the point is that I see enough to join you, to follow you, perhaps lead you, as my answering laugh seems to say.

My response means more. It dives as far as it can go in the direction of your meaning, then shoots along the rest of the way by the impetus of faith. God only knows exactly what your joke means to you. He knows far better than you do. He also knows exactly how much my answering laugh understands. In Him, and only in Him we ultimately meet, and it is our more or less enlightened consciousness of this absolute but hidden union which makes the joke a success. We intend to meet, and because of that intention we do meet, by faith, which takes here one of its protean disguises, — an all-encompassing good nature. We laugh, partly at the point of the joke, partly out of pure good nature which pardons inanities and supplies missing links, because it is determined to make the joke a success, at all hazards. Such good nature makes mutuality possible in fun.

In simpler words, laughter is partly contagious, not purely intelligent. We often laugh from general sympathy or because some one "sets us off," not because we see the joke. The general upshot of his laughter hits us, whether we catch the point or not. Sometimes this contagion in fun happens without any effort on our part. Sometimes it is impossible without an effort, first to see what the joke means and then to project ourselves into the mirth any way by hook or crook. In lifeless moods we fail. We find the doors of our sympathy tight shut against the warmth of most people's fun. Their words and gestures penetrate but leave us frigid unless we can summon good nature enough to feel their spirit.

Without a free gift of good nature there can be no mutual understanding, especially in love. Congeniality, physical, intellectual, emotional, or spiritual, can never be perfect as long as we remain human growing, imperfect beings. Lock and key can be made to fit each other perfectly because they are dead, but if they were alive they would never fit. Only the less-than-human or the more-than-human can fit each other perfectly or answer each other's love in complete mutuality. Yet in love, as in laughter, faith can do wonders. Love meets love to some extent by spontaneous sympathy, but far more by intention and contagion.

Because of this "justification by faith" well-meant failures are infinitely touching and mutually endearing to many a faithful couple. Only Omniscience holds the whole of what a kiss or a blunder can mean, but when two mates know *that*, there is no end to their power to bear, to forgive, to supplement, to take for granted, in love and word.

Mutuality, then, is attained not because a preëstablished harmony brings together exactly the right people at precisely the right time and gives each of them identical thoughts, identical joy, or identical affection which flame up simultaneously but independently in each. We meet and answer one another burdened by a double imperfection; neither can express what he means, neither can precisely understand even the bit that gets expressed. But love excites love in part, as laughter begets laughter, by the contagion of its intention. Granted that we are determined once for all to play the game and to meet somehow; then we play into a common intention as court-tennis players play against the same wall, not directly at each other. Practice makes us apt to anticipate our fellow's position. Mutuality in love is an "art" in which proficiency is attained by labor rather than by preëstablished harmony. But the labor draws us into adventures, into danger and daring, which is in itself enough to explain our incurable tendency to find love romantic and so perpetually to anger Mr. George Bernard Shaw.

Shaw, and all who strive for literalism in love, set to work first to take the uncertainties and the infinities out of it. Marriage, they say, shall be a contract for specified purposes under state control. Love is "a ridiculous exaggeration of the difference between one

person and another." These differences are in truth
so slight that there can be no romantic adventure in
finding one another, no danger of losing one another,
no mystery anywhere, but only confusion and muddleheadedness.

Now, romance, I take it, is the sense of mystery,
beauty, danger, and infinity in love. We find these
blessings in love as we do in night. Mr. Shaw finds
them, too, wherever he is especially interested; for instance, in the "hallucination" out of which his writings (as he now tells us)[1] spring.

To ignore the romance in love, in history, in games,
in music, or anywhere else, is one of the easiest things
in the world. One has only to slouch because one is
sick of standing erect, to refuse the task of looking
behind the obvious and relapse into sleepy literalism.
As one's eyes grow fatigued with reading, the letters
cease to be symbols and become letters only. Meaning,
interest, and beauty die out of the words on the page.
They are only printer's type, no longer signposts to
infinite meaning.

There is no sin in this sort of blindness, provided
one recognizes that one's fatigue and not the letters
are at fault. But to sneer at the letters because they
are only ridiculous black scratches, to sneer at all who
find wisdom or beauty in what these scratches mean, is
simply to stagger and lurch because one is too bored to

---

[1] In an answer to the inquiry of the Modern Historic Records Association, quoted in Boston *Transcript*, June 15, 1912.

walk straight. Every one finds romance in what he loves. He cannot keep it out. No one finds romance when he is too indifferent to look for it or too tired to translate symbols into meaning. A baby is a lump of flesh, a symphony is a long, confused noise, a picture is a bit of discolored canvas, and man is an ugly, featherless biped to any one who has not interest enough to see more.

To all of us, when we are sleepy or seasick, the world presents itself in these terms. Now and then Mr. Shaw attracts notice by loudly exclaiming, in print, that a man can see best when his eyes are too sleepy to open, and that under these conditions he sees no romance in the world. Romance is not a surface quality. It is, therefore, no more visible on the surface of the sleepy man's world than excitement in the pages of the sleepy man's book.

By being just a trifle more *blasé* than Mr. Shaw one can wipe science, mathematics, color, and shape out of the world. All the experiences of our devitalized moods are flat, colorless, meaningless, and stale, and it is as easy to let ourselves get devitalized as it is to drop our end of the load which we are helping to carry. If we give up the effort of attention which sustains the world of romance in love, then science, commerce, and social life simultaneously collapse and we progress towards savagery. But tell me what most vitally interests a man and I will tell you where to look for the saving romantic grace of his nature.

Mystery, beauty, danger, and a prehensile affection spring up in many a modern's mind when he thinks of his new automobile or of the wildcat stocks which he manipulates. Romance crops out in strange places, but better anywhere than nowhere, for without it we creak like dry sole leather.

CHAPTER XXIX

MARRIAGE

In this book marriage means such a union of one man and one woman as is described in the Christian marriage service. For various reasons such an ideal union is not always attained in modern "civilized" communities. But of late we have been told by certain "advanced" writers that it ought not to be attained, or retained, any longer. Other institutions, they say, — the State, the Church, — have been radically transformed; but marriage, at least in theory, has retained its old-fashioned shape, which, according to G. B. Shaw, suits only a small minority of the (English) people. Is it not time for matrimony to join the march of evolution and be brought up to date?

Moral and spiritual growth certainly ought to take place in the marriage relation, but it is often forgotten that change and growth are not the same. Change may be so radical as to destroy growth. Forest fires and popular crazes are changes which abolish development. Nothing grows unless it has a central core of identity which does not change. A tree can be changed into parlor matches, but it cannot grow parlor matches like leaves. The State can grow only so long as some idea of government persists. It can decay into anarchy,' but it cannot grow into anarchy, because no "it" is left to grow.

So marriage will not grow but decay if it "outgrows" its fundamental purpose. But before considering radical changes, would it not be well to give it fair trial? We can hardly say that marriage has been fairly tried, as long as man remains so fitfully and imperfectly monogamic as he now is. Let us call to mind what can be said, first in defense, then in praise, of the plan to make it a fact instead of — as now — an ideal.

That monogamy is enjoined by Christianity and by modern Judaism, that it is the law of the land, that public opinion supports it enough to make frank polygamy a disgrace, that the history of marriage seems to tend on the whole towards monogamy, in theory if not in practice, — all these are important facts. But to my mind they are not a final justification of monogamy. For the current interpretations of religion, law, tradition, and public opinion are subject to change, and may be modified by the conscience of a later generation. The torture of law breakers was once supported by religion, law, tradition, and public opinion; in fact, it is only within a century that these currents have been reversed. Marriage must have a foundation deeper than any tradition or enactment.

Against secret polygamy and violation of the marriage vow it may be urged, first, that such secrecy involves lying and sneaking about back streets; second, that jealousy and marital bitterness are almost sure to poison the lives of those concerned; and third, that a family racked by any such strain makes a poor nest for any children who may be born. These three reasons for monogamy are more important than those derived from shifting tradition or enactments. Yet they do not seem to me final. If public opinion changed, the restraint of secrecy might be removed and lying would become unnecessary. If every one willingly agreed to polygamous and polyandrous relations, there might be no bitterness or jealousy in them, and it seems at least possible than any arrangement which suited parents might be made to suit children. They might not object to being brought up by the State according to the platonic principle.

George Bernard Shaw and other Socialists appear to think that economic reasons are basic in the support of monogamic marriage. If wealth were justly (i.e., socialistically) produced and distributed, no one, they think, could afford the expense of plural marriage. But if all parents worked and the birth of children were prevented, I do not see why plural marriage need involve increased expense.

If monogamic marriage is to continue in theory and to be steadily approached in practice, we must have better reasons than any of these. Our belief in it must be founded on something more fundamental than economy. The temporary codes of Church, law, and public opinion must have something back of their fiat.

A sound defense of monogamy must justify first of
all its exclusiveness: — "Forsaking all others, keep
thee only unto her so long as ye both shall live." Of
course this does not mean that married people shall not
make friends among both sexes. It can only mean that
there shall be in marriage a core of primary intimacies
shared with no other human being. The law insists
only upon the physical and economic side of this primacy. So long as a man does not commit adultery, so long
as he supports his wife and is not cruel, or, in variously
defined ways, intolerable, to her, the law is satisfied.
It makes no attempt to buttress the spiritual privacy
of the marriage, but on the physical side the law stands
for absolute privacy. Whatever else is shared, this
shall not be shared. It is for the public good that the
marital relation shall not be public or promiscuous.
So says the law.

Yet such exclusiveness is contrary to the general
trend of the times. We are less and less tolerant of exclusive rights and private ownership. Hence it is natural that a considerable wing within the Socialist party
should be opposed to all legal sanctions for the exclusiveness of marriage.

The justification of any sort of exclusiveness is its
fruits in character. Tradition, law, and public opinion
have been guided thus far by the belief that character,
service, and happiness are best built up through affections which are to some extent exclusive because they

:are loyal to the objects of their own free choice. Is this reasonable?

Let us draw some parallels from outside the field of married love. It is generally agreed that in the choice of a country, an occupation, or a residence there should be, if possible, finality. A man who wanders from country to country soon becomes a "man without a country." He is usually unhappy and amounts to little. It is hard for him to form lasting ties of interest, friendship, and service or to become a happy and growing creature. Law backs up this conclusion to a certain extent. Sometimes it forbids a man to emigrate or immigrate. Invariably (so far as I know) it forbids him to hold citizenship in one country and then act against it in the interests of another. Such laws are violated, but the sentiment that each man owes loyalty to one (native or adopted) country is still strong enough to resist overt internationalist propaganda. Most of us believe that, while we should be friendly with all countries and open-minded towards their ideas and customs, such a brotherhood of nations ought not to mean fusion of nations. Like the "Jack of all trades" the "Jack of all nations" is too superficial in his acquaintance with any to serve it (and through it, all of us) well.

Very rare in my acquaintance are the people who have changed from trade to trade and yet succeeded in any. The rolling man gathers no skill because he is not faithful to any job long enough to learn the soul of it, or to get its best rewards. May it not be the same with the

"free lover"? While attracted to one mate, he perceives the counter-attractions of others. He is not
narrow-minded. He recognizes beauty and goodness
everywhere and wishes a generous share of both. But
precisely similar counter-attractions offer themselves
to every man who has set himself to do a piece of work.
The other man's job, like the other man's wife, often
looks more attractive than his own. Few men stick to
their work because they are perpetually in love with
it and never in love with any other. They stick to it
because they have learned to believe that nobody ac-
complishes anything unless he binds himself to resist
his momentary impulses and to learn one trade as
thoroughly as he can. Moreover the best rewards of
work, financial and personal, usually come late. To
leave one job for another usually means to leave it
before we have got the best of it or given it our best
service.

To go from city to city within one's country is probably commoner in America than elsewhere, and no
one deprecates changes made before we have chosen a
place to live. The preliminary survey of many places,
if one can afford it, is as wise as it is to see many possible mates before one marries. But when the choice of a
place to live has once been made, every one regards it
as an evil, though perhaps a necessary evil, to move
away.

These choices — of country, residence or job (or
mate) — are usually exclusive. In taking one we reject

many, and often find the rejection very painful. Like a polygamist we want to grasp several of the alternatives offered. But we have learned the necessity of sacrifice, not only for moral reasons, but from pure prudence. If we try for several, we lose all. Moreover, most of these choices, since they are final, involve not only exclusiveness and sacrifice at the start, but devotion all the way along. No man likes his business every day: sometimes he loathes it; yet he knows that to throw it up and try another, or to drift about, would be crazy. He learns to disregard or to crush his impulses of repulsion for his job. He must "make good" in it whether he feels like it or not.

All this we Americans have learned in business because work is the thing we have learned best. But in love a wave of indifference or dislike is taken very seriously, perhaps interpreted to mean "time for divorce" or "right to be unfaithful." We are foolish enough to expect constancy of feeling in love, though we know that in everything else our feelings vary like the weather.

One reason for greater stupidity in affection than in business is this. You have one business and not (as a rule) a dozen near-businesses besides. But though you have rightly but one mate, you have many friends of her sex. A close parallel to the difficulties thus suggested and to the right solution of them is to be found in painting. The landscape artist does not welcome to his canvas all the beauties that he sees and loves as he sits down to sketch. The laws of his art force him not only to reject much that fascinates him, but to choose one point of delight for the focus of his picture and subordinate all else. It is torture sometimes for the amateur, this enforced sacrifice of rival beauties, all of them desired. But the sacrifice (unlike that of monogamy) is enforced by no convention, by no law of State or of religion, but only by the nature of his own original choice. If he tries to combine all that attracts him he will do justice to nothing. When he chooses a subject, he pledges himself to one interest, forsaking all others; but unless he is a saint or a simpleton he is tempted a hundred times, while he paints, to combine rival beauties, loved but incompatible. Why incompatible? Because his picture, like his life, must contain a center of interest, a graded scale of values and of devotion. Without that center it falls to pieces.

So in our human relationships, whether religion, law, and custom say so or not, each of us must try to establish a center. Our faithfulness to friends and acquaintances must be subordinate to one primal loyalty, and what is owed and received in that primal loyalty must decide what can be given to others in the same field.

It appears, then, that in many other fields of life we have convincing proof of the principle on which monogamy rests. In science, in art, in practical affairs, in patriotism we habitually select a single interest to which all else then becomes secondary. Would it not be strange, then, if there were no need to establish by marriage such a center?

A plausible attack may be made on monogamy by picturing it as slavery. If monogamy is inviolate, one person seems to some extent to *own* another. In this twentieth century and in a land of freedom are we to admit property in persons? Certainly. All loyalty is binding as well as enfranchising. It is voluntary surrender of one's freedom in the service of a cause. Our country owns us enough to punish us for treason if we are unfaithful to our citizenship. Any one who binds himself legally or morally to a business, a college, or a science is in some respect owned. Nothing is less free than art or thought or love. Each undertakes to construct something which needs time, perhaps eternity, to complete it. Each is going somewhere, and is bound, therefore, upon its journey. That journey, that desire, which is the kernel of individuality, certainly limits freedom, but it does not in any proper sense enslave. It is not slavery to bind one's self to fidelity because one wants something supremely.

In support of these reasons for partial ownership of one person by another and for such surrender of freedom as is implied in loyalty to the marriage vow, consider this: Whatever other basis there may be for private ownership of land, tools, or persons, it is generally agreed that the labor which a person puts into anything gives him some right to it. A stethoscope that I have long used fits my ear and trains my ear until the two belong together; no one else can use that tool or serve the community as well with it as I can. Hence the community is interested that a durable bond between me and my tool should be established. Only long practice brings swift, skillful, and economic use of anything. In short periods a man and his tool cannot grow to fit each other. It pays, then, to let the workman keep his own tool (as he probably prefers to do) and not to share it impartially with others. It shall belong to him because he can probably do better work with it than any one else can.

An unfinished manuscript or picture naturally belongs to him who began it, because he can probably bring more value out of it than any one else. One need not insist that no one else could have done better with the subject had he started independently to bring out all that was in it. One need not insist that all marriages are made in heaven and could not have been better arranged. But is there not every reason to suppose that in marriage, as in work, it generally pays for partners to stay together and finish the structure of family life which they have started? Each has begun to bring something out of the other. Each has become used to the other, more or less, as tool and hand, writer and subject, are constantly shaping each other. As time goes on, husband and wife each acquire a hold upon the other like that of the musician and his violin. Each stimulates the other, now and then at least, to his best work, his best citizenship, his greatest happiness. Outsiders can rarely do so much.

Beyond the field of personal relations there may be

still more fundamental loyalties which call one away from wife, from friends, and acquaintances alike. At the call of the country we rightly interrupt all personal relations. At the call of science and humanity it may be any one's duty to give up his life as uncounted American physicians have given theirs. The call of conscience or of God may be so clear that a man may rightly leave wife, friends, country, and bury himself in a hermitage or in study that is without any known human benefit.

These are rare calls, and partly because of this rarity they may bring grievous conflict of one loyalty against another. But when the final choice is made, it involves none of that disloyalty which monogamy forbids. "Forsaking all others" does not mean ignoring country, science, art, or God. It means that as long as we are loyal to personal claims at all, — as long as there is no call to give up all persons (including, it may be, our own) for a supra-personal good, — one must keep a central primacy and privacy.

Within the field of personal relations one should be loyal to each of one's subordinate ties, to friend, business associate, official superior or inferior, mere acquaintance, each after his kind. The artist may need as much delicacy of touch to deal with a subdued accessory in his picture as to finish its focal center. Each of the less intimate personal relations is likewise a fine art in itself. None can be confusedly mistaken or mistreated for any other without harm.

I do not say that married people should belong to each other only so long as they bring out each other's best. The fundamental reason for continuity in marriage is not this mutual inspiration. It is the need of a primacy among our affections of various degrees. But when for this and other reasons people persevere in marriage despite many temptations to break away from it, they often reap in later life a harvest of mutual responsiveness which only years can bring to maturity. Some of the best traits of marriage, — the subtle understanding of what need not be spoken, the instinctive habit of filling in one another's deficiencies or anticipating one another's needs, — these never have time to develop unless man and wife resist some of the storms and shocks of their earlier years.

It is fashionable nowadays to talk of marriage as a contract between husband and wife. This is something like calling violin-music a contact between fiddle and bow. It is not untrue; it is merely foolish. There is a contract in marriage and there is a contact between bow and strings. But there is so much else that no one in his senses should pick out this subordinate element to characterize the whole.

What sort of contract is marriage? How does it differ from a contract between a housebuilder and a (prospective) householder? First of all in this: Contracting parties are not usually drawn together by any mysterious and elemental attraction. Employer and employee exert, as a rule, no subtle fascination on each other. Their differences have to be adjusted, while the differences of married people are often their most effective bond. Give the complementary differences of sex a chance and they will work for each other's benefit without pay, without effort and even without capacity. In marriage, when mind and conscience sleep, our subconscious elemental energies may be busily serving the common good, despite our ineptitudes and even despite our sins. Of course this is not the whole truth. No matter how devotedly a man is attached to his wife, he does not want to be fastened to her beauty, any more than to her apron-strings. He wants to be rationally as well as magically linked to her. He wants to be led by her experience and her nobility as well as by charm. It is good to be thus linked by bonds of many colors, as we are in marriage, rather than by one dull instrument, a contract.

For the many-sidedness of marriage gives it strength. Even *two* interests shared throw light on each other and on those who share them. Each reflects and multiplies all, like a group of mirrors. Married people share, as a rule, more and more diverse interests with each other than with any one else. Houses, children, sorrows, relations (poor and not so poor), finances, reputations, meals, beds, opinions, prejudices, sickness and health, — who but mates can share so many and so richly varied realities? Who else has the chance to realize with soul and with sense how each reënforces the rest?

Contrast with the many-stranded union of marriage the feeble bond that holds two philosophers met in argument. With only their professional studies to join them, is it any wonder that they so rarely convince each other? If philosophers were really serious in their desire to comprehend each other, they would live together, cook, eat, and sleep together like pioneers, share their gawky pre-philosophic past with each other, plan some romantic, some strikingly extra-philosophic adventure together, study each other's behavior in money matters, love-affairs, games, and family tiffs. It would take time — just as marriage does; it would try each of them sorely — as marriage does; but it might well bring to them and to their opinions some fraction of the mutual conversion, the mutual enlightenment, intimacy, and esteem that bless marriage.

Any one who wishes to strengthen his basis of agreement with another, to appropriate all he can of another's greatness or to communicate his most cherished aspirations, must, I believe, do what he can to ape and copy marriage, humbly imitating the conditions it so richly furnishes for all these supreme achievements. It is because employer and employee, radical and conservative, plaintiff and defendant, are in contact at so few points, share so few of the benefits of long and close association, — are, in short, so bereft of the trials and blessings of marriage, — that they waste so much vigor in fighting each other.

Theoretically our form of government ought to make us experts in marriage; for we are supposedly familiar with the fact that in union there is strength. But in fact we shall learn more of what the national unity-in-variety should be, by recalling how in marriage, sorrows explain and justify creeds, how children and other responsibilities explain expenditures, how children and other miracles teach tolerance, how words are interpreted by personal history, and hands grow beautiful in their remembered use.

Of course I have not done justice to the richness of the marriage union: only music gives me the parallel that I need. There, the interweaving strands of melody and harmony—each carrying its own spirit and meaning, each modifying and enriching the rest, all blended in the current of a single utterance — seem to me the fittest of images to suggest the interweaving and reënforcing of interests in marriage. Not a note in the chord or a phrase in the melody is itself without the rest. United they stand and give life each to each. Divided they fall and scatter like seeds, until some one plants them once more in fruitful company.

Perhaps the greatest blessing in marriage is that it lasts so long. The years, like the varying interests of each year, combine to buttress and enrich each other. Out of many shared years, one life. In a series of temporary relationships, one misses the ripening, gathering, harvesting joys, the deep, hard-won truths of marriage.

The unmarried can rarely follow so many strands of interest at once. They share food with one friend, work with another, play with a third, travel with a fourth, failure with a fifth, quarrels with a sixth. But with no human being can they share the light shed by each of these experiences on all the rest.

The ripening of money by compound interest is slow and feeble compared to the ripening of compounded interests in married life. God forbid that I should belittle the sacredness of first love because I hold just now a brief for enduring marriage. But there is fascination in familiarity as well as in the first glimpse of a new world. A love that can remember its own development, can look down the lengthening vista of its adventurous past and project its future, has perhaps less quivering intensity but surely more volume and richness than its opening days could possess. Such elastic strength comes only with time. Early love may be incomparable in its creative brilliance, but in maturer love we win the fruits of security.

I know well that this very security may be base and slack. People may become so sleepily content with their marriage that they cease to care much about anything, even about each other. But there is another security that is not base; I mean the reliance on one's footing that nerves one to a bold leap, the firm foundation which gives time to think and plan, opportunity to serve, to appreciate, and to grow. Even business needs some security if it is to get in motion at all. Even the bomb-thrower must be relatively safe while he prepares and throws his bomb.

Not tamely secure are the blessings and fruits of marriage. They must be rewon again and again. But well-grounded reliance on our right to try for them, and on our hope of rewinning them as often as we sincerely try, — that we surely need and find in marriage.

All security ties some future's hands in order that we may risk something else. Fortified by good health, one may risk money; buttressed by money one may perhaps risk health. In marriage, the security ordinarily attained is this: there is some one who forgives us more often and more freely than the unmarried can expect; some one who makes God's infinite forgiveness more credible. There is some one who loves us long after we have forfeited any natural right to be loved and long before we have won any. Supernatural in this sense marriage almost always is; thus it prepares and enfranchises us for religion.

In the forefront of my tribute to marriage I have put forgiveness, because I know nothing that we need more. We need it not merely to lighten the burdens of discouragement, but to stir us out of the apathy of habit. Fresh impulse to our work, fresh heart for the impersonations which every art and every game presuppose, new love of life and its author, — such are the issues of forgiveness. Your better half forgives not only your more obvious sins, but your awkwardness (behind which

she sees some grace quite hidden to other mortals),
your foolishness, your dumbness, your blank and un-
inspiring face. Despite all these drab exteriors she sees
something worth while in you, and because she sees it
she helps it to be born.

Forgiveness is to the spirit what home is to the
householder. It is the assurance that in the house of
the spirit some one waits for our deed, — the deed
never yet done, but always due. That expectation is a
stronghold to which we return at night, from which we
carry vigor to our morning's work. Such security ener-
vates only when it no longer nettles us to deserve
it and, by this effort, to reëstablish it. "Thy face a
home, a flying home to me," says Chesterton to his
wife. There is no ignoble torpor about a flying home.
Unless we make shift to fly a bit ourselves, we are left
behind.

There is a bracing negative aspect to the marriage
vow. It commits us more or less irrevocably to forsake
all others. It cuts off the freedom to act on the spur
of the moment. Unmarried, we are like the riderless
horse who allows only for his own height when he ducks
under low branches in the forest. In marriage we must
choose our path more carefully. But this is just what
the vast majority of us need. We need to be fenced
into a narrower field than of ourselves we should even
find. We need to be harnessed and given a bit of road
to cover. In the end we put out more power and win
more happiness when our choice is thus restricted and

our path narrowed by a promise, given and taken. We get somewhere because we are no longer so free to change our course.

Any responsibility gives us direction and continuity, but marriage brings us in addition some of the choicest adventures that the world has in store. Certain of these adventures, or tests, every modern must meet and conquer, as the mediæval knight met the enchanters and dragons of the forest. If he misses them, he will slip out of life like a boy entering college heavily conditioned. Can you remember? Can you imagine? Can you be a good winner, a game loser? Can you resist satiety? Such questions form part of the examination which, early or late, every one must take. For some of these questions marriage gives us the best-known preparation and the fairest marking system.

Take the last question as a sample. Can you resist satiety? Only by miracle, it seems; for every day you and all of us pay cool insults to the clouds, the trees, and the cities, to pictures and books, to fire, rain, and nightfall. You turn upon them the ignominy of your neglect and upon yourself that ignominy returns a thousandfold. With shame you discover that the picture on your wall is practically invisible to you after the first few months. Just with the tail of your eye you brush across its surface now and then. Yet it has done nothing to deserve such treatment. It has not degenerated. It is you who have degenerated, your color and freshness that have faded, your mental structure that has collapsed. Part of you has been killed to avenge the slur you cast upon an artist's child.

Familiar and humiliating enough, — this defeat. In everyday life we have almost given up the hope of avoiding it. But in marriage we sight a better chance to win at least partial victory. For there, the well-nigh immovable body of our dullness meets an awakening force as nearly irresistible as any that human life encounters. There the test, "Can you resist satiety?" is squarely put up to us and we are given an un-equaled chance to win a victory or to duck under to one of the devil's most soul-destroying blows. Nothing in creation less deserves our neglect than the soul and body of the person we are pledged to for life. Nothing has so good a chance to rouse us and to save us. Trees and birds speak our language far less clearly. If they love us and forgive us, they are usually silent about it. When they serve us it is far from clear that they were meant so to serve. If they summon up the past and call in the future to refresh and to defend us, we are none the wiser. But the one soul that has a fair chance of saving us from the ignominious death of satiety, by warming our dull life with greater life, is the faithful soul called our better half.

Victory here gives us hope of victory elsewhere. In-asmuch as we learn to see the perpetual novelty, rest, and charm which marriage offers to all, we have mas-tered one stage in the art of unsated happiness and of unchecked growth. Successfully married people have more news to tell each other and more capacity to hear it eagerly than any less closely, less durably united couple can have. The habit of seeing and hearing freshly can be acquired in marriage if anywhere, and once acquired here, it may be gradually extended into more difficult regions.

So it is I believe with most of the other tests with which the world invariably confronts us. If in marriage a man cannot learn to see himself as others see him, he will probably never learn it at all. If there he learns nothing of the art of vicarious living, he will never have again in all human probability so easy and inspiring a teacher. If family life does not spur him so to envisage the distant and the future that he expresses himself and controls himself somewhat as the present demands, he is apt to remain a donkey to the end.

So far I have written mostly of strength and of the trials of strength in marriage. So much for the deep root of it. Now for its shoots and branches.

Everybody wants to be understood by somebody; but in the natural course of events everybody is more or less misunderstood or distortedly understood by most of his friends and acquaintances. They have no "call" to pay special attention to him and are rightly engaged in their own business. In heaven, scripture tells us, we shall know as we are known, wholly; but to most of us this perfect knowledge would be inconceivable but for the glimpses and tastes of it in marriage. Marriage gives us the best chance in sight to grasp our share of complete mutual comprehension. I believe that any benedict among us, the "pick-and-shovel" man, the shipping-clerk, the plumber, or the railroad magnate, is more apt to be understood by his wife than by any other human being. The bachelor and the maid (old or young) are less often appreciated with that ripe mixture of favoritism and keen sight which the married enjoy.

Enjoy it they certainly do. Almost every one wants to pour out his joys, his troubles, and his plans to some-one who will meet him halfway. The number of re-served people dwindles towards zero in the intricate understanding of marriage. Most of them were re-served before marriage because they feared to be laughed at, quoted, or misunderstood. There remain a few who can never quite trust themselves and their secrets to any human being. They become monks (or their equivalent); or missing that outlet are apt to be-come dry and brackish. An outlet for free expression is the only way of insuring an inlet,—an intake of new power. Friends and acquaintances give us precious bits of their confidence and their attention, but except for our mate there is seldom any one who cares to hear all that we would say and to say all that we would hear. Others are more keenly interested elsewhere. No one else has so good a reason to be interested; no one else is so often interested (and interesting) beyond reason.

The intimate commingling of new thoughts and plans too fragile and tender to be grasped by any save one, is as intense and peculiar a joy as any form of union can give. It is mutual creation, and all the leaping wonder and holy fear of creation attend it. The "marriage of two minds," in those who are also married in every other sense, is full of adventure and the pioneer spirit. I know well that this can be missed in marriage. But where else can it be so often found? Its perfection of swift give-and-take, heightening each personality by inflow of the other, is equaled perhaps when two musicians in some miraculous hour make and interpret music together. But it is only in the occasional raptures of nascent music that they can enjoy themselves in this heaven-glimpsing way, while husband and wife can sound each year the chords of a myriad newborn thoughts.

Wonderfully close to the most sacred purpose of marriage is its greatest danger, — idolatry. But in this respect it is like all other good things. From marriage, as from every great gift, we are meant to learn something greater, something more vital than itself. But we may miss its spirit and stick fast at its letter, like pupils who fasten upon the master's fascinating tricks and foibles instead of plodding past him to seek from God their own share of beauty and truth, unshared before. All human teachers are dangerous but necessary. We are tempted to depend upon them, not merely at the start, but so permanently that they pauperize instead of enriching us. Their finite stock of food exhausted, we starve. By the same fatal error, business which should be our symbol becomes our life, art degenerates into conventionality and marriage love, which should acquaint us with divinity, is worshiped instead for its own sake.

Have you never watched the debasement of a beautiful voice under training? Its own original glimpse of beauty is soon lost and the image of another's mannerism becomes indelibly fixed on it. So I have seen people lose their religion in marriage. The great teacher spoils them, because they have failed to go behind his teaching to the sources of his wisdom. Yet some such teacher we all must have. We may avoid the idolatries of marriage only by exposing ourselves to the same dangers in some other form. For, married or single, we learn mainly by imitation.

How, then, can we best guard ourselves from the dangers besetting every attempt to appropriate the blessings of a great teacher, a fascinating symbol, like marriage?

The chief dangers and failures of which we must take account are two: idolatry and "*hifalutinism.*" The idolatrous marriage is slavishly content with its material and spiritual conveniences. The hifalutin marriage is a bungling of sentimental amateurs who will not learn their technique, who try to play the game without knowing the rules. It is too high and mighty to notice plain, or even beautiful, facts. It parallels the amateur artist's attempt to enjoy the spirit of his art when he has never mastered its materials or acquired its technique. It tries to loll in the second-story balcony of love's home before it has put in the underpinning.

All that I can say of the defenses against idolatrous failure I have already said. Of the hifalutin I have something more to say. I have insisted, perhaps too often, on the need of piercing through the letter of experience to its spirit. For in this attempt it is easy to forget that what we want is the spirit of this letter — precisely this letter — not something like it. If we want to interpret the meaning of a text, the first essential is to catch our text, and to read it word by word. Then — only then — comes the leap of interpretation.

One can miss the best happiness of marriage because one travels through it in kid gloves, Pullman cars, first-class staterooms, and grand hotels. Rich, city-bred, voluntarily childless, one can mince through marriage as sightseers promenade in a forest on a graveled path with hand-rails, signposts, and seats. On the other hand, one may know marriage as Kipling's Mowgli knew the forest, because he traveled as well in the tree-tops as on the springy ground. No one knows a tree unless he has climbed it, tasted its bark, felt out the spring and thrust of its limbs with pencil on paper, cut into it with an axe, clung to high branches in a rain-storm, as John Muir did in the High Sierras, studied minutely its cells, its osmotic currents and tropisms. After such knowledge of a tree one is fit to treat it as a symbol, not before. So it is in marriage. Knowledge and skill should precede as well as follow that vision without which we perish.

In the chapter on "The Glory of Raw Material" and in the paragraphs on the good loser, I tried to acknowledge my reverence for the hard, raw surface of things because it is through just *this* surface, out of just *this* unique tang of crudeness, that a true vision of deeper meaning, wider truth, richer happiness is to come. Horror of the lapdog view of life, — fear of the amateur's bungling vagaries, recoil from the lie of conventional piety and chromo-colored enthusiasm, brings me back to the same theme as I try to base the idealism of marriage broad on the roots of things.

Marriage, then, as a great teacher and symbol, bids us, first of all, study the facts, learn our technique faithfully, and play the game for all it is worth, with no shirking of its hard knocks, no fatuous assumption that we know it before we have learned it, no quailing before the twin giants, — Success and Failure, — who are to be enemies or friends as we shall decide. We follow the game wherever it leads. Good winners and good losers we are schooled to become, in marriage as in sport. Then from the springboard of reality and skill comes the leap of faith. "Thy God shall be my God." We say to the beauties and puzzles of marriage as Ruth said to Naomi and as the Christian says to Jesus: "Where thou goest I will go." What thou teachest I will learn.

PART IV: WORSHIP

CHAPTER XXX

IT is a favorite trick with those who pretend to read the palm or the handwriting to say, with special emphasis and secrecy to each customer: "I can see in your hand that the deepest and best of you has never yet found expression. Half unconsciously you are repressing a flood of power which pushes ever for freedom. To set it free will be the deepest joy of your life."

The beauty of this ever-successful trick is that what the sharper pretends to discover in this individual, he knows to be true of every living being. We are piteously unexpressed. We differ only in the means that can set us free. How many in whom we least suspect it are longing to sing, — not to interpret a genteel melody, but to let themselves out in song! The efforts expended in business, in sport, and even in affection seem comparatively impersonal and indirect. They do not free the breast, they do not tell the tale.

How many in whom we least suspect it are longing to pray! How many who hardly suspect it themselves! I believe that the craving to sing is but a partial and imperfect image of the craving to pray. What song is to prosy speech, that prayer is to song. It is the supremely personal and direct utterance for which creation longs, for which hard toil prepares.

Yet worship is out of fashion. The average man thinks of it as something mediæval or obsolete. He may excuse it like any other fondness for what is old-fashioned; he may find it interesting, amusing, even endearing, in those who throw themselves into it sincerely. But in any case he looks on at it as a spectator; it is not for him.

This is not horrifying or even surprising to one who believes, as I do, that worship is a permanent and necessary privilege of the human spirit. There are plenty of loafers and drudges who never learn to work, plenty of workers who cannot play, and whole nationsful of people who have only the most elementary acquaintance with love. A vital organ of the soul sickens and shrivels; yet the person survives in some sort through the marvelous compensatory readjustments unconsciously wrought out within him.

More serious than dropping prayer altogether out of sight is the tendency to dilute it by bland and innocuous additions which make it more acceptable to the fastidious, but less' nutritious. Thus Du Maurier tries to make us think that we are all more worshipful than we had supposed: — "Trilby sang a song of Béranger's and l'Endormi said: 'C'est égal, voyez-vous, to sing like that is to pray and thinking is praying very often (don't you think so?), and so is being ashamed when one has done a mean thing, and grateful when it is a fine day. What is it but praying when you try to keep up after losing all you care for, and a very good praying, too? Prayers without words are the best.'"

"Yes," one might add, "and so are poems without words, and music without notes, and landscape without color or modeling, and life without consciousness." Doubtless the acts which Du Maurier so cheeringly puts forward as prayer are steps, perhaps long steps, in the right direction. They may prepare us as kneeling and other symbolic acts prepare us for prayer. But we must demand more of ourselves, because our deeper selves demand more of us. Emerson[1] asserts that "The prayer of the farmer kneeling in his field to weed it, the prayer of the rower kneeling with the stroke of his oar, are true prayers, heard throughout nature, though for cheap ends." I doubt it.

The farmer may have been cursing the weeds. Yet his kneeling and Trilby's singing might well have been preparation for prayer. We must recognize the value of symbolic and habitual acts like kneeling. Physical attitudes help us to think and to feel as well as to pray. When we want to concentrate our thoughts we relax the larger muscles and fix the eye. Emotion has also its physical symbols and accelerators, all the more useful because habit links them up with the emotion they last accompanied.

There is nothing more ceremonious and superstitious about kneeling and closing the eyes before prayer than there is about lying down to promote sleep.

[1] In his essay on " Self-Reliance."

In both cases the action initiates and promotes the state of mind which we desire, especially when habit and association reënforce the connection. We need such symbols just as we need the symbols called "words" or "atoms." However dry and meaningless in themselves they yet preserve and clarify the meaning which we give them. The fact that worship surrounds itself with beauty, with symbols, symbolic acts and rites, means simply that it is sensible and well-planned like baseball or business. For athletics and commerce have their own symbols which every one uses as a matter of course. We moderns are indifferent or averse to worship, not because it employs ceremonies and symbols, but largely because of our clumsy shyness in the use of this particular set.

But though many of us are now adrift and far from the land of worship, the shores of that great continent are vast and deep-cut and the wind of the spirit blows perpetually toward them. We may not land and explore, but we can never tack very far from shore. To-day we veer away from some jutting cape, but to-morrow we wake to find ourselves in the shadow of some deep fiord, or catch a glimpse of snow-capped peaks as the land-fog lifts. Whenever beauty overwhelms us, whenever wonder silences our chattering hopes and worries, we are close to worship. Dumb impulses toward it haunt us in the pause before battle. To follow thought nearer and nearer home in lingering meditation is to grope for God. The deep joy of mutual love or parenthood, the decisive victory of the right in national life or in ourselves, brings us that wistful, wondering pause, that "orbed solitude" which is close to prayer.

So, unless we are blind to beauty, deaf to the call of righteous battle, incapable of prolonged reflection, a stranger to the poignancies of joy and sorrow, incapable of wonder, we are in perpetual danger of falling into worship as the tired mortal falls asleep.

Worship renews the spirit as sleep renews the body.[1] Our souls as well as our bodies get drained, now and again, of available energy. We "go stale" as Hamlet did, and to our jaundiced view the world too becomes "stale, flat, and unprofitable," or "sicklied o'er with the pale cast" of our own low-grade cerebration. This is not always the result of physical fatigue; for people who never did a stroke of work in their lives are as prone as any to the symptoms of spiritual fatigue.

Those symptoms consist for the most part of "staleness" in various forms. They may be acute, chronic, or recurrent. In the normal growing man they return with each cycle of his growth and could be traced in his soul like the rings of a severed tree-trunk. The tired spirit finds a waning interest in familiar tasks; even

[1] Throughout these chapters on Worship I have borrowed freely from Professor W. E. Hocking's book, *The Meaning of God in Human Experience*. Yale University Press, 1912.

contempt may be bred by this ingrowing familiarity. What's the use? What is it all for? we ask ourselves. Minor waves of spiritual fatigue, daily, weekly, or monthly, are often dully borne because custom has mistaught us to assume that all novelty must wear off, that familiarity necessarily blunts the keenness of appreciation, and that no love can last forever. The appetite for life, the zest and pleasure in recreation decline or disappear. In the acute and extreme cases a positive nausea of existence may seize us.

Moreover, spiritual fatigue shows itself in loss of *power* as well as in a lack of *feeling* for life. We see neither straight nor far. We magnify trifles and ignore the universe. We pin our faith on the success of a party. We expect mathematically exact justice for our deserts. We cling to the letter of the law and demand our pound of flesh. We exaggerate the purity of our own motives and the impurity of others. Like a tired body heading for the elevator, we drift into thought-sparing devices, such as physical explanations of crime or economic conceptions of history. We demand quick returns on every expenditure of love or labor. The gambling habit, the cynical spirit, incredulity of goodness, timidity before new action, restless craving for new sensation, betray that irritable weakness which is characteristic of fatigue in the spirit as in the body.

This suffering and impotence are natural enough because the efforts of work, the cramped application that is symbolized by bending over a desk and confining the attention to a single point "provide for their own arrest," as Professor W. E. Hocking has so beautifully shown. As the growth of a colony of bacteria is checked by the chemical products of its own way of living, as there is something in the very nature of work that calls (through fatigue) for rest, so there is that in all Godless living which tends to draw us (through the pain and paralysis of spiritual fatigue) back to God. "Worship is the self-conscious part of the natural recovery of value" in life, when it has grown stale. For worship is the conscious love of the Spirit of the Universe, and we need it regularly like food or sleep.

We need it to cure us of absorption in the fragment, to free it of lonely isolation. All good work implies concentration on detail, and all such concentration involves temporary blindness, like that of the unused eye of the microscopist, who looks at a bright, narrow, intensely interesting field with one eye; his other eye is wide open, but voluntarily blinded. It actually sees nothing because it intends to see nothing. Searchlight vision is strong and keen within its own field, powerless outside it. Taken alone, it is false because it ignores much. The mind is hungry for truth and for the whole truth; it grows weak and restless when it has only fragments to feed upon.

We who can give ourselves wholly to the whole alone, are perpetually trying to give ourselves whole-heartedly to this piece of business, to that reform, to this patient, to this picture. We are not built so. We cannot get the whole of ourselves into our daily work, not even into our play or our love. The fruitless attempt results in a cramp of the soul which hardens into permanent contracture, unless we relieve it by a soul-stretch, such as a tired man gives when he opens arms and legs wide and extends himself like a starfish. Prayer has been often and rightly described in metaphors of opening a shuttered and darkened existence to let in the light of Heaven. The figure implies that normally we are in open communication with the whole spirit and purpose of life, just as our bodies are in open communication, through the interchange of breathing and the radiation of heat, with the whole physical universe.

Nevertheless we attempt again and again to shut ourselves off in spiritually unventilated corners. There we stifle and droop. Play and love revive us partially because they take us into better-ventilated, less cramped activities. Worship fulfills what play, art, and love attempt.[1] "Pleasure, recreation, friendship, the companionship of men and women, beauty, — all these recall the outgoings of ambition and moral effort and unite a man with his natural appreciation. Worship is the whole which includes them."[2]

Because worship is a renewal of our depleted spiritual

[1] "Worship is ideally capable of fulfilling all the functions of the other means of re-integrating selfhood, whether of love, of recreation, or of sleep itself (witness the exploits in comparative sleeplessness of Madame Guyon, of Philip of Alcantara, and of many another)." Hocking, p. 563.
[2] Hocking, p. 418.

energies, it is naturally intermittent. One need not jeer
at the worshiper for spending so little time on that
which he declares to be his salvation. For it is in work,
play, and love that he must earn the right to pray as
he earns the promise of sleep. No one can find out
except by trying whether he needs prayer once an hour,
once a week, or less often. The rhythm of its recurrence
should be governed like that of any physiological function, varying like food, sleep and recreation, with our
expenditures of effort and energy.[1]

We often advise each other to "think it over and see
what *on the whole* seems best"; or we say, "*All things
considered*, I have decided to go." Any one who did
this would be near to prayer. Such phrases are loosely
used, but they suggest that once upon a time, in the
morning of life, when the phrase and the phrase-
maker were new, some one verily tried to shape his
decision after considering all things that lay within his
range of vision. Preserved in that phrase is somebody's
revulsion from snap-judgments, some one's determination to get a view of the background and middle distance of his life as well as its foreground, and to shape
his course accordingly. We live in choked and con-
fusing foregrounds, full of noise and fury, but crammed
with significance. We must not miss the message of the

[1] There is, however, another type of prayer-like consciousness which,
like breathing, should be in perpetual operation. Perhaps something
more like aspiration than prayer is what St. Paul had in mind when he
bade us "pray without ceasing," something which I shall try to describe
more fully below.

moment. The present is full of brand-new events, each bearing in its hand a letter personally addressed to you and another to me. These messages must be read and promptly answered, else we miss our chance and disappoint many hopes. But if we are not to be batted about like clowns in a circus, we must now and then pull out of the stress and see what it means, after "considering all things" that are past and distant, or future and shadowy, but still alive and at work in our minds.

"Considering all things" is turning from part to whole, from brilliant near-seen views, all foreground, no perspective, to a vision like that from a mountain-top. Whoever tries to "see life steadily and see it whole" by retiring to a viewpoint detached from the current quotations and the latest news has moved in the direction of prayer. Your soul and mine are parts of God. We forget this. Prayer reminds us.

It is especially when we are confused and uncertain what next to do that we turn from partial to wider views. When lost in the woods you climb the highest tree in sight. From the top of it you may be able to see where you have come from, where you are, and where you should go next. Such a view is precisely what prayer gives. It orients us. As we look over our stumbling, circuitous past we see where we have veered from the track that we meant to keep. We see just where our mingled success and failure have landed us. We look ahead and shape our course afresh.

It takes time, this tree-climbing, and in any party of woodsmen there is usually one who begrudges that time. The evening is pressing on. Tree-climbing does n't get us ahead. It may give pretty views, but while we are waiting idle here we might, by ranging about, have hit upon the path. Similar reproaches are directed at prayer and worship. The immediate utility of the rites and ceremonies of worship is as little as that of painfully shinning up the tree. We are not then or there getting ahead with our jobs. We have turned away from the world; we seem to be getting "other-worldly" and monkish.

But it is the greenhorn, not the old woodsman, who chafes at the halt for a look around. The best way to get ahead is sometimes to stop short and see where we are. The best way to advance our work is, sometimes, to lay it aside and go to bed. On the whole, all things considered, we may find ourselves on the wrong track. Then our pause has been time well spent.

When the captain takes an observation at sea to settle the ship's position, her run and her course, he gives up for the time being the task of sailing the ship. Whatever he has been doing to earn his pay and get the ship ahead, he must quit while he is taking his daily observation. His detachment from ordinary work during that observation, has a parallel in the apparent uselessness of prayer. It bakes no bread; it cuts no ice. It leaves the present and the foreground of life for others to attend to. It retires for a fresh look at the whole,

More truth on Prayer & Worship

as a painter stops and backs away from his canvas, now and then, to get a truer impression of what he has been doing, and has still to do. "Why don't you stick to your painting?" an outsider might say. "You'd get along much faster if you kept your eyes open and painted steadily, instead of stopping so often and squinting through your half-closed eyelids." Smart but false.

There are many other familiar acts which suggest the value of prayer-pauses in the zealous practice of our vocation. The locomotive engineer, peering about the vitals of his engine during a stop, has often reminded me of Sunday worship. The shopman who periodically closes shop and refuses customers, while he takes account of stock, knows better at the end of the pause where, on the whole, he is and what he should do next. The factory engineer knows that his machinery, like his help, needs to rest one day in seven. When the power is turned off, he can carefully go over his machinery, find flaws and weak spots (as any one of us finds them in himself when he prays), and thus true up the whole.

CHAPTER XXXI

RECOLLECTION: DISENTHRALLMENT: SOLITUDE AND
SINCERITY: THE REËNFORCEMENT OF ASSOCIATION

No one is armor-proof against forgetfulness. Most of
the facts and faces that we meet, soon become as dead
as if they had never lived in our experience. We do
not keenly regret their death. But our plight becomes
more serious when we forget what we had intended to
remember. To me the stupendous total of our unin-
tended forgettings is one of the tragic and humiliating
facts of existence. Most serious of all, however, is the
kind of forgetfulness acknowledged by a boy of my
acquaintance who, after shirking his music lesson,
very truthfully explained that, though he had not forgotten the lesson, he had *forgotten the importance of it.*[1]
It is this sort of forgetfulness that really disintegrates
personality. A little more of this and a man splits into
"multiple personalities," a polite way of saying that
he has "gone to pieces."

The double and triple lives that we lead may trans-
gress no law of conventional morality and yet may dissipate our force and squander the spirit's patrimony
more than riotous living. Home life, business life, and
recreation dwell in compartments so separate that each
forgets the others and may contradict them. This
division and mutual estrangement of our energies surely

[1] See *Every Day Ethics*, by Ella Lyman Cabot. H. Holt & Co., p. 217.

calls for some effort to pull ourselves together, to introduce the different sides of ourselves each to each and
see them at least coöperate instead of competing.

When we set ourselves to this work of collecting or
re-collecting the scattered pieces of ourselves, we begin a task which, if carried to its natural conclusion,
ultimately becomes prayer. We are driven to something of the sort when the shock of illness, war, bank-
ruptcy, or death has shaken us out of the rut of habit
and brought us face to face with the mess which we are
making of our years. It was after such a shock Lincoln
called the whole nation to prayer in his message of
December 1, 1862: "The dogmas of the quiet past are
inadequate to the stormy present. The occasion is
piled high with difficulty and we must rise to the occasion. As our case is new, so we must think anew and
act anew. We must disenthrall ourselves and then we
shall save our country."

Recollection leads now and again to disenthrallment.
But innocence preserves us perpetually free of the en-
thrallments of habit and falsehood. In Hans Christian
Andersen's story, "The Emperor's New Clothes," two
rogues offer to weave for his majesty a suit of extraordinary beauty, which, however, will be invisible to
all who are stupid and to all who are unfit to hold their
present offices. The sharpers are awarded the contract
and set to work with nimble fingers pretending to
weave a fictitious fabric on empty looms. Courtiers
and high officials visit the weavers and see nothing,

but dare not say so, since such a confession would prove them dull or unfit for office. For the same reason the king pretends to see and to admire the invisible fabric on the empty looms, puts on the imaginary clothes, and sallies forth to exhibit them amid the hypocritical applause and fawning enthusiasm of his courtiers.

"*But he has nothing on!*" said a child, who saw him from its doorstep.

Ah! what cheers and whooping should now be echoing down the centuries, what rockets and Bengal lights should light up the heavens to applaud that magnificent act of disenthrallment! With a child's miraculous strength he pulled himself out of the entangling net of human prejudices and saw the whole fact, as Jesus did when he stood by the woman of Samaria. To see straight, to speak or write truly we have first and chiefly to get ourselves cleansed of the encrusted deposits of other people's ideas, and of our own caked habits.

"Suitably clad externally, but mentally clogged with a thousand irrelevant thoughts, I go to visit a friend."[1] To be worthy of this friendship I must first cleanse and disenthrall myself by "full imaginative recall of that friend's life and my relation to it. This is the beginning of a "prayer before action," the preliminary purification which tradition has so long prescribed for us.

When one gathers himself for a leap, poises and focuses his energies, quelling internal conflicts, banishing

[1] From an unpublished paper on Prayer, by Ella Lyman Cabot.

irrelevant twitches and tremors, he acts out a physical analogy to the prayer before battle. He may go beyond analogy. A college football player earned some newspaper notoriety and much ridicule a few years ago when it became known that he was accustomed to pray before a match game. The idea of begging God to favor his team and to weaken the rival team naturally excited derision and contempt, for "Prayer that craves a particular commodity, anything less than all good, is mean and vile,"[1] as Emerson says. But I know from team-mates of the derided player that his prayer was essentially like Lincoln's: "I am not trying to find out whether God is on our side, but whether we are on God's side."

He was pulling himself together, trying to get in touch with the ultimate sources of his strength, and, not being unduly influenced by the modern fad of atheism, he naturally turned to God.

But it is with the disenthrallment which initiates the prayer before action, and all other prayers, that I am just now concerned. If you make a failure of your visit to the friend from whom you have been separated for months, if you fill up the precious minutes with chat about superficialities which neither of you wants to recall, and if you leave untouched the deeper or more fruitful interests in which your friendship has been built up, it is usually because there has been no preliminary cleansing of the surface of your mind

[1] Emerson's *Essays, First Series*, Riverside Edition, p. 76.

where are accumulated all sorts of riff-raff, news and happenings, gossip and comment, which have stuck there from your miscellaneous contacts with uninvited experience.

These clogging impurities confuse you like the thickets in which the woodsman loses his way. Your mind must be free of them before it can see its course. Such disenthrallment is essential in attempts to rid ourselves of the curse of indecision. All prayers for direction spring, I suppose, out of the misery of indecision. Opposite courses of action are balanced evenly; we are drawn to each and repelled from each. A classical instance is Emerson's doubt about leaving the ministry. There were no heretic hunters on his trail. The pressure was all directed toward inducing him to stay. Only his own conscience urged his breaking away from the church whose traditions he loved; he was by no means certain that his scruples (about his fitness to perform the rite of the Lord's Supper) were of importance. He dropped his work and went to the mountains to find help in his indecision. I do not know that he prayed. What interests me now is his act of disenthrallment, his decision to put distance and new surroundings between himself and the tangled situation. He wanted a fresh view from a height; he got it, came back, and resigned his pastorate.

I have strung together these familiar experiences of spiritual fatigue, of mountain-top views, nautical observations, stock-taking, re-collecting our scattered selves, and of disenthrallment in the pause before decisive action, because I want to show that we are again and again in a state of mind close to the shores of prayer. We usually sheer off, it is true; but it would be just as natural to land, and just as common, were it not that modern fashions and modern education have made us half unconsciously dislike the sensation of touching this firm ground. Disenthrallment, for which Lincoln appealed to the nation in the early threatening months of the Civil War, is an attempt to go back to first principles, to free ourselves of prejudices which check growing insight into a new situation. It is perhaps the most important of the approaches to prayer, and I want to illustrate it further.

We often say to each other that the person who has lost, or never acquired, the capacity for *wonder*, is bound to dry up. Premature senility is always threatening him if his mind cannot rest in admiration. If he cannot surrender himself to pure wonder in the presence of a child, a crystal, a skyscraper, a starry night, or a leaping salmon, he does not get that bath of spiritual refreshment which keeps us young. Wonder rejuvenates us first because it floats off the load of responsibility; for the moment it washes the mind clean of all thoughts, good and bad, sad or pleasing. Thereby wonder brings our ordinary mental life to a standstill. It makes one stop talking ("struck dumb with astonishment") and even suspends the ordinary uses of thought. The mind comes to rest without going to sleep. It draws in its strained projects, recalls the scattered flocks of thought, and rounds itself up like the resting amœba. The soul stares as the eye stares, and stands stock-still like the body.

But wonder, with its disconcerting and arresting mystery, disconnects us as well. To be rapt in amazement means by derivation to be snatched out of the orderly or disorderly sequence of our ordinary behavior. In our amazement we no longer notice what else besides the wonderful apparition is around us. We are deaf and blind as well as dumb. This quenching and isolation of the soul is but half, the negative half, of wonder. The other half is an effortless absorption in the marvel which is before us. We see, hear, and remember what astonishes us; it stamps itself photographically upon us. Then, freed from ourselves and our ordinary thought-harness, we dive into the heart of something better.

Wonder does not always lead to prayer; it may lead to stupefaction. I suppose we can waste as much time in watching a child as in any other way. Our wondering gaze may degenerate into automatic and fruitless staring. Like all disenthralled states, like all prayer and worship, it is to be judged by its results. Refreshment, new plans of action, more energy, more adaptability, more sympathy, should issue from the momentary monastic retreat into which wonder tempts us. Wonder at a child makes for mental soundness and vigor, because it may shock us out of our "anxious consistency" with our previous little ideas about children. But it may simply suspend all mental progress and leave us drifting and swinging in vacancy, as boys swing on a gate, half hypnotized by the motion. For wonder, like beauty, is a gate that we are not meant to swing on. We are to open it and pass through into prayer or into action.

The danger that wonder may degenerate into "mere wondering" is parallel to the risks of æstheticism. The average man believes by instinct that there is something of namby-pamby in the career of any one who devotes himself to beauty. This is a healthy instinct For the disenthrallment which beauty achieves for us ought to be brief and brilliant, a "cool silver shock of the pool's living water" which sends us bouncing back to some definite task. While it lasts, nevertheless, beauty ought to be one of our surest and swiftest aids to disenthrallment, to worship, and through them to action.

I have already tried to describe the miraculous power of beauty and affection to whirl us about, turning our backs to the working world, and directing our delighted eyes to a vista of refreshment. In that vista I cannot tell where love and recreation cease and worship begins, for I do not believe that the man most conscious that he is praying is always the most prayerful. But whenever we begin to recognize that our "beholding and jubilant soul" is directly continuous with the Soul of the Universe, we have begun to worship.

That saturation with beauty brings us nearer to prayer has been instinctively realized in planning the outlook, the architecture, the decoration, the music, and incense of many churches. But our perception of this analogy and our consequent recoil from the barrenness of our grandfather's "meeting-house" has made us forget that there are types of beauty that do not promote worship at all. Operatic and amorous music is often sung in churches in a style fit to secularize and suppress any movement towards prayer.

I have given up trying to believe that in sorrow and failure we can always find blessings disguised. I now think that such blows may contract, harden, even crush, a soul until it has, so far as we can see, no power to react. Just as beauty, and even love, may spoil a child by soothing it into a lackadaisical and flabby acquiescence, so frustration, and disappointment, though they brace and stimulate some of us, certainly seem to hammer the life out of others. Yet, though I do not believe that it is always a good thing to be balked and thrown back upon ourselves, I cannot doubt that it *may* be just what we need. It depends on what else there is in the sufferer and around him.

But whether the final outcome of sorrow and failure is good or bad, their immediate effect is certainly to

pull us up short. "No farther now in that direction,"
they say to us. "Give up these hopes, shut that desk,
lay down those tools." One of the results of this arrest is to make us look ourselves squarely in the face,
and a rueful sight it is for most of us! We are eager to
recommend such a mirror to others, but rarely feel the
need of it ourselves. Even if we do feel the need, we
may be incapable of turning to face it. Then ill-fortune
takes us by the shoulders and twitches us about with a
whirl that has all the suddenness and externality of
the revolution wrought by beauty. Despite the agony
and wasted effort by the way, such a revolution may be
salvation. For to array one self against another in
bitter civil war may be the only discoverable way of
saving both. We rarely do any thinking unless we
have to; one of the forces which most often knocks us
out of self-contentment in a round of conventional or
unconventional habits, is misfortune. When forced
to reflect and be reflected, I may be driven to ask,
"What am I here for?" "What have I been doing?"
Then I touch the solid ground of repentance, near to
prayer.

"When half-gods go, the gods arrive." Thinking is
not worship, but if it is initiated by a wrench of sorrow
which banishes the half-gods of our superficial existence,
God may appear. That is why we need the wrench.

In some of us the difference between serious thinking
and prayer is the difference between half speed and
full speed. Thinking *plus* agonized questioning of the

scheme of things which has rolled me in the dust, has not the confident appeal of the believer to his God; but if it is serious it will probably come to that.

I have tried to picture disenthrallment, the initial stage of worship, springing from experiences of recollection, of danger and decisive action, of wonder, beauty, sorrow, and failure. I have still to write of joy and success as disenthrallments.

"A man of average capacity never feels so small as when people tell him that he is great," said Professor G. H. Palmer, after listening to a torrent of eulogy at the dinner celebrating his fortieth year as a Harvard teacher. Joy and success tell us that we are great. We may be foolish enough to believe it; but sometimes we are plunged into humiliation by the staring contrast between our own insignificance and the splendor of the opportunity with which happiness crowns us. One looks so paltry and mean under a crown fit for a demigod. I lifted a six-year-old girl off an electric car the other day because her father had the baby in his arms. She did not distinguish me from the machinery of the car till she had reached the sidewalk and got a grip of her father's hand. Then she turned and sent after me a flash of smiling recognition that made me feel like the tinker who was carried to the king's palace while asleep, dressed in magnificent clothes, and saluted as prince when he awoke.

So she saluted me, whom she had never seen before,

and her look almost crushed me beneath the weight of
honor, blessed but painfully undeserved. Such a mingling of abasement and exaltation gives one for the moment a new heaven and a new earth. Familiar objects
look strange and new, old problems soluble. We are
in Lincoln's phrase disenthralled, — free for the instant
to see truly, as Hans Christian Andersen's little boy
saw the truth. But every bit of pure truth has in it
the quality and aroma of the whole, wherein honor, humor and pathos, victory, pain, and defeat are wonderfully mingled. Linked with that perception of our own
littleness which is pressed home upon us in any moment of entrancing joy, is the contrasted majesty and
beneficence of the universe. We could not feel so small
and at the same time so richly blessed, unless we felt
that we are *placed*, given a home in the world. The
spiritual essentials are for an instant clearly isolated by
the experience of disenthrallment; and whatever gives
us clear sight of these brings us close to worship.

Before battle and before any action which we are
alert enough to perceive as decisive, there is a natural
impulse to pull ourselves together and look over past
and future with an ingathering sweep which prepares
us for prayer. I suppose that many a man who has
rarely tried to pray at other times finds himself groping
in that direction when the sense of impending action
descends upon him. Responsibility and danger are
closely linked in their power to turn us toward the

Eternal, to make us "theotropic." Any responsibility vividly felt calls the risk of failure to our minds and at the same time centers those risks around our own decisive action. We see how small is our ingenuity compared with the incalculable chances of disaster. But we also see that just here and now the universe has put it "up to us."

Like other prayer-compelling forces, responsibility is always close to us. Opportunity is always now or never for us, and every day is Judgment Day. But whatever makes us feel this afresh — appointment to office, marriage, parenthood — gives us a simplicity at once humble and bold, disentangles us from the trees and lets us see the forest. To find these nodal points of concentrated insight and recollection is also vital to the growth of friendship, and it is in this sense that prayer is as valuable before a visit as before a battle.

As an axe-blow upon a tree, shaking the ground in which it is rooted, shivers through the entire globe and out through every part of the universe, so any act spreads outward through a network of endless consequences. Responsibility is my thread of connection with this infinite labyrinth. I should be mad if I attempted to follow it to an end. But worse than madness is the spiritual near-sightedness which leads us to think, feel, and work as if we had no such connections with the infinite. Such short-sightedness is a species of insanity perhaps more widespread than any other. To go as far as we can into the network of thoughts re-

sulting from any thought or of consequences following
any act, and then to see that our part permeates and
is permeated by the whole life of the universe, is the
path of practical wisdom, of spiritual hygiene, but also
of worship. For there is that in every thought and act
which tells us all we need to know of the whole universe, just as any foot of space and any minute of time
stands for the whole and mirrors its nature.

Is this still disenthrallment? From our workaday
associations, yes. To be launched in responsibility
brings us into wider and deeper connections by snapping
the narrower ones. We withdraw from people, from
work, and from all the half-gods of ordinary existence,
into a solitude wherein we can be sincere.

Many of us put on for company an artificial manner,
a forced expression or a "society smile." This mask
need not be false or fraudulent in the ordinary sense.
It may be only the expression of that decent self-respect which makes us stand erect instead of slouching,
or dress ourselves properly before appearing in public.
Yet propriety is a mask which may hide us from ourselves, if it becomes habitual. We forget to take off our
"society" thoughts with our "society" clothes. The
habit of keeping up with the moods and demands of
the others may dampen and finally quench the desire
to be sincere with ourselves. It may keep us from
asking ultimate questions or entertaining ultimate
doubts.

Furthermore, all moral effort involves the kind of pretense which I have already described as "impersonation." Long before they fit us we have to take up the responsibilities and put on the manners of adult life, of bread-winning, parenthood, salaried work, truth-telling, and chastity. We have to act as if we were fit and competent in order to make ourselves so. We have to assume a virtue when we have it not and thus painfully to acquire it. This is as it should be, but sooner or later the accumulated fatigue of impersonation, the heat and weight of our moral costume, grow oppressive, and should be thrown off, like any other fatiguing burden. To strip away the disguises of moral strenuousness and of social compliance as the actor plucks off his wig in the greenroom may lead only to moral laxity or to sleep; yet it is through this same gate that we must pass to that solitude and ultimate sincerity which is one of the approaches to prayer. For our best as well as our worst may be buried under the disguises of moral and social effort.

Woe to the man who cannot stop acting; who makes no difference between stage and greenroom, and who is afraid of solitude! Mob-contagion, the automatic registration and reproduction of actions which no one starts but all transmit, needs no crowd. Two or three can create it, spread it and magically transform each other into helpless puppets, dangling on strings and twitched by the dread hand of Nobody-in-particular. Lowered on our wires to such a marionette stage we surely "descend to meet," as Emerson said, for any value that there is in us splits into a hodge-podge of gregariousness.

Make this state of things bad enough, and with the instinct of self-preservation we react; we feel a salutary hunger for solitude and renewal. Unfortunately this reaction may not be fierce enough to carry us farther than unabashed hygiene prescribes. We retreat to the mountains, the sea, or the country. We "go abroad" in search of health, distraction, or "art," and unfortunately we often partially succeed. These palliative remedies may so far satisfy us that we fail to retreat into ourselves. We do not burrow back to our origins; we reach no original and life-saving insight. We stop on this side of prayer.

A dread of solitude is often partially responsible for the abortiveness of this recoil toward prayer. We hear of solitude most often nowadays in connection with vice or imprisonment. The dangers and the abuses of solitude are uppermost in our minds. And solitude in its literal sense, which we do not often face, is really hell. If in solitude you meet no fresh thoughts which lead you back to the sources of healing and forgiveness, if instead you meet only the tortures of helpless loneliness, then solitude is your worst foe. But in the populous solitude of disenthrallment, the noises which drown God's voice are stilled.

While describing the aids and approaches to worship I have ignored some that have proved historically most helpful; I mean the reënforcements of association in churches and church ceremonies. Crowd-contagion, as I have just sketched its evil influence, is headless and blind. It leads to monarchy or to murder; it exalts or destroys a man or an institution, with as little intention as an earthquake or a drought.

But in church we see the possibility of directing and marshaling the gregarious impulses of mankind so as to concentrate and reënforce our theotropic power. The forces that make soldiers steadier and bolder when they can touch shoulders, may also magnify in every member of a congregation the timorous impulse toward worship. For the crowd is not simply gathered together, but gathered together in the name of Christ, under the leadership and unifying influence of a revered personality.

Many who feel *gauche* or irritable in church can share the enthusiastic church-member's experiences by recalling a college commencement or the meetings of some professional society or political club pervaded by a genuine instinct of membership. I believe that many college graduates get their nearest approach to the experience of public worship in the surging feelings of devotion and loyalty called out by Commencement songs, exercises, and speeches. Few of us go to Commencement as a duty; we take the day as a privilege and an opportunity. We forget for a day the claims of naked utility and the restraints of self-consciousness. There is aroused in us a powerful emotion of gratitude and loyalty to an institution, very little of which is visible or tangible. It is genuinely *a spirit* to which the graduates are loyal, a college spirit to which they contribute and from which they draw new inspiration for the coming year. They have funded there their best ideals for the country and for young Americans. Yet they do not feel that they have made or invented the spirit of this institution as skeptics say men invent God. They were born in it, nourished by it, and love to think of its permanence through past and future, through civil war and through the passing crazes of the time.

This is the spirit in which we ought to go to church, if we go at all, because we love it and find there our chance for service and for refreshment, a renewing of tarnished standards, an outlet for reverence and aspiration. All this men do find in Commencement Day, and that day is therefore the nearest approach that many of them ever find to worship. Some results of worship, the reënforcement of loyalty, devotion, and self-abasement, one certainly does achieve in these half-secular gatherings for the praise of an institution.

By incorporeal aid, as well as by visible comrades, we rise above our common level, both in church and in non-ecclesiastical gatherings. We are companioned by the many-colored memories of former gatherings, what is left to us and what is gone, what has leaped up anew in us and what has changed almost beyond recognition; all reënforce and renew the sacredness of the experience. We feel the unseen presence and the instant sympathy of many who have sat or knelt beside us in troublous or in jubilant days long past, "*als knieten viele ungesehen und beteten mit mir.*"

CHAPTER XXXII

WHEN a child wakes in the grip of a nightmare, sobs and stammers it out to his mother, and finds that its horrors have swiftly vanished, he has discovered the value of confession. Through expression something confused and inarticulate has lost its terrors. By confession he marshals his troubles in consciousness and spreads them out in form and order; thus he gains command of them and of himself.

Confession in more or less secular forms, confession to a doctor or a chum, gives some relief to the tortures of internal strife, — duplicity and fraud, the burden of lies, thefts, treachery, or concealment, or, it may be, the more subtle duplicity of warring ideals, curiosities, and doubts. In any case we seek instinctively through confession some inner peace or at least some truce to inner war. We make these secular confessions primarily because we cannot hold in any longer. We confess not so much because murder will out, but rather because the tension between what we are and what we seem has grown intolerable.

An interesting variety of confession, rediscovered and reapplied by the German neurologist S. Freud, forms part of his "psycho-analytic" treatment of functional nervous disorders. People suppress and try to bury a disappointed hope or an evil desire; but accidentally they bury it alive, so that it struggles and shrieks beneath the weight of daily life piled on top of it. This is, I think, the essence of the Freudian doctrine. Now and then the struggles of this fragment of buried existence shake the surface of everyday life and emerge in a fit of weeping or of rage. "You begin to cry," said a small boy of my acquaintance, "for the thing that made you cry, but you go on crying for all the sad and sorry things that ever happened." You had never quite laid the ghost of these ancient sorrows. From the deeper inconsequent strata of your existence it rises to haunt and oppress you.

So in rage: we begin to be angry with a companion for some trifling annoyance, but we go on into a "fit of rage" because our momentary anger is reënforced by the renascent memories of a multitude of other injuries, long half-consciously brooded, never quite forgiven. All this submerged corruption boils up to the surface, sometimes with our own aid; we may work ourselves into a passion for the sake of the vent it gives to our repressed and smouldering resentment.

A better vent is given by full confession. To see clearly that we are abusing our fellow for his part in spats which both should have forgiven and forgotten long ago, shames us or makes us laugh. The air is cleared; the ghosts of past quarrels are laid. To tempt the sufferer into confessing what he did not know enough to confess, is the substance of psycho-analysis, though Freud has misled many into supposing that all such confessions must deal with one topic, sex.

The assisted and guided confession of half-conscious troubles, and the more spontaneous outpourings for relief of tortured and desperate memories, are of obvious value in moral hygiene. But what is their connection with worship? The answer seems to be this: We confess because of a hunger for soundness. "What," we ask, "can heal the divisions of this wounded spirit? What shall make us whole?" It is confession. But the healing of one wound makes us aware of other and deeper suffering, and of an unsatisfied hunger for friendship, not only between the hostile parts of our own personality, but between that personality and the social order which nourishes it. We claim our right and duty to take a man's part, not a parasite's, in the society around us. We want to lift our part of the load and to deserve some portion of the good things that come to us.

But this is not enough. We are conscious — fitfully and in glimpses — that our deepest gratitude and service cannot be paid to any visible institution like the State, the progress of science or civilization. Behind these are the universe and its Spirit, which made them and will unmake them if they fail. Fundamentally we want to get down to bed-rock. We long for harmony, not only with the better part of our own selves, not only with the quite fallible and temporary institutions of society, but with the bottom principle of things.

If we follow home the impulse, it prompts confession to One who knows better than we how to frame that confession and hears what we mean but cannot say.

I have now described as well as I can the steps by which one may reach prayer in its usual and traditional sense, namely, *petition*. I shall not try to prove that our minds are given their nourishment and their sense by sharing in a Total Mind through which, as through an atmosphere, we speak to each other and deal with nature. That proof, as I believe, is abundantly supplied in other books, and lives in the deeds of all noble people.

But many who are aware of God, and try to live according to what they believe to be his will, still feel that petition is a relic of barbarous or of naïve ages, something not to be taken seriously by reasonable people. Prayers for rain, for victory in battle, for the recovery of the sick, — what are these but frantic attempts to break the laws of nature? And even if they could succeed, would they not be grossly selfish? For my victory is often another's despair. The rain which falls on my crops leaves my distant neighbor's all the longer in drought. But if we admit that "all prayer that craves a particular commodity — anything less than all good — is mean and vile," do we eliminate all the prayers that any needy mortal wants to make? "All good" is a pretty large order and a tolerably vague one.

In answer to this question, which often troubled me

in past years, Christ's words in the garden of Geth-
semane now seem wholly satisfying: "If it be possible
let this cup pass from me. Nevertheless thy will, not
mine be done."

No one who believes in God, and thinks of duty as
the increasing approximation to his will, can absolutely
desire any particular commodity or immunity. Every
wish becomes conditional and "has a string to it."
Strange though it sounds, a conditional wish is not
absurd or even uncommon. You want to win your football game, — yes, but you don't want to win by any
means or unconditionally. You want to win if you
can do so under the rules of the game and with no more
luck than is compatible with the dominance of skill and
science. In other words, what you want above all else
is good sport, a well-played game, and an antagonist
worthy of your steel. To win by a fluke, as yacht-
races are sometimes won, to win by undetected violation of the rules, or to win over an antagonist half your
size, is not what you want. Your desire to win is limited on every side. If it be possible I want victory.
Nevertheless let the best man win. Let the traditions
of good sport be maintained whoever wins or loses.
If I can only win by a fluke or a fraud, then I want
to lose and to lose well.

A scientific investigator wants his experiment to
succeed; he wants to be known and promoted through
success. He is looking, perhaps, for a cancer cure. But
if it turns out that he is looking in the wrong place,

he wants nature to tell him so decisively. He wants no fame and promotion that are based on a fluke or a misunderstanding. He would rather fail and waste the time and money which he has spent on his research than publish as *fact* any "may be." Behind his intense desire, there is for him, as there was for Christ, a "nevertheless."

Any high-minded man wants prosperity for his party, his nation, his race, or his cause. But he wants it conditionally. The "rules of the game" still govern him. If his nation can survive only by sucking the vitality of other struggling nations, then he wants his nation to go down. Our devotion to any cause becomes conditional as soon as by sympathy and foresight we see that our cause can only win by breaking the rules of the game.

Whoever, by religious instinct or religious philosophy, has come to believe that the universe is a team of which he is a member, wants the success of the team unconditionally and with his whole heart, and wants nothing else, save with the condition, "provided this does not contravene the needs of the team." Such is the spirit of Christ's prayer. Obviously, then, conditional wishing is part of our daily exercise. The babyish tendency to "want what you want when you want it" is squelched or modified in every piece of concerted work, in every advance of science, and every harmonious family. To revise and subordinate our wills until they are conditional on the success of a city, a party, or any other team to which we are loyal, is among the most familiar and unheroic necessities of civilized life.

We take the further step, from loyal team-work in business, science, or politics, to world-loyalty whenever we realize that we are part of the world and not merely part of our own town. When one is driven by the necessities of thought or drawn by some swifter process to recognize the living universe beyond the city limits, one has no longer any absolute desire except that the Will expressed in that universe shall prevail. This desire is the perpetual though often half-hearted prayer, "Thy will be done." My own conditional will is not wiped out, unless it hopelessly conflicts with itself, i.e., with my unconditional will for the success of the universe. Loyal citizenship is thus one of the approaches to religious loyalty and to prayer.

Since we are so bound together that we must succeed or fail together, each at bottom wants each of the rest to succeed in his own way, so far as he can find it. For the same reason, each nation not too blind to see the facts is interested in the national success of the whole family of nations. To crush out a single nation or a single will is to weaken the world-team.

Whoever "craves a particular commodity," unconditionally and without consulting, as well as he can, the interests of all concerned, is not praying. Before prayer he must confront his desire first with all the visible objections to see if they can be harmonized with it. Then finally in prayer he binds himself, absolutely

and in advance, to modify or wipe out his will so far as
this may be necessary in order to meet any objections
now unknown to him and so to harmonize it with the
Will of the Whole.

Any one who sincerely wants the truth, even when it
wrecks his other desires, is in the attitude of prayer.
If a man is sincere when he asks you to tell him the
truth about his fitness for a certain office, he will take
his medicine, even though the verdict is "utterly unfit." On the whole, all things considered, he does not
any longer want the office, since he is unfit.

But it takes time and struggle to get to this point.
It is hard to squelch the rampant energies which tell
him to grab the office anyway, to get the honor and
profit of it and cover up the traces of his unfitness.
All sorts of sophistries rise up in him to defend his will
against his Will. "Some one equally unfit will get the
office if I don't. I need the money for my children's
education. Surely I must n't neglect my family." To
struggle against these sophistries is the struggle of
prayer. For the sincerest people may be unwilling to
ask advice of any living man in such a dilemma. They
fight the problem out "alone," seeking the truth in the
presence and before the tribunal of the best they know.
If there is a genuine fight, if the man's native desire for
the place is given a fair hearing, not simply brushed
aside without consideration, and if the judge is not in
the pay of native desire itself, but is chosen because
he represents the squarest judgment available, then

something very like prayer is going on whether the name of God is mentioned or not.

If he is sincere he means to find the Truth, or the nearest available approach to it, and to correct his decision as often as new light appears. This desire, like all desires to find the solid fact or the True Course of action, is really an infinite desire. The presence of such an infinite desire judging our finite cravings is the presence of God in our prayer.

Petition, then, is not a mean whimpering for favors; it is the only honorable and manly act for any one in doubt about his belief or his course of action. All straight thinking means asking for the truth and getting the best answer that we can find. Petition is merely one expression of sincerity and of clearness in thought.

There is a superficial resemblance between conditional wishing and a cowardly or a fatalistic submission to whatever comes, just as there is a certain likeness between humility and the slimy "umbleness" of Uriah Heep. Sincerity is the touchstone which decides. If you sincerely want a true judgment about the worth of your desire for office, you will give fair consideration to the possibility that despite all your sins and limitations you may really deserve that office yourself. Your crude desire may be wholly right. You do not intend always to duck your head to others, nor to crush and forget your desires by keeping busy about something else, nor to avoid the responsibilities and reproaches of taking the best berth in sight. You want to be fair to your own elemental cravings as well as to the claims of other people. Hence prayer does not always mean renunciation. It means perpetual readiness either for victory or for renunciation, whichever is the verdict of the best judgment in sight.

So far as we achieve this readiness, we achieve as deep a peace as any human being has a right to. We are on more solid ground than when we simply hustled along and tried to forget our desires for the much coveted or the apparently unattainable. For desires controlled only by the pressure of work and concentration spring up again when that pressure slackens. Even while we are working they color our outlook and tend to make us sour, or at best merely stoical. After facing a desire with the best wisdom which we can reach, after thinking it through with absolute sincerity, which is the presence of God, we can begin to work again whole-heartedly because there are no longer any rebels in camp. We have expelled both the doubts about our right to success and the sullen misgivings about the need of our renouncing it.

Such decisions cannot often be made once for all. They drag along indefinitely. In every wide-awake person I think there must be such trials, prolonged for years because the evidence is not all in. It may take one a long time to make sure that he is in the right profession, or to decide whether he ought to give up all for a cause. Here "the readiness is all," — the readiness to change just as soon as the evidence is sufficient to

demand a change, and the equal readiness to keep on
waiting and hunting for new light until sincerely convinced, or until it is clear that further indecision is in
itself a decision and the wrong one. Meantime we play
the game under the rules for all that it is worth.

This is, I suppose, one of the meanings in St. Paul's
phrase, "Pray without ceasing."

What about prayers for others? One may agree that
there is petition in all good thinking, and petition to the
Absolute Spirit by all who aspire in the spirit of absolute sincerity. But when we pray for another's safety
or success, are we not asking for a change in the laws of
nature? When President McKinley was sick, it certainly seemed as if some prayed for him with a gambler's superstition that it could n't do any harm and
might do good. Is not this to play fast and loose with
sacred things?

Again Christ's words set us straight. "If it be possible let this cup pass from me," — *or from him*, we can
say with equal right, if we add as all Christians must:
"Nevertheless thy will, not mine be done." Our friends,
if we love them, make up so large a part of ourselves that
our desires include them. Such desires, like all others,
are crude and need to be purified in the fire of the
thought of God. Prayer is, then, a struggle for mutual
accommodation between one of my desires and the
Judge of all my desires, a struggle born of our need to
live at peace together. Can I think of any way of help-

ing my friend in his trouble without making matters
worse, without neglecting prior claims? If not, I can
at any rate drive out panicky impulses to despair and
curse; for if before God I clearly picture the situation
and my friend in it, these childish tendencies drop
away.

In a crude and vague form, something that is akin to
the *praise of God* celebrated in hymns and church services, often breaks out in the midst of rejoicings over
college victories, success in politics, love, or war, and
especially in the presence of overwhelming natural
beauty. But such jubilations are often formless and
thoughtless. Even in Emerson's magnificent definition
of worship as the "soliloquy of a beholding and jubilant soul," the jubilant soul appears a little indefinite.
It does not seem to know quite what it is rejoicing about.
Somehow its gratitude and exultation spread beyond
the event or spectacle in the foreground, to "everything else." It is not merely that

> "Morning's at seven,
> The hillside's dew-pearled";

but that, moreover,

> "God's in his heaven,
> All's right with the world."

There is the same vagueness in the enthusiasm of
people who sing hymns with real fervor, but do not
notice the meaning of the words, or, if they do, are
repelled. Yet I believe that the religious sentiment

intended by the composer of the hymn does reach many who sing it in this vague way.

The weakness of such enthusiasms is that they forget for the time the blind cruelties of nature, the undeserved sufferings of children, the famines, the prisons, and the insane asylums. To deserve the name of worship and the praise of God, our enthusiasm must be such as to remember, include, and surmount these evils. This requirement is hard to fulfill and must compel most of us to confess that we know very little of such experiences. James Russell Lowell counts but three in his lifetime, and somehow we resent his arithmetic because it seems that so great an experience ought to change the color and texture of one's life so radically that another such experience would be as incommensurable with the first as odors are incommensurable with mathematical equations.

I have nothing of my own to report here, though I think the experiences of exaltation and gratitude which have come to me, as to thousands, in the hymns and liturgies of the Christian Church are somewhat more definitely religious than the expansive enthusiasm for things in general which springs out of us after a plunge of ecstatic delight in art, nature, love, or victory. But any one who has been carried away from his usual moorings by a wave of intense gratitude for opportunity, for human nobility, or for beauty, must have noticed the painful internal pressure of the desire *to repay some one* while at the same instant the impossibility of adequately repaying any one stares him in the face. Something has to give way when an irresistible force meets anything less than an immovable body. We should be torn to pieces or made silly by the effort to express our endless gratitude, or to spend it on some finite object, were we not dimly or clearly aware that benefits received from any one of God's creatures can be repaid to any or all of the others. Indirectly through them, directly through the praise of God, we can utter in infinite time the full force of our gratitude. What I owe to A, I can repay to some extent through love and service to B, C, and D. But how can I get even with the rainbow? What can express the torrent of thankfulness I feel to Christ? Worship is the only answer. Through worship the stored residue of our unexpended gratitude, all we could never pay, all men ignored when we tried to pay it, flows straight or deviously back to God, who sees the whole.

By tracing out the full meaning of gratitude, I believe one might trace the full outline of belief in God and in immortality. For gratitude, like love, is by birth and lineage an infinite emotion, satisfied with no finite service or praise, exhausted by no measure of effort and expression. It implies an infinite object and an infinite life as one end of a stick implies another. Meantime inarticulate gratitude is tolerable only because we are aware, vaguely or less vaguely, that some one understands and receives what we cannot express in word or deed. Without that awareness gratitude would be like a wild beast in our breasts. In worship or the praise of the Almighty and All-comprehending Spirit continuous with ours, we conquer at last our inarticulateness and are relieved for the time of our burden.

By overflowing enthusiasm and by gratitude, then, we are enticed near to the shores of prayer, and no human being can ever deny to another the right to believe that in some moment of joy and thanksgiving he has actually landed and knelt.

Reverence is a familiar and manly emotion and few are ashamed to confess it; yet it stops this side of worship only when it is too shy and timid to recognize its own thinly disguised meaning. Take it for a moment from the other fellow's point of view. No one can stand reverence paid to himself or fail to see that the billet is addressed to some one else and by a most lovable blunder delivered at the wrong house.

"Farther up the same road — in fact an infinite distance from here," one must call out to the messenger. "Your direction is all right, and I know the Person whom you are after, in fact I am a poor relation of his, but He does n't live here."

Yet we reverence others. Can we, then, go on purposely paying unto others that which we know could never conceivably be paid to ourselves without blasphemy? Every one of us knows that no amount of added virtue or subtracted sin would make him fit to receive reverence. For the trouble is not with our particular incapacity and littleness, but with the inherent

unfitness of *any* finite being to contain the outpourings
of an infinite impulse. We must pass it along as we do
gratitude expressed to ourselves; we pass it to others so
far as we can, but chiefly and most directly to God.

Any of us not wholly devoid of modesty and curiosity
must sometimes have been set to wondering at the profusion of valuable goods which *nature* leaves at our
door, obviously not meant for us. How disorderly and
capricious, it seems, on nature's part! How humiliating
and embarrassing for us to find at the breakfast-table
a crown we are quite incapable of wearing, to find in the
sunset a poem we cannot read, to have gratitude given
us in a smile for work we never performed. Rewards
fifty sizes too large for us, five hundred times greater
than what we bought and paid for, are delivered to
us daily.

That sunset, that magnificent thunderstorm, What
are they really meant for? Whom or what do they help
in the struggle for existence? They were there before
man came on earth. They surely do not fit me; they
humiliate and overwhelm me. They are meant for
some one else, yet I, too, understand a bit of them. They
are not addressed to any being who contradicts my
aspirations.

I say that they are aimed, like all reverence, toward
God. They hit you and me on the way, because we are
on the path to Him.

CHAPTER XXXIII

THE *gaucherie* and shamefacedness, the scorn or revolt of the up-to-date man invited to take part in worship, reaches a climax when we approach communion. Rapture, ecstasy, and the mystic states associated with them, are to the minds of most of us either the fakes and hysteria of "mediums" or the fanaticism of dancing dervishes. Part of this instinctive discredit is due to our distrust of emotionalism and all that goes with it. Good citizens are alarmed at the idea of being "carried away" by music, acting, athletics, politics, religion, or anything else. "When was Lincoln ever carried away?" they will ask you. "Did n't he chew his straw, smile or frown a little, tell a story or two, and maintain his steady composure throughout all the crises of his maturer life?"

I do not know how far this tradition does justice to Lincoln, but in any case I think it represents a truncated ideal of a man. The person who cannot be "carried away" by any music is to be pitied, not admired, on that account. He probably lacks a musical ear or an acquaintance with the human experience which music portrays. He is blighted and numb like one who cannot fall in love. But if one is more fortunately endowed on the emotional side and has never become sour and *blasé*, then he can be rapt and entranced by art as much as any devotee by religion. He will look as ridiculous and behave as unsocially as a dervish; or he may look utterly passive and dreamy, although in truth his outward "passivity" is a mask concealing intense activity, "like the motionlessness of the rapid wheel or the ease and silence of light." [1]

Any one who cares for music is able to follow sympathetically, even if he cannot share, the accounts of the religious experience called "communion with God." He knows what is meant by an intense but "effortless attention." It is a concentrated mental activity comprehending a multitude of present facts without dropping stitches by the way, coursing over wide realms of memory and anticipation as people do when in great and sudden danger. In this *conspectus*, one gets beyond trying; one wakes to an experience that is not less but more definite than our ordinary consciousness.

Of course such states of entrancement are justified only by their results. Partial intoxication with ether or nitrous oxide gas produces moods which feel much the same as religious ecstasy; but they differ in that they have no beneficial or lasting effects. If we do not reap new explanations, new clews to action, new powers of self-devotion and self-control, new appreciation of others' strength and of our own weakness, then our worship has been fruitless; in the end it may degenerate into self-indulgence, a wallowing in emotion for

[1] Hocking, p. 384.

emotion's sake or a slavish engrossment in details of habitual rite.

Though nothing can be plainer or more terrible than sin, the shameful and intentional violation of our own standards, it is now fashionable to ignore it. This will not do. The attempt to dilute and modify sin by calling it "unintentional mistake" or "an infraction of unconventional rules" means muddleheadedness or sophistry. No one loses the consciousness of sin unless he loses it on purpose, that is, by sinning until he has calloused himself.

In prayer we seek *forgiveness* for our sins. But what can that forgiveness mean? Christ has told us to look for its meaning in our own struggle to forgive those who trespass against us. To forgive those who have wronged us is not to forget the injury. For some people forgetting is as easy as it is inane; for others it is impossible; for all it is valueless or harmful. In forgiveness there is always struggle; in forgetting there may be none. We struggle to regain through forgiveness our regard or affection despite the culpable weakness which we recognize. "Nevertheless" is the crucial and victorious word in forgiveness, as it was in Christ's prayer that the cup might pass from him. Our affection is not unchanged, but nevertheless we make a new venture of hope and faith.

So Christians believe that the world-spirit gives us another fair chance whenever we sincerely repent of our sins. This is a miracle like all forgiveness, for it implies that the laws of cause and effect are not the only factors in the workshop where character is moulded. According to the law of cause and effect we get "an eye for an eye and a tooth for a tooth," since action and reaction are equal and opposite; every sin leaves an indelible mark not to be wiped out by repentance and reform. This is true as long as we deal with the arithmetic of finite quantities and closed circuits. A ball batted against the walls of a closed rectangular room takes mathematically predictable directions, at velocities that depend on the rigidity of the walls, the elasticity of the ball, and the force with which it is driven.

But by forgiveness an unmeasurable power is discovered. We may cut away virtue from character by sin, yet, through the infinite quality of forgiving love, we may have left a chance of achievement still infinite. A similar miracle happens when one cuts off a bit of a line. In the piece which has been cut away there was room for many points, yet in the piece which is left there is still an infinite opportunity to find more points. So for love, even for our human love, there are still infinite "points" to be found in a person whom we forgive, even though by sin some possibilities have been cut away.

This miraculous fertility in the infinite resources is opened to us sinners only by the sincerity of our prayer for forgiveness, the sincerity of our repentance. For sincerity has in it always an infinite quality like that of love and reverence. It may be an absolute sincerity, prepared for endless trial and sacrifice. One who sincerely devotes himself to the service of truth wants truth at whatever cost of labor, humiliation, and reform. He is prepared with an answer to all possible objectors, however numerous, each plausibly presenting him as a substitute for truth something "just as good for less money." Sincere repentance is likewise infinite because there is no end to its sorrow and no limitation to what it is ready to perform in the way of expiation. If to any right demand for sacrifice or humiliation a repentant soul can answer, "Ah, no, not that, anything but that," then his repentance is so far insincere and forgiveness is so far helpless.

Absolute obedience is a virtue not highly prized in America to-day. But whatever be our belief as to the need of it in other fields, there can be no question that absolute forgiveness presupposes absolute obedience. If we are to be forgiven we must be beaten to a standstill: "Lord, here am I: what wouldst thou that I should do?" St. Francis of Assisi attained this spirit and trained his followers in it.

"A certain poor and infirm man came unto him. On whom having much compassion, St. Francis began to speak to one of his followers of the other's poverty and sickness; but his follower said to St. Francis: 'Brother, it is true that he seems poor enough; but it may be that in this whole province there is not one who *wishes* more to be rich than he.' And being at once severely reproved by St. Francis he confessed his fault"; — the fault of uncharitably imputing sin. Then comes the test of true repentance. "Blessed Francis said unto him: 'Wilt thou do for this sin the penance which I shall bid thee?' Who answered (in unconditional obedience), 'I will do it willingly.' Then Francis said unto him, 'Go and put off thy tunic and throw thyself naked at the poor man's feet, and tell him how thou hast sinned against him in speaking evil of him in that matter and ask him to pray for thee.' He went, therefore, and did all the things which blessed Francis had told him."

We moderns are proud to say that we owe absolute obedience only to our consciences, but I wonder how many of us possess a conscience that is quite uninfluenced by a desire to be easy on the culprit whom it judges, a conscience that is as ready as St. Francis was to demand of us the expiation that really expiates?

The forgiveness of sin is perhaps the whole of the *answer to prayer*, its all-inclusive result. For [the attainment of spiritual peace, the quenching of uncertainty, the freeing of shackled powers, and all that one could hope to obtain through prayer, can, I suppose, be properly included under forgiveness. That we are as dull, as habit-bound, and unoriginal as we are is doubtless largely our own fault. If so, the divine forgiveness will mean a burst of originality in thought, word, and deed.

To be original, in musical composition, in scientific

hypothesis, or in the control of one's temper is a miracle, like all novelty. Whatever is really new, is something uncommensurable with former experiences, unpredictable as the face of a new baby. One veritably original thing each man does. He gets born, and the mother's assurance that there never was such a baby as this is literally and absolutely correct. Every birth is a miraculous birth, because no two individuals are alike, and novelty is always inexplicable. The birth of a new thought, a new habit, a new leaf, a new day, is just as miraculous, because its newness is the one thing that all law and all previous experience cannot explain.

When saint or sinner asks with all his might: What shall I do next? What does this puzzling experience mean? What will best express this idea? — he is not reaching for a dictionary or thesaurus in which to find ready-made what he needs. He is reaching for the truth and the right. Ultimately he is reaching for God's help, and when his question is answered he gets all he can hear of the answer to prayer.

Intense wondering, determined groping after the truth, seeks the new, not for novelty's sake, but because nothing else is true to this minute's and this individual's need. We want the new in order to save our lives, to save us from dying away into habits of vegetative existence; to save us from petty picking and stealing among the trite old words and deeds which lumber up the world.

In composing music to a song, if a melody doesn't

come to one ready-made, by the free and miraculous grace of the universe, one dives again and again for the pearl of sincerity. "What do those verses mean to me? What *is* the music that properly belongs with them?"

But what does one dive into? In what direction does one stare when he is striving for the true musical expression of a verse? Surely he is staring into the face of the deepest truth he knows or can reach. The veritably right phrase is the one he peers after. We are here vitally interested not so much in what he attains as in what he faces, — the infinite vista down which he directs the infinite longing of his gaze. Surely he is straining towards the Origin of all things. He is pleading with the Creator for his one mite of creativeness! He is trying to prostrate himself before the Absolute Truth upon this theme, for that Truth is all that he wishes to express.

So far as I can see, no prayer for light or strength does anything else than this. As one struggles in earnest talk to hear the new from one's comrade, and to find the accurate phrase for one's own meaning, one stares with the mind as intently as one fixes the muscles and the eyes. Then what does the eye of the mind seek to envisage? What else but the invisible Truth in which men who seek with all their heart find more than they deserve?

Here, then, is another way of obedience to Paul's "pray without ceasing." The effort to be original defeats itself, but the effort to be sincere, the desire to say what one means without too shamefully wronging the beauty of the truth that one looks off to on the mind's horizon, is a perpetual seeking of God's presence, a prayer ever joyfully renewed.

Originality of thought and speech is perhaps the least important of the sincerities which are the goal of all earnestness. To brace up one's standards in any sorriest corner of their tattered and disreputable substance is to be original, and that in the most arduous and honorable way. Why should n't a man stop beating his wife's long-suffering soul with the cudgels of his inconsiderateness? To be more decent to her would be a perfectly original work of art, doubtless hung upon the line in the gallery of man's humorous or pathetic approximations to the beauty of holiness.

The need of worship reflects an intense weariness with what is old and habitual, a hunger for what is radically new and untried. In the pain of spiritual fatigue, it is the "impulse for spiritual self-preservation," and renews the worth of life as we see it, by reminding us of our ultimate Good.

The conscious approaches to worship, like the effort to dispel prejudice in scientific and dispassionate judgment, are largely negative. By beauty, joy or sorrow or danger, we are detached from the habits and associations which, like the shell of a crustacean, both register our progress and limit it.

In worship we seek to know our God by absorption and contagion, as we catch the spirit of a commanding gesture, or feel the sweep of a national crisis. We throw ourselves into worship, as we dive into the ocean, confident of its well-tested power to lift and refresh us, but no longer balancing, sustaining, or directing ourselves by step and step as we do on the land of ordinary thought and action.

The answer to prayer is in the forgiveness of sins, conditioned by the sincerity of our repentance, and in a heightened power of fresh or original vision, which is the servant of reform.

CHAPTER XXXIV

ALL TOGETHER

I HAVE sketched four pictures of "real life," the world of healing, refreshment, and strength. I hope they do not all look alike. The sharp contrasts, the vivid individuality of each should never be merged. For in all the range of creation nothing is more vitally interesting than its differences of mood and tone, of light and dark, of right and wrong. In fact, there is nothing comparable to the fascination of these contrasts except the opposite, — their unity.

Most people that I meet or read about seem to find the contrasts more obvious than their unity. The talkative, plastic, sociable people are amazed at the silence of the laboratory and the mechanical rigidity of the workshop. Serious professors and mill treasurers look askance at play and art, or revile it as foolish frivolity; the clergy, who have been beaten into toleration, are wistful and puzzled at the thought of the total inefficiency and uselessness of whist, chess, or polar exploration. Most of all unreasonable and blank seems to most moderns the worshiping mystic and his retreat from the world. To workers, players, and lovers alike this monkish withdrawal from the living interchange of society and of nature seems incomprehensible, — at best something to be borne with a shrug or a pitying smile for its mediævalism.

Thus we are split into camps and cliques which are perhaps more dangerous in their smiling or sneering toleration than they would be in open warfare. For war might bring about a contact close enough for mutual comprehension — in the end. Toleration may mean a lazy acquiescence in contradictions that ought to arouse. We may bear the conflict between what I think right and what you think wrong so equably, so peaceably, so amiably that we come at last to tolerate a similar conflict within our own breasts, — which is disaster and damnation. When my act says "right" and my conscience says "wrong," and I all the while look tolerantly down upon the conflict as from some height of Olympian calm, — then God have mercy on my soul! Even the peaceful toleration of a similar difference between my standards and my neighbor's is dangerous unless it is a truce or a pause in prayer for light.

It is the same with our camps and cliques. We do not march behind fighting banners of play, of love, or of worship, as organized labor and organized capital march and countermarch behind their standards. We sit in little offices, shops, and kitchens, content not merely to mind our own business, but mindlessly to ignore its kinship with other business. We each keep our eyes and our minds at home. The result is that the devotees of Work, Play, Love, and Worship are suspicious of each other. They do not touch shoulders or act together as a team.

I should be sorry to aggravate these puzzles or to

sharpen still further these divergences and mutual
suspicions. For just because Work, Play, Love, and
Worship diverge so sharply each from each, they must
have a common root. Things can only differ when they
differ *in something*. Races differ in color, habits, morals,
and cookery because they all possess color, habits,
morals, and cookery. So it is with the sustaining
powers by which men live. All varieties spring from
likeness. Hence it is the task of any one who exploits
the variety to pounce speedily upon the unity, — if he
can. What is it, then, to live?

To live is to talk with the world. Work, Play, Love,
and Worship are four good ways of keeping up the
conversation. The experiments of the working scien-
tist or philosopher are the questions which he puts to
reality. The answers come in the form of reactions,
results, or readings. The dialogue need not be noisy,
but it must be active. A science which cannot think
of a question or get an answer when face to face with
nature is unproductive. Even a working hypothesis
must earn its pay by asking more and more insistently
for the answer called verification.

In agriculture, mining, or navigation it is still question
and answer that busy us, — but now in a rougher,
noisier exchange. We wrestle with the elemental, ex-
changing blows or benefits, issuing commands and
watching for signs, like an officer, or more often like
a private.

All the earth plays this game. Strategic moves (like chess play) are made by the bacteria as they search out our weakest tissue and by the bacteriologist who tries to foil their attack. Within a decade Paul Ehlich put a question to nature 606 times, each time in slightly different language:— "Will you or you or you," he said to one newly made chemical compound after another, "carry arsenic in lethal dose to my enemy the *treponema pallidum*, without harming on your way any human cell?"

At the 606th attempt he heard an answer that suited him better than any nature had given him thus far; the great drug salvarsan was christened forthwith.

The army of science has many men listening for answers to the questions asked by each. Sometimes the answer to your question is heard after your death by a youngster with keener hearing. Sometimes a friend (or an enemy) with better gift for language will reshape your question, modify your experiment so that a clear "yes" or "no" comes back from nature, hitherto quite silent.

But the natural sciences are no more talkative than the rest. All good thinking, all faithful research, whether in history, philosophy, mathematics, economics, or any other branch of knowledge, takes the form of question and answer, as it interrogates the material which it studies. To sit speechless before nature is to drowse; to ask questions that find no answer is to fail. Often the *tête-à-tête* is hard to maintain. The student runs dry of topics. He hears no answer and wonders (like the worshiper) whether any answer is on its way. Or he fails (like the uninspired artist) to put his desire into definite form.

This is natural and familiar enough in the laboratory or the studio, as it is at the breakfast-table. But table talk is simpler than art or science because the great conversations of work and play allow us no graceful retirement. No genteel silence will do. For all the live forces in the world are chattering away. Money talks; music speaks; the vessel answers your hand upon the wheel; the soil responds or fails to respond to your cultivation. To be deaf or dumb is to be entranced, stage-struck, or paralyzed.

Out of this slough, training and the inspiration of others' example are the best roads. We must be trained for all sorts of intercourse with our world, taught to play, to love, or to pray, as well as to work. Our shyness in the give-and-take which is life, can be trained out of us by hard knocks, our coldness mitigated by the radiant warmth of good friends. But we must anticipate our dangers and be fore-armed. To all of us comes the temptation to be less than alive, to pull out of the talk, to stop listening, or to go on using the same phrases long after the poor, bored universe has ceased to attend. That is a weak game, a brutalizing job, a languid affection, a formalistic worship full of "vain repetitions such as the heathens use," or "those wanton revels in mere perception which are at present the bane of our art, of our literature, of our social ideals and of our religion." [1]

If it is true that initiative and response are the necessary framework of *all* life, then the sociable woman with a silent husband may take comfort in the thought that perhaps he is as loquacious as any one, but in his own way. Conversation in its ordinary form, she then perceives, is but one of the living world's perpetual interchanges. There is a similar give-and-take in the games her husband enjoys, in the business that seems to submerge him, and in the wilderness where he takes his solitary vacation. If she and all of us can believe that our different roads converge toward one goal, we are less lonely each upon his own.

Of special importance, as I believe, is a reiteration of the ancient truth that the solitary worshiper or ascetic leaves men and nature behind him *because he is seeking better company.* Of course worship is not always solitary, but there are times when the conditions for intimacy of appeal and clarity of response which man just then needs are not to be had in the parlor, in the market, or even in a church. Hence he forsakes the world in order to get closer to the World. He is not doing something wholly different from his busy, playful, and sociable brethren. He is in touch with reality and with facts. He aims to be as busy as the laborer, as creative as the artist, and more ardent than the lover. Yet he does not attempt any fusion of these

[1] Josiah Royce, *The Problem of Christianity,* vol. II, p. 163.

separate activities. He seeks, above all, to orient himself and to get his sailing orders before he goes farther.
For he *is* going farther. Unlimited and exclusive worship is to him an abomination like unmitigated drudgery, perpetual diversion, or unremitting domesticity.

Yet worship is not strictly correlative with work,
play, and love, for it balances and supports them
all. Without them worship would have, so far as I see,
no significance. But each and all of them tends toward
spiritual fatigue from which worship alone can revive
us. I will not say that worship is the climax and cul-
mination of all that is most active in daily life. For God
can be reached through many channels outside worship. But to it man returns from all other activities
as he comes back to his home, — the common goal and
starting-point of every fresh endeavor.

Thus far I have found in all the deeds by which men
live, one salient feature, — the responsive interplay
between purpose and fulfillment, between initiative
and return. But this exchange is not a mere shuttling
of rigid materials across the world's loom. In all forms
of vital reciprocity something new emerges. Even the
shuttle is not a *mere* shuttle. It helps to create a fabric. So our shuttling questions, conversations, barter-
ings, experiments, political actions and reactions, must
build something if they are to give us new spirit and
take up our spirit into themselves. Service given and
knowledge received must be continuous and construc-

tive, else they are no better than idleness or sleep. Conversation becomes gossipy and desultory unless talkers pursue some quest together.

Look at the negative side of this idea. A desperate consciousness of anguish or of oppression is no life-giver, because it is static or revolves in a circle. It may be as full of sensation, of passion, of intimacy and intensity as the trashiest modern novel or the yellowest modern journalism, and yet contain as little of truth or worth. Passion cannot hear. Anguish cannot speak. Neither can create, though both are often linked, more or less unconsciously, with some greater power which makes them take part in creation. Paderewski strikes the piano with the fire of passion, but without its blunders and deafness. If he struck with his fist instead of with his fingers we should get the fruits of passion pure.

Is it not true that we rightly desire to abolish from the earth whatever lacks creative interchange? I recently heard a patient declare that not for anything would he have been deprived of the experience given him by a year's illness, not yet ended. But what we *would* willingly be deprived of, what we strive to banish, is the sick man's desperate or fruitless struggle with overmastering pain, the immigrant's forlorn, bewildered wanderings in an ill-managed port of entry, the prisoner's soul-numbing walk up and down his cell, the child's suffering under punishment which he believes unjust or cruel, the fruitless aridity of the desert, the torpor of the tropics, the paralyzing cramp of poverty, the exhaustion of industrial overstrain.

The four essentials which I have been describing throughout this book are united, then, by their root. They are rooted in one deep fact which seems to be as fundamental in the natural as in the spiritual world. They all create something new out of an interchange which can be called give-and-take, initiative and response, adaptation to environment and by environment, or simply conversation. They all sprout symbols, like leaves, as soon as they grow up, and through these they draw their nourishment. This means that absolute faithfulness, in work, in play, or in love, brings us into contact with God whether we know it or not. Whatever we do "for its own sake" looking to no ulterior reward, we are treating in fact as a symbol of what-is-best-worth-while-in-the-world. Ultimately, if we think it through, this means what our forefathers meant by God.

The divinity of work, play, and art is in their absolute faithfulness, their care for a degree of perfection which cannot be recognized or rewarded by men. The same faithfulness expresses much of the religion which is love; beyond that, the endless power of forgiveness that is in any pure devotion, points to its share in the infinite fertility and resource of the divine. To be conscious of the divinity which is directly continuous with our own effort whenever we do our best, enhances the effort and the joy in it. But the continuity and the contact are there whether we recognize them or not. We cannot get away from God, though we can ignore him. When Him we fly, He is the wings.

Because the four heroes of my tale are thus intimately related through their common ancestor in man's need, it is but natural that they should support and shape each other by their difference as well as their likeness. They do not fuse or drop their individuality, but play into each other, work toward each other, befriend one another, and send each to the other's shrine.

Recall some examples of this interchange. Unsatisfied with the best we can do at our work, we turn (if we are wise and healthy) to the lessons to be learned from play, — from Franz Kneisel's string quartette, for instance. That quartette plays with the dash, the precision, the reserve which we want to get into our work. The artists in that quartette have carried their music through the laborious and painful to the playful stage before they let us hear it. After the concert they will set to work again upon some new and sterner task, in turn to be mastered and transformed to something fit to play in public. The working side of life seems to belong more properly in private, where we prepare and whet ourselves for play. Every new game or art requires work before we can learn it. The shapeless silly games which can be mastered without labor and cannot be improved by practice, are fit only for the feeble-minded or for the feeble-minded hours near to sleep.

Love, like beauty and play, brightens and strengthens us for work. We labor to deserve the miraculous gift. We work to prove our devotion, to express our gratitude for what is given us, to pass along and fix its inspiration in permanent form. One suspects the genuineness of any affection that does not issue in work. "If ye love me," says the vision at the heart of every affection, "keep my commandments," carry them out in work and in joy. Every strong emotion ought to be worked off or worked out somehow, as William James and others have told us, — the emotion of love above all. "Do you love your country? Well, then, what work are you doing for it?" You say that you care for poetry. "Did you ever master any or learn it by heart? If not, your head, not your heart, is in it."

When love springs up between people who have not known hard work their union lacks something that labor would have taught them. Such an affection lacks the patience, the long foresight, and tenacious memory which work trains, while in the process it knocks some of the nonsense out of us. So work teaches us to love.

On the other hand, love teaches us how and why to work. To attach one's self to a task "for better, for worse" may seem impossibly quixotic and barren unless one is already learning through love in marriage that total commitment is a joy which makes all half-hearted and temporary contracts look cheap.

In the love of those who cannot play one suspects **no** lack of fidelity. Fruitlessness is a more probable fault. Play gives us the rest, change, fresh surfaces, new lights, and tastes by which to keep our affections fruitful. Play and the renewing of our minds and bodies by beauty, as well as by worship, make our love creative. The minor art of humor is especially quickening and restorative. Until we can laugh at each other as well as with each other, our love is vulnerable. It lacks the comradeship and equanimity that even shallow acquaintances may possess. It is topheavy.

Work, love, and play make a strong team together. They brace and reënforce each other. Yet they all leave us rudderless and unsatisfied without prayer. They can attain creative power only in worship, which — inchoate or full formed — is the source of all originality, because it sends us to our origin. The harder we work and play and the more intensely we devote ourselves to whomever and whatever we love, the more pressing is our need for reorienting, recommiting, refreshing ourselves in an appeal to God.

Yet worship is itself refreshed and supported by daily life. One mistrusts the sincerity of all religious expression by those whose lives do not furnish a large proportion of performance to a relatively small amount of prayerful pledge or petition. For religious expression is our superlative, and becomes cheap and weak unless through stored and gathered efforts we earn our right to use it. The most religious people are not those who talk and write the most about God, but those who best prove their love in faithful performance of what they believe to be his will.

Each of the foods by which our spirit lives makes us hungry for the rest. We may ignore or misinterpret the desire, but unless it is satisfied, we shrivel. Each of the four languages in which we may talk with our neighbor, the world, falls on deaf ears and fails of response unless it is spoken with creativeness, with symbolism, and with loyalty to a central motive. Work falls flat, play and art become sterile, love and worship become conventional, unless there is originality, personal creation in each. I must do my job in my own way, find an individual outlet in the symbols of art or game, and an individual answer in love and prayer if I am to feel at home in the world. Yet this individual note is no cry in the void because it claims brotherhood with all future and distant notes.

By originality and by symbolism, then, the home of our spirit is consecrated, but still more truly, perhaps, by our free and final allegiance. Our will is needed to invest the world with its own divinity. We hoist a flag and take possession once for all with a sort of "cosmic patriotism," grateful for our escape from chaos and the dark.

THE END

INDEX

INDEX

BOOKS BY RICHARD C. CABOT, M.D.

The Christian Approach to Social Morality
    National Board of Young Women's Christian Associations, 1913,
    600 Lexington Ave., New York City

Differential Diagnosis
    W. B. Saunders Company, Philadelphia. Two editions, 1911,
    1912

Social Service and the Art of Healing
    Moffat, Yard & Co., New York, 1909

Psychotherapy and its Relation to Religion
    Moffat, Yard & Co., New York, 1908

Case Teaching in Medicine
    W. M. Leonard, Boston. Two editions, 1906–1912

Physical Diagnosis
    William Wood & Co., New York. Five editions, 1901–1912

Serum Diagnosis of Disease
    William Wood & Co., New York, 1899

Clinical Examination of the Blood
    William Wood & Co., New York. Five editions, 1896–1904

DATE DUE

AUG 1 1 1972		
DE 14 '80		

GAYLORD   PRINTED IN U.S.A.